SOLITUDE IN SOCIETY

Solitude in Society

A Sociological Study in French Literature

ROBERT SAYRE

HARVARD UNIVERSITY PRESS

Cambridge, Massachusetts, and London, England

1978

*Publication of this book has been aided by a grant from
the Andrew W. Mellon Foundation*

Library of Congress Cataloging in Publication Data

Sayre, Robert, 1943–
    Solitude in society.

    Includes bibliographical references and index.
    1. Solitude. 2. Alienation (Social psychology)
3.   French fiction—20th century—History and
criticism.   I.   Title.
BJ1499.S6S37   843'.03   77–16265
ISBN 0–674–81761–3

To the Memory of
Georg Lukács
and
Lucien Goldmann

Preface

This book is the culmination of a long personal, political, and intellectual itinerary. Its origin lies in the direct experience of the modern form of solitude in my own adolescence. Near the end of that period, as a student in Paris in 1963, I first read Flaubert's *L'Education sentimentale* with a tremendous shock of recognition; I immediately identified my own frustrations in those of Frédéric Moreau. This discovery, that my personal experience had been of central importance in the work of a nineteenth-century French writer as well, only reinforced my belief that the essential solitude of the individual is a universal of the human condition.

It was only several years later, in the latter half of the 1960s, through the process of political engagement, activity, and education, that I began to question the "existential" posture with which I had grown up. It began to dawn on me that the larger political and social struggle of which I had made myself a part had as one of its profoundest meanings the overcoming of the specifically modern condition of alienation and solitude. My political engagement, which originally seemed to have little to do with the earlier experience of isolation, had in fact everything to do with it—with my search for a solution to the paradoxical dilemma of solitude in society. When I first read Marx's *Economic and Philosophical Manuscripts of 1844* in 1967, what had remained hidden from my view suddenly appeared clearly for the first time: the *sociohistorical* nature and limits of the phenomenon within which I had lived totally immersed and had elevated into a timeless category. In the context of a praxis of social transformation this new consciousness became possible; with it I embarked on the doctoral thesis upon which this work is based. The personal trajectory—from a passive, individual, and immediate *vécu* to collective social action and an intellectual analysis associated with it—is similar to those through which many others have passed and corresponds, on the level of theory, to the passage from existentialism to Marxism.

In an important sense, then, one of the primary contributions to this study comes not from an individual but—in the most general way—from the collective social movement whose goal is the transcendence of human alienation.

I wish to acknowledge the more specific contributions, however, of those who have read parts or all of my text in its various stages, who have engaged me in discussion, elaborated critical comment, lent me their erudition, provided stylistic suggestions. Some of these share my general perspective, others do not. I carry, of course, full responsibility for the analysis developed. But I wish to express gratitude to the following people for the various kinds of aid they have offered me in this endeavor: Paul Bénichou, Jean Bruneau, Gilbert Chinard, Steven Halliwell, Fredric Jameson, Marion Leopold, Justin O'Brien, Bertell Ollman, Paule Ollman, Daniel Penham, Richard Raskin, Léon Roudiez, Norman Rudich, Edward Said, Sylvie Weil Sayre, Maurice Shroder, Allan Silver, Carl Singer, and Susan Suleiman.

A version of Chapter Five first appeared as "Solitude and Solidarity: The Case of André Malraux," *Mosaic*, 9.1 (Fall 1975).

Permission to quote from the various texts has been kindly granted by the following: *Remembrance of Things Past: Swann's Way* by Marcel Proust, translated by C. K. Scott Moncrieff, reprinted by permission of Mrs. Eileen Scott Moncrieff, copyright 1934 by Random House, Inc.; *The Diary of a Country Priest* by Georges Bernanos, translated by Pamela Morris, copyright 1937 by Librairie Plon and Macmillan Publishing Co., Inc.; *The Fall* by Albert Camus, translated by Justin O'Brien, copyright 1957 by Hamish Hamilton Limited and Alfred A. Knopf, Inc.; *The Planetarium* by Nathalie Sarraute, translated by Maria Jolas, copyright 1960 by George Braziller, Inc.

A note on translation: Except in the few cases where seeing the original language is essential to understanding the point I wish to make, I have provided translations for all of the quotations from sources in foreign languages. In some instances, when I felt that it would be useful for the reader to be able to refer to the exact language of an important citation, I have reproduced the original in an endnote. Also, I have left in the original language some quotations that appear only in a note. Whenever the reference does not name a specific translator, the translation is my own.

Contents

SOLITUDE IN SOCIETY

Introduction

I

In this study I will attempt, through an examination of French literature as one manifestation of Western culture, to investigate the relationship between the modern phenomenon I shall call "solitude in society" and the socioeconomic system of capitalism. Solitude in society—that is, a generalized and radical social fragmentation that causes the isolation of each individual within the social framework, his inability to communicate adequately with others—is one aspect of the fundamental crisis of capitalism: "alienation."

Much has been written about solitude and alienation, so much in fact that the terms have tended to become vaguely defined clichés. The literature on the subject is vast and motley.[1] Although the material on alienation and solitude is too extensive to review in any detail here, it is possible to define several characteristic approaches. The least interesting of them, from our point of view, ignore or deemphasize the general cultural phenomena and direct our attention toward marginal cases of alienation, such as the aged, the handicapped, the criminal, or the "deviate."[2]

In a recent sociological study Robert Weiss presents evidence that loneliness is an extremely common experience in contemporary society, but then focuses on those particular situations in which individuals are "more likely" to be lonely—situations such as divorce, death of a loved one, displacement from one community to another, and so forth. Loneliness is defined as "a response to the absence of some particular type of relationship or, more accurately, a response to the absence of some particular relational provision." [3] Loneliness is shown to result from the lack or loss of intimate relationships and a sense of community in an individual; but Weiss never asks whether there may be generalized impediments to realization of these "relational provisions" in the very nature of the society he is observing. Other studies are similarly circumscribed by "one-dimensional" behaviorist and empiricist conceptions of human activity current in American psychology and sociology. [4]

Some works describe and analyze—sometimes with insight—the general cultural phenomena of alienation and isolation in modern society; often these analyses contain an historical dynamic as well. But when their authors do not possess a sufficient theoretical tool of analysis, they are unable to explain fully the nature and genesis of alienation. David Riesman's classic *The Lonely Crowd* is one such study. The socio-psychological discussion of inner-direction and outer-direction is useful, but the explication of historical shifts in character types in terms of population curves is not, as Riesman himself has since recognized. [5]

Studies of solitude and alienation which do not base their historical dynamic in the economic structure—the conditions of production for basic human needs from which all social forms arise—are sometimes accompanied by prescriptive suggestions for amelioration of existing social structures, or individual therapy, or a combination of the two: social, group, or community therapy. [6] In my perspective, these proposals for application of sociological theories to the problems of bettering relations among men within the framework of existing society only show that the theories themselves are unable to define the root causes of alienation (which lie in the very definition of the society itself).

The other important body of literature on alienation is philosophical: the modern "existentialist" tradition from Heidegger and Jaspers to Sartre, Tillich, and Marcel. Although there is much diversity within such a broadly defined tradition, the existentialist viewpoint generally tends toward an atemporal interpretation of alienation, or "estrangement" (both translate *Entfremdung*), and solitude (*Einsamkeit*). [7] Estrangement is the tragedy of the human condition, man's fate. Either there is no salvation from that condition, or salvation can come only through revelation and the grace of divine love—outside of Time. Thus the Christian existentialist Nicholas Berdyaev writes, "From the ontological standpoint solitude implies a longing for God as the subject, as the Thou"; [8] human bonds exist only through union with the divine subject. The existentialist viewpoint often also includes the idea that in modern, secularized, mass society the sense of estrangement is more acute—men are more deeply aware of their fate than in the past. Yet the categories and the analysis remain basically atemporal.

To the above approaches to alienation and solitude—the empiricist and the metaphysical—I will oppose a Marxist interpretation. Several important recent studies have demonstrated the central importance of the concept of alienation in Marx's theory.[9] For Marx, alienation is a multifaceted phenomenon, involving at the same time alienation of man from nature, from his labor, from his "species-being," [10] and from other men. It is with this latter aspect, the alienation of human relations, that I am primarily concerned here.

For Marx one of the defining characteristics of man in general is sociality: "Man is in the most literal sense of the word a *zoon politikon*, not only a social animal, but an animal which can develop into an individual only in society." [11] Men become what they become only together, in relationship to other men. The idea of the "natural" individual existing at man's historical beginnings is a bourgeois myth of the eighteenth century. The earliest stages of humanity are, on the contrary, characterized by total identification of individuals with "a definite, limited human conglomeration"—family, tribe, and community.[12] On the one hand, the individual is fully integrated within the primitive community; on the other hand, that community is severely limited geographically and in size, and itself is not united with the sum of human societies, indeed sometimes exists in an antagonistic relationship to other communities. Moreover, the individual still has no partial distance from the collectivity that would allow him to define and develop himself as an individual; the concept of the individual, in fact, has little meaning in this context.

The primitive community, after the nomadic stage, is based on land and the common ownership of land as the means of production. The individual defines his personality as part of both land and community. This integrated relationship continues to persist in the several pre-capitalist economic forms that develop out of primitive communalism.[13] The prerequisite for the first development of the individual—in ancient Greece—is exchange as a significant factor in the functioning of society. As Marx states: "Man is only individualized (*vereinzelt sich*) through the process of history . . . Exchange itself is a major agent of this individualization." [14] In spite of this beginning of individualization, however, strong social solidarities continue to surround the individual in antiquity.

In the feudal period, as in earlier economic forms based on land, the individual is bound to and defined by the land; he is also bound in a direct, personal relation to the feudal lord. Thus: "In feudal landed property the lord at least *appears* as the king of the estate . . . It appears as the inorganic body of its lord . . . Similarly, the rule of landed property does not appear directly as the rule of mere capital. For those belonging to it, the estate is more like their fatherland." [15]

Only with the advent of capitalism in the sixteenth century—and culminating in its dominance in the eighteenth and nineteenth centuries—is the individual set free from previous social bonds, thus creating the preconditions for his increasing isolation. Under capitalism the exchange of commodities and money becomes the dominant economic form, and the worker becomes a wage laborer whose labor is itself a commodity. Competition of each individual against all others, following their private interest, is the general rule; competition separates both workers and bourgeois. In the marketplace worker and bourgeois meet as isolated and competing individuals indifferent to each other; the impersonal and antagonistic relationship of exchange constitutes the basic network of bonds in the social fabric of capitalism.[16] Human relations become "reified"; they come to be mediated through the process of exchange of money and commodities, in which money, ever expanding, is the dominant factor. "If *money* is the bond binding me to *human* life, binding society to me, binding me and nature and man, is not money the bond of all *bonds*? Can it not dissolve and bind all ties? Is it not, therefore, the universal agent of separation?" [17]

Under capitalism the primary collective entities are false, "illusory" communities. The community of class (with the exception, in Marx's view, of the modern proletariat) "was always a community to which these individuals belonged only as average individuals . . . a relationship in which they participated not as individuals but as members of a class." [18] The same is true of the community of "cooperation" in work. Workers are isolated individuals in the marketplace, then an alienated mass in the workplace: "Being independent of each other, the laborers are isolated persons, who enter into relations with the capitalist, but not with one another. This co-operation begins only with the labor-process, but they have then ceased to belong to themselves." [19] And all individuals in capitalist society participate as abstractions, as nonconcrete "citizens," in that "substitute for the community," that "illusory community"—the State.[20]

There can never be any question, however, of returning to a Paradise Lost of primitive communalism. That community was based on severe limitations: fragmentation of general humanity into small, separate social groups, a primitive level of development of productive means that allowed for only the most restricted expressions of human powers and needs, and the total identity of the individual with the limited social group, rendering impossible any development of the individual as individual. Capitalism creates "for the first time a system of general social interchange, resulting in universal relations, varied requirements and universal capacities." [21] Local disjunctures are broken down and a world system of relationships develops. The evolution of cities and communications concentrates and universalizes social relations. Through this process the isolated workers become more and more a unified proletariat, with the role—different from that of all previous classes—of abolishing the existing illusory communities and actual isolation, and creating the conditions for the true community of communism. In the Marxist conception, community will at the same time give full expression to the individual; true individuality can exist only in true community, following the alienated development of the isolated individual in the capitalist period.[22]

But capitalism creates only the material basis for the universal community that is the *telos* of human history—the full elaboration of man's social nature. While it creates the most complex and universalized social relationships, it at the same time alienates them. Thus the contradiction of solitude in society: an increasingly generalized society of solitary individuals. Marx locates the point at which men became fully conscious of social isolation: "It is only in the eighteenth century . . . that the different forms of social union confront the individual as a mere means to his private ends, as an external necessity. But the period in which this view of the isolated individual becomes prevalent is the very one in which the interrelations of society . . . have reached the highest state of development." [23]

By the mid-nineteenth century the privatization of the individual achieved its full realization with capitalism itself, as the capitalist mode of production extended its influence throughout social existence, eventually leaving no domain untouched. Whereas the basis of earlier production was land, the locus of industrial capitalism, and consequently the situation in which the isolated individual attains its most absolute form, is the city. Engels observes this end result of an historical process, in his observations on London in 1844:

The hundreds of thousands of all classes and ranks crowding past each other, are they not all human beings with the same qualities and powers, and with the same interest in being happy? . . . And still they crowd by one another as though they had nothing in common, nothing to do with one another . . . The brutal indifference, the unfeeling isolation of each in his private interest becomes the more repellent and offensive, the more these individuals are crowded together within a limited space. And however much one may be aware that this isolation of the individual, this narrow self-seeking is the fundamental principle of our society everywhere, it is nowhere so shamelessly barefaced, so self-conscious as just here in the crowding of the great city. The dissolution of mankind into monads, of which each one has a separate principle, the world of atoms, is here carried out to its utmost extreme.[24]

II

Corresponding to the rising awareness of alienation in modern society, a plethora of theses and books have appeared in recent years—mainly in the 1960s—on alienation in literature. These works almost all reflect a common source: the existentialist tradition. In fact, they are sometimes directly inspired by the philosophy of Nietzsche, Heidegger, Berdyaev, or Niebuhr. Colin Wilson, in *The Outsider*, one of the first studies of alienation as reflected in modern literature, recognizes his indebtedness to the Christian existentialist perspective.[25] For this point of view, alienation and solitude are the eternal dilemmas of existence, and as such are present in all great literature.[26] At most, contemporary artists have a sharpened consciousness of them. As with the existentialist critics of modern society, the analysis, based on the individual and sometimes the supernatural, remains essentially nonhistorical. A passage from the introduction to *Rehearsals of Discomposure*, by Nathan Scott, summarizes a point of view tacitly accepted by many later critics:

This renewal of concern about the nature of man which has taken place, outside the confines of academic philosophy, among poets and novelists, has been accompanied and, in large measure, prompted by the crisis of modern civilization, in relation to which all things of the spirit in these past years have taken their form. But these writers have not merely been journalists giving prosaic reports on social and political dislocation, for their experience of the insecurities of the modern world has been deepened into an experience of a more perennial and a more ultimate dimension of human insecurity from which there is no escape. They have tended increasingly to spell this basic intuition out in terms of a metaphysic of alienation or estrangement, and it is with certain representative statements on this theme of spiritual isolation that I am concerned in this essay, for I believe them to contain insights into the nature of man.[27]

The existentialist critic often defines the "crisis of modern civilization" in terms of secularization and the Death of God,[28] without inquiring what has caused secularization in history; or, in a more historical vein, he defines it as the malaise that has resulted from the "cataclysms" of the twentieth century: the two world wars, Nazism, the atomic bomb. Thus Scott sees writers as affected not only by the "disintegration of traditional faiths," but also by wars and "demonic hierarchies of power and wickedness in high places." [29] As Fritz Pappenheim points out, this view is characteristic of existentialist social philosophy:

> It attributes the rise of alienation to a few isolated and almost fortuitous occurrences which have broken in upon the lives of the present generation —so to speak—from the outside. Such a premise is of dubious merit because it tends unduly to limit the scope of inquiry. It leads us to ignore from the outset significant developments which . . . show that alienation is manifest in all realms of modern life.[30]

By so limiting the scope of inquiry in literary studies, this view is indeed unable to explain the existence of the themes of alienation and solitude in nineteenth-century literature, *before* the wars, Nazism, and so forth, or to trace the dynamic of their transformation. For the existentialist mind they are static: an event strikes an artist's life from without and sets in motion a meditation on man's essential nature.

My premise is that literature grows out of a *total society*, not autonomously or out of isolated events. Both Georg Lukács and Lucien Goldmann have based their sociological methods of literary study on the proposition that, like all human phenomena, literature is comprehensible only as part of a larger "totality," which is the history of men in society. If literature is, in Kenneth Burke's terminology, a "strategy" for dealing with a "situation," that situation is social and is in historical flux: literature is indeed an expression of "attitudes toward history." [31] It follows that the criticism of literature must include consideration not only of the strategy but also of the situation—social and historical—without which the strategy is meaningless. In the Marxist perspective this socio-historical situation is always, in the final analysis, economic.[32]

For dialectical Marxist thought, literature is neither entirely transcendent nor entirely determined by socio-historical structures. The dialectical position sees man as neither totally free nor totally determined, but as a subject working himself out in history to create his freedom. Literature incarnates both the protest of men frustrated in their aspiration toward the full realization of themselves and their ideological adaptation within the present socio-historical framework. Literature then, if we reconsider Burke's definition, is a strategy (both protesting and adapting) which encompasses a concrete situation (the socio-economic reality, itself torn by the contradictions of man-in-history, protesting and adapting).

In modern society the contradictory reality of alienation and radical solitude engages man-in-history; it is from within this situation that the artist must work out his strategy. The present study is an investigation and history of the strategies to encompass solitude—solitude as a perspective on alienation central in literature: alienation in human relations. Consequently, although the study is strictly limited to one national literature, it has the status of a case study. Just as there are *décalages* in national histories, with the same basic forces developing at different speeds and in different configurations, national literatures also develop unevenly and idiosyncratically. Limiting the field to French literature will allow us to come to general conclusions without being obliged to deal with the problems of "synchronization" implicit in a comparative study.

It is hoped that a study of solitude in such a perspective described above will contribute to the ongoing enterprise of Marxist criticism, an enterprise that was carried forward, although with important limitations and even distortions, in the 1930s in the United States; it was almost totally eclipsed by the formalistic New Criticism in the McCarthyist and Cold War period, but has since the late 1960s been significantly renewed. Since the categories of alienation and solitude are central to the Marxist understanding of man under capitalism, a study of the category of solitude in literature is of considerable interest to Marxist criticism. Conversely, it is supposed that the bringing of Marxist tools of analysis to bear upon the thematic study of solitude will contribute analytical categories and a broadening of the scope of inquiry, allowing for a more global understanding than is possible without those tools.

My study is in two parts, with differing critical approaches. The first is historical and extensive, or "horizontal." It traces the social history of solitude as a literary theme from its beginnings to its radical transformation in the nineteenth and twentieth centuries. This approach allows for a scope of inquiry broad enough to encompass the dynamic of the theme and the genesis of a new vision: solitude in society. It has, however, the limitations of an overview. Part Two is, on the contrary, analytical and intensive, or "vertical." It consists principally of depth studies of the expression of solitude in five twentieth-century French novels extending from the beginning of the century to the 1950s. Through the study of individual novels over this time span, we may embrace the "microscopic" dynamic of solitude *within* one historical period—the modern period of monopoly capitalism.

The novels were chosen with several critieria in mind. First, they make a chronological spread: one novel from the pre-World War One period; two from the *entre-deux-guerres*; and two from the 1950s. In addition, they generally are "representative" in the sense that their authors developed "strategies" which are parallel to other strategies of the period. The literary strategy of Malraux, for example, is parallel, though not identical, to that of Saint-Exupéry and the early Montherlant. Finally, the novels were chosen as the most important and comprehensive of the given author's works; in these novels their vision of the world is most fully articulated. In cases where an author's vision evolves in the course of his novelistic career (Malraux and Camus), an added dimension of *devenir* will be part of the analysis.

PART ONE

A Social History
of Solitude

1

ᕤᲰᕠ

Antiquity
and the
Middle Ages

I

In its earliest meaning, solitude designates a location: areas beyond the bounds of the societies of men. Forests, wastelands, deserted islands, open seas—the *eremia* of Greek literature is dangerous and forlorn. It is the Scythian wilderness in which Prometheus is bound to his lonely crag, the isolated island upon which Philoctetes is abandoned, the woodland haunt of the Bacchae.[1] When a great city like Troy is razed to the ground, it lies bereft of the men who once made it a populous center, reduced to a desolate "solitude."[2] Human beings are "solitary" (*eremos*) when they are obliged to live outside society. One of the worst fates for a Greek citizen is exile, to be cast out of the polis, far from family and friend, an unprotected individual in the dangerous wilderness-solitude or in another polis in which he does not have the rights of citizenship. It is a potent curse to wish eternal exile upon one's enemy.[3]

Thus Philoctetes berates Odysseus bitterly for having stranded him, "aphilon eremon apolin": destitute without friends or city on Lemnos.[4] He is like a dead man, he says, and, indeed, to the Greek mind one is truly alive only within the context of one's city. Similarly Medea, carried off from her homeland and then betrayed, complains to the women of Corinth:

> Thine is this city, thine a father's home,
> Thine bliss of life and fellowship of friends;

But I, lone, cityless, and outraged thus
Of him who kidnapped me from foreign shores,
Mother nor brother have I, kinsman none,
For port of refuge from calamity.[5]

Even within the bounds of his polis a man may feel the solitude
that comes with loss of family or marriage ties—the network of
relationships that surrounds, aids, and protects the individual. It is
quite as strong a curse to wish the extinction of a man's family as
to wish his exile. The proud warrior Ajax hesitates before throwing
himself upon his sword; by committing suicide he abandons his
mistress Tecmessa, leaving her a widow among his enemies, and his
son an orphan.[6]

Thus also at the death of Alcestis, her son Eumelos throws himself
upon her body and bemoans his orphanhood. He and his sister are
henceforth to be alone like ships without escort (monostolos) on the
voyage of life. Returning to his palace after the funeral, Alcestis'
husband Admetus is overcome with sorrow at his loss; the palace
becomes a "solitude" without the presence of Alcestis. In spite of their
abandonment, however, there are solidarities that mitigate the solitude
of Admetus and his children. The loyalty and sympathy of the larger
community of Pherae (as represented by the chorus) is an aid to
Admetus. Moreover, the family is not entirely dissolved; the father
and two children will remain to share their suffering. Finally, Admetus
believes that when he dies he will be buried with his wife, that he
will descend to meet her again in the nether world where they will
make a new home together.[7]

Electra is destitute of both polis and family ties. She is an outcast
from the polis because of her hostility to Aegisthus, the usurper of
her father's throne. Treated like a foreigner or slave (and thus a non-
citizen) in the royal house, she lives as if exiled. She is abandoned
also by her family: her mother rules with Aegisthus the new state
created through the murder of Agamemnon, and her brother is exiled
in a foreign land. She and her sister are without husbands and sons
who might avenge them and are robbed of their paternal inheritance.
Without family aid Electra is powerless to assert her rights within
her own city. Thus orphanage and loss of family ties within the polis
is in fact closely related to the solitude of exile. To be an orphan without the aid of male kin and without inheritance is to be precariously
on the fringe of society.[8]

Electra continues, in spite of separation and death, however, to feel
a close solidarity with her kin. She has awaited for years Orestes'
return to avenge their father's murder, and when she is told that
Orestes is dead she turns to her sister for help in killing Aegisthus.

Her sister's refusal leaves her alone, but alone as representative and defender of the family honor. She does not think of herself as existing apart from her lineage. Her destiny was linked with Orestes' (as avengers) while he lived, and now in death they will live together under the earth. Orestes is not dead, however; he has returned to protect his sister and fulfill the family destiny against the usurper who rules the polis.

This older clan solidarity, then, may stand in conflict with polis loyalty. Antigone (who returns to Thebes after the incidents of *Oedipus at Colonus*) is more radically alone than Electra against the city, for her father and brothers *are* all dead; no Orestes finally returns to aid her. Only her sister remains, who, like Electra's, refuses to help. Nor has Antigone any sympathy from the chorus of Theban elders; like their king, Creon, they condemn her independence in going against a state decree. Yet she is only independent in relation to the state; she stands united with her kin in defense of the ancient burial customs for her brother's desecrated body. The death sentence is meted out for her refusing to replace this clan solidarity with the more modern loyalty to polis. In death she will rejoin her kindred, to live with them forever.[9]

Thus Antigone and Electra, while they feel destitute of family support in a hostile city, are in a more fundamental way united with all of their family. For their entire being is defined by its participation in a lineage. They have no individuality except as an expression of the larger group's destiny. They illustrate Lukács' contention in *The Theory of the Novel* regarding Greek civilization:

Man does not stand alone, as the sole bearer of substantiality, in the midst of reflexive entities: his relations with others, and the structures resulting from them, are actually full of substance, like him, in fact more truly filled with substance, because they are more universal, more 'philosophical,' closer and more kindred to the archetypal Homeland: love, family, city-state.[10]

The sixth century B.C. saw the growth of a new economy based on commerce and exchange in Greece; with it the *individual*—free to make, buy, and sell on his own account—began for the first time in human history to exist with relative autonomy from the social group.[11] Yet strong solidarities—social and religious—continued to enclose and protect this individual. He was not yet, and would not be for many centuries, a monad isolated within the human community.

The experience of the chosen people of the Old Testament, and of the brothers in Christ of the New Testament, is one of community with God and with the people of God. God directs the theocratic society of the early Hebrews in its wanderings and struggles with surrounding peoples, as he directs missionary efforts of the Christian brotherhood throughout the Roman Empire. Only at the extreme limit of personal distress does the Hebrew mind feel abandonment—from God and fellow man. In the Psalms we find, among the hymns of praise, prayers and laments in time of personal danger from enemies (particularly false accusers) or serious illness. Most often in these laments, although the sufferer feels the hostility or abandonment of his fellow men, he continues to feel a bond with the Lord who will finally save him.

Thus in Psalm 38 a sick man, spurned because of his disease, calls out for aid which he knows will come:

> My friends and companions stand aloof from my plague,
> and my kinsmen stand afar off.
> Those who seek my life lay their snares,
> those who seek my hurt speak of ruin,
> and meditate treachery all the day long.
>
> . . . . .
>
> But for thee, O Lord, do I wait,
> it is thou, O Lord my God, who wilt answer.[12]

Distress occasionally reaches such proportions that the believer feels total abandonment and separation from God, as in the well-known Psalm 22 lamenting a very grave illness:

> My God, my God, why hast thou forsaken me?
> Why art thou so far from helping me, from the words of my groaning?
> O my God, I cry by day, but thou dost not answer:
> and by night, but find no rest.
> Yet thou art holy,
> enthroned on the praises of Israel.[13]

This passage expresses the same revolt as Job's: a sense of abandonment by God when he does not make his presence felt through justice.[14] Yet the last verse shows us that, like Job, the psalmist never puts the existence of his God in question, even in the depth of his despair and revolt.

The book of Psalms contains, on the other hand, hymns of thanksgiving for deliverance from sickness and enemies. Indeed, the dominant feelings in the Psalms, in spite of moments of destitution, are praise and trust in God's covenant, as in Psalm 23:

> Even though I walk through the valley of the shadow of death,
> I fear no evil;
> for thou art with me;

thy rod and thy staff,
they comfort me.
Thou preparest a table before me in the presence of my enemies;
thou anointest my head with oil, my cup overflows.[15]

Jesus' life in the synoptic gospels is also one of absolute faith in his mission to the people and in his continuing communion with God. Only in the final moment of agony do gospel accounts suggest he feels abandonment. It is indeed Romantic reinterpretation that leads us to associate Gethsemane with tragic solitude; the gospels themselves do not express it. All the accounts tell us that Jesus prayed to God in the garden, putting himself entirely in God's hands. "And going a little farther, he fell on his face and prayed, 'My father, if it be possible, let this cup pass from me; nevertheless, not as I will, but as thou wilt.'" [16] The Lucan account adds, "And there appeared to him an angel from heaven, strengthening him. And being in an agony he prayed more earnestly" (Luke 22:43–44). When Jesus returns to find his disciples sleeping, he does not wish them to be awake to aid him in his solitude, but rather to pray themselves, "that you may not enter into temptation" (all versions). And when one of Jesus' disciples strikes a priest come to arrest him, Jesus has not, according to Matthew, lost his faith in the powerful presence of God and the heavenly host: "Then Jesus said to him, 'Put your sword back into its place; for all who take the sword will perish by the sword. Do you think that I cannot appeal to my Father, and he will at once send me more than twelve legions of angels? But how then should the scriptures be fulfilled, that it must be so?'" (Matt. 26: 52–54).

Luke reports that on the cross Jesus tells one of the criminals, "Truly I say to you, today you will be with me in Paradise" (Luke 23:43), and that Jesus says as he dies, "Father, into thy hands I commit my spirit" (Luke 23:46). In the more somber versions, Matthew and Mark, Jesus quotes in his final agony the lament of the psalmist: "My God, my God, why hast thou forsaken me?" (Matt. 27:46; Mark 15:34). Like the psalmist's, however, his cry of abandonment implies an ultimate faith in God's presence: he *addresses* the God whose will he can no longer feel.

Thus, as in classical Greek literature, biblical writings do not express the theme of man's tragic isolation from his fellows and in the universe. On the contrary, man partakes of an intimate community with God and his people. The central meaning of solitude in the Bible, on the other hand—and here solitude reaches important thematic proportions—is the *desert*. Solitude again is a place outside society. In Greek literature we saw the man alone as the exile without a city, condemned to wander or live in strange lands without protection. In biblical literature, on the contrary, the desert is the privileged place of retreat where direct communication with God is achieved, and where the persecuted Hebrew people are free from the oppressive yoke of pagan society. It is in the wilderness that God speaks to Moses from the burning bush, that the chosen people are saved from slavery in Egypt, and that Moses receives the laws which will serve as the basis for the new nation in Palestine. There also the prophets receive the word of God.

The *Theological Dictionary of the New Testament,* in its section on *eremos, eremia,* and related words, traces these roots in the Old Testament:

Emphasis on the saving aspect of the wilderness period creates in Judaism a tendency to ascribe to it everything great and glorious. The characteristics of the last time, e.g. that the Israelities see God, that the angel of death has no power, etc., are carried back into it, and its special features are also linked with the Messianic age, e.g. the blessing of the manna. There thus arises the belief that the last and decisive age of salvation will begin in the *eremos,* and that here the Messiah will appear. This belief led revolutionary Messianic movements to make for the *eremos* . . . The community of Christ is to remain hidden in the wilderness until Christ comes again and ends the assault of Satan.[17]

John the Baptist, who announces the coming of the Messiah, is a wilderness recluse, perhaps associated with or influenced by the Essene community living in the desert by the Dead Sea at about the same time. A proto-monastic colony, the Essene ascetics left the corrupt cities and temples to renew the faith: "The members of the community conceived of themselves as repeating in a later age the experience of their remote forefathers in the days of Moses. When they left the cities and villages and repaired to the desert, they pictured themselves as going out into the wilderness to receive a new Covenant." [18] There, far from the societies of men, they could commune directly with God, and not only await but also prepare for the coming of a new Prophet who would usher in the new age. Their "manual of discipline" quotes the same passage from Isaiah quoted by John: "Prepare in the wilderness the way . . . make straight in the desert a highway for our God" (Is. 40:3). Finally, although Jesus himself refuses to retire to the desert, and accomplishes his mission among the people of the villages and cities, "the 'place without inhabitants' is one where nothing separates Him from God and which He therefore seeks when He wants to escape the crowds." [19]

The desert is, then, the sacred retreat of both communities and individuals, and these biblical solitudes contain in germ the later monastic ideal of Christianity. In the first centuries after Jesus' death, the belief of the early Christians in his imminent return and the institution of the Kingdom on earth caused them to work enthusiastically at proselytizing within the cities of the Roman Empire—preparing for his coming and the Last Judgment. As late as the beginning of the third century A.D., Tertullian is still able to assert that Christians are not "dwellers in woods" or "exiles from life." [20] During the period of persecutions (second half of the third century), many Christians fled to the deserts, but usually did not remain. It was Anthony, in the early fourth century, and the widely circulated *Vita Antonii*, which created the eremite ideal. As Herbert Workman comments in *The Evolution of the Monastic Ideal*: "The *Life of Anthony* was produced at the psychological moment. With consummate art it presented Monasticism as the one adequate solution of the difficulties of life." [21]

For with the end of the persecutions and the institution by Constantine of Christianity as a state religion, the Church began more and more to adapt itself to the world. The Church put an increasing emphasis on outward forms—the sacerdoce—and on ecclesiastical hierarchy; ecclesiastics competed for the wealth that high position offered. The Church thereby reflected within itself the class distinctions and the competitive, mercenary mentality it encountered in the "world"—that is, the society within which it integrated itself. In Workman's view, "The hermit fled not so much from the world as from the world in the Church." [22] It might be more accurate to say that he fled from both, for it is evident that early ascetics were revolted by the life of the industrial and commercial centers. The solitude of the desert was a welcome return to a simple, agricultural way of life closer to the rhythms of nature. Jerome writes in one letter, "O desert enamelled with the flowers of Christ. O solitude where those stones are born of which in the *Apocalypse* is built the city of the Great King! . . . how long, brother, wilt thou remain in the shadow of roofs, and in smoky dungeon of cities? Believe me, I see here more of the light." [23] Thus the hermit abandons the corrupt, artificial, and ugly life of cities, ruled by the antagonisms of men grasping after wealth, for a simple and direct communion with God, with the heavenly host of God's angels, and with all of God's creation—more humbly with the beasts and birds.[24]

This communion of the individual hermit, however, gives way to another kind of communion. Although the first form of monasticism was an individualistic affirmation by the hermit of direct, spiritual communication with God, nature, and men over against the corrupt, spurious communities of Church and society, it almost immediately—

with the first monasteries of Pachomius in Egypt, around 305 A.D.—
was replaced by the new ideal of community in the desert-solitude.
Workman rightly attaches great importance to this development:

> Undoubtedly, as the meaning of the word "monk" shows, Monasticism
> started with the individual hermit, seeking by himself to save himself; the
> monk was strictly the anchorite . . . But so quickly did Monasticism pass
> through its merely individualistic stage, that we find, almost as soon as it
> emerges out of the mists of romance into the light of history, the solitary
> hermit—the *monachos* strictly so called—joining himself unto others, seek-
> ing to adapt his life to a common rule. Hermits and anchorites, it is true,
> still survived, especially in Lower Egypt . . . but only as the exceptions for
> whom new names had to be found, inasmuch as their own name had been
> appropriated by the conforming majority . . . monachism gave place to
> cenobitism, at first the loose organization of the laura, or cluster of cells
> around some common centre, later the stricter rule of a monastery. Thus,
> by three stages of development, the "monk" becomes the brother of the
> common life, the mark of whose life is not so much his isolation as his
> socialism.[25]

Already in the history of monasticism we can see that the flight from
society is at the same time a search for and creation of a new community. One flees society to create the true Society.

The fifth century saw the spread of monasticism to Gaul, where
the monastic ideal and reality was to have enormous importance
during the Middle Ages. But before turning to the beginnings of
French literature, we must take a step backward to consider that other
influence on French culture: Rome.

In Roman literature, to be sure, the older meanings of solitude continue to occur. There is the solitude of orphans and widows (and, in
general, those bereaved of or separated from family), the solitude of
the man who is without or who is abandoned by his friends, although
this usage is rare, and the solitude of exile. There continues to appear
also the wilderness-solitude, the dangerous wastelands and barbarian
countries through which the exile must wander.[26] Ovid's *Tristia* and
Epistulae ex Ponto, written from exile in a barbarian country while
he was abandoned by friends and separated from his wife, resume
these sorts of solitude. A far more important meaning, however—a
new form of solitude outside society—becomes a major theme in Latin
literature. Indeed, on his way to exile over wintry seas, Ovid recalls
not only the urban pleasures of Rome, but the pleasant solitude of
his gardens outside Rome. The new solitude of Roman times, then,
is the country house, estate, or farm of which many Latin writers were
proprietors.

We must first examine briefly some socioeconomic developments surrounding the phenomenon. By the end of the Punic wars, the small landholders or peasantry who had been the basis of the early agricultural economy were decimated. Forced conscription had taken them from their fields, and losses in their ranks were heavy. Moreover, many farms were destroyed by the movements and battles of opposing armies. In this situation large landowners and wealthy entrepreneurs were able to consolidate vast latifundia that were farmed by slaves, also a product of the continual wars. The dispossessed peasantry was obliged to look for work in the cities, especially Rome, where with other slaves from the wars they joined the growing mass of urban workers. At the same time, Rome was seeing the growth of commerce and industry, an influx and movement of capital, the rise of banking and speculation—developments stimulated largely by Roman imperialism.[27]

The latifundia were farmed for profit. Alongside the large holdings, medium and small properties existed, often near the cities and owned by the urban middle classes:

Around the urban centers, the country in many provinces of the empire was populated with villas and farms, country seats and farm buildings. The master of the demesne would usually come there to reside during the pleasant season, either for his personal pleasure or so as to superintend the harvest of grapes and olives, the making of wine and oil. A steward, several slaves, sometimes also emancipated laborers . . . were sufficient for the cultivation of these modest demesnes . . . Horace's villa in the Sabine country "was not only a little garden for the man of letters, or a lizard's hole as Juvenal expressed it . . . it was also a real demesne, with meadows, grounds, woods, and an entire agricultural production. It was a fortune as well as a pleasure."[28]

From within this context Horace writes in the *Epodes* and *Satires* his classic expressions of *procul negotiis* ("far away from business cares"); the pleasant solitude of the country estate has become a way of escape for the urban middle classes from the evils that already are felt to be integral parts of city life: ambition and cut-throat competition, avarice and luxury. In the *Satires*, Horace inveighs against men of the city who seek only to be richer than the next man and who make friends only for advantage. In the well-known fable of the country and city mouse, he shows that in the city the mouse need always fear the dog: the smaller are always menaced by the greater, and riches and luxury are always in danger of being snatched away.[29] Over against city life Horace pictures the simple joys on a small ancestral farm.

> Happy the man who, far away from business cares,
> Like the pristine race of mortals,
> Works his ancestral acres with his steers,
> From all money-lending free;
> Who is not, as a soldier, roused by the wild clarion,
> Nor dreads the angry sea;
> He avoids the Forum and proud thresholds
> Of more powerful citizens.[30]

These first lines of the usurer Alfius in the second Epode make clear the basic set of oppositions. Business (in particular monetary transactions) and the usurer's interest are contrasted with "ancestral acres"—the farm passed on from generation to generation. Further on in the poem Horace invokes Priapus, the garden god, and Silvanus, guardian of boundaries. The heart of the contrast is in the idea that money is never stable; it is always growing, diminishing, changing hands. The boundaries of the paternal farm remain, making the farm a haven of peace from the flux and precariousness of urban business. Other specific evils of modern urban life are then enumerated: the dangers of war and maritime commerce, the animosities of the forum and the client system. Another basic contrast, however, is implied between the "pristine race of mortals" and the new situation. As we have seen, rural property was changing hands in Horace's time. The peasant working his land, as in the ancient agricultural society, was disappearing. Horace hoped that with peace and prosperity under Augustus after the civil wars, Rome would return to the older ways. Nonetheless, although he pictures nostalgically here the happy life of the peasant plowing his fields with oxen, he of course was not a peasant himself and did not work his own land. His life is more accurately evoked in one of the *Satires:*

> O rural home: when shall I behold you! When shall I be able,
> Now with books of the ancients, now with sleep and idle hours,
> To quaff sweet forgetfulness of life's cares![31]

Horace is one of the many owners from the city of medium-sized properties. His only wish is for "a piece of land not so very large."[32] This is what he possesses, and he insists he will not attempt, like the wealthy landowners, to buy up his neighbors' plots. Yet these medium holdings are, just as much as the latifundia, dispossessing the peasantry.[33] In spite of his nostalgia for the peasant life, Horace's situation and ideal were part of the syndrome of his time: the growth of new economic forms in both the city and the country, which drove the urban middle classes to obtain land for profit farming *and* as a retreat from city life. Such was the safety valve, so to speak, of the system.

In the country one found some measure of the peace and stability of olden times, while at the same time receiving an income.

At the end of the second book of the *Georgics*, Virgil praises country as against city life in much the same terms as Horace. The rural life is described as one of leisure and secure rest as opposed to war and the turmoil of cities; it does not deceive men, as does the life of luxury always under threat of ruin. Rural life retains the ancient religion, austere virtue, and the stable, patriarchal family; Justicia, when leaving the earth at the end of the Golden Age, left traces (*vestigia*) in the country. The farmer does not have to pity the poor and envy the rich as in the city; for all is abundance where he lives, and he picks the fruits of the trees which the earth gives willingly and unaided (as in the Golden Age). The concluding lines begin by asserting that this rural life was the one led in the early days of Rome, but finishes by going further: even before the reign of Zeus, during Saturn's Golden Age, men lived as they now live in the country.[34]

In the first book of the *Georgics*, Virgil had described the Golden Age: man did not work the fields, for the earth produced everything willingly and unaided. Honey dropped from leaves and wine ran in streams. Moreover, fields were not divided into property; crops were held in common. Only when Zeus instituted the Iron Age were men obliged to work—with iron plows. Yet Virgil still associates country life in the modern era with the Golden Age. And in the fourth eclogue he predicts that under Pollio's consulship the Iron Age will give way to a new Golden Age of paradisiacal agricultural abundance; although at first cities, commerce, and rural labor will continue as vestiges of the Iron Age, by the time Pollio comes to maturity all of this will disappear: "every land shall bear all fruits." [35]

Several implications should be drawn from this brief account of Horace and Virgil's poetry praising country life. First, there is a tendency to see country life–which the poets lived as landowners—as a nostalgic, idealized image of the happy peasant or shepherd as in the *Eclogues*. This trend will continue in the pastoral tradition. Second, there is a tendency for the olden-day peasant image to "slide into" an image of the Golden Age, that is, of an anti-urban paradise lost. The monk and anchorite, as we saw, escape urban society to a desert associated with the Kingdom of Heaven, and there they create fraternal communities. Similarly many of the Roman middle classes flee to their country estates, associated with the ancient, communal Golden Age. The first important literary expressions of solitude—solitudes situated outside urban society and as an escape from it—are directly linked with notions of ideal community.[36]

Later Roman writers develop and modify the theme of country

solitude. Pliny the Younger was an extremely wealthy landowner. Most of his fortune was in land; some was in capital, which he lent at interest. A part of his lands were inherited, others acquired. Thus he did not share Horace's contentment with his own boundaries. In one letter he speaks of his desire to annex a neighboring property which is for sale, and asks advice how best to raise the money.[37] His Laurentian and Tuscan estates—winter and summer retreats respectively—are large and elegant villas, not at all on the scale of Horace's. These villas, however, are his *secessus* or *solitudo*,[38] where he cultivates his mind with study and his body with hunting. In solitude one is not obliged to belong to the community of animosity and rumor which exists in Rome: one converses only with oneself and books. Such solitary leisure also brings liberty (*libertas*) for the individual: freedom to do what he wants, for he is no longer constrained by the obligations of business, public office, and the network of social relationships about him.[39]

In Pliny, then, the theme is given a more individualistic direction. He does not call upon either the peasant or the Golden Age associations that were present in Horace and Virgil. Country solitude becomes the landowner's cultivation of his own mind, free from the affairs in Rome to which he must often return. Seneca, another immensely wealthy landowner (both men are representative of the later Roman period, when the large estates slowly swallowed up the medium and small [40]), also recommends and practices country retirement as most conducive to stoical detachment from the blows of Fortune and a cultivation of the self. But he criticizes the Romans who run away from the city simply because of lack of success; they bring with them their cupidity, envy, and so forth, from city to country. What is important is the creation of a state of quietude in one's mind: "The place where one lives . . . can contribute little towards tranquillity; it is the mind which must make everything agreeable to itself. I have seen men despondent in a gay and lovely villa, and I have seen them to all appearance full of business in the midst of a solitude." [41]

Thus both Pliny and Seneca express the theme of country solitude in terms of the individual and his self-cultivation. Similarly the Christian hermit expressed the individualistic trend of monasticism. Although the hermit's retreat involves a far more complete rejection of society, impelled as it is by a total religious engagment, nonetheless it represents a parallel revolt to that of the Roman landowner-philosopher. The latter, though, as a member of the ruling classes, both escapes *and* participates in the social system.

I have sketched briefly the dominant solitudes of the ancient period: the solitude outside society, first of the exile, then of the hermit-monk and country gentlemen. The ancient period does not know solitude within society in the sense of prolonged and generalized psychic isolation. At most the ancient mind feels loneliness at the death of a loved one (kin, other close relations), or at the unusual and extreme hostility of other men; but even these feelings are mitigated by larger social and religious solidarities. Moreover, these kinds of solitude, although within society, result from *separation* from others; the solitary individual is deprived of an important human contact he had hitherto enjoyed. But the functioning of human relationships themselves is never put into question.

Seneca, writing near the end of the period, when urban-industrial forms have developed to a high point but have not made the crucial advances that the Industrial Revolution will later effect, illustrates the far limits of the ancient awareness of solitude within urban society. He writes in one letter: "Thus a mob of friends surrounds prosperous men; around ruined men is a solitude, and friends flee from it." [42] This does not mean that the ruined man is necessarily lonely; it literally means that around him is a deserted area—that is, there are no friends crowding around him. And this solitude of men who have lost their fortune—which results from friendship being treated as a business deal (*negotiatio*) [43]—is not carried into the general nature of social relations. It has not yet become a comprehensive cultural phenomenon. Thus Seneca prizes true friendship, which is not a business relation, for it brings perfect communication even in separation: "A friend should be retained in the spirit; such a friend can never be absent. He can see every day whomsoever he desires to see . . . we should be living within too narrow limits if anything were barred to our thoughts. I see you, my dear Lucilius, and at this very moment I hear you; I am with you to such an extent that I hesitate whether I should not begin to write you notes instead of letters." [44]

II

In many countries under the Roman Empire, in Gaul for one, agriculture made significant progress and converted to cultivation vast forests, swamps, and other waste areas. With the barbarian invasions of the fifth century, however, much of the new cultivations became forest and desert again; farms and cities were razed and abandoned to return to their wild state. The second wave of invasions in the ninth and tenth centuries again wrought havoc upon rural life. Peasants fled the invaders, leaving their farms and villages. The period is characterized by a general desolation of the countryside, sparse population, and small towns.[45] Thus the bishops of Reims lament in 909: "You see the wrath of the Lord break out before you . . . There are nothing but depopulated towns, monasteries torn down or burned, fields reduced to solitudes." [46] In the high Middle Ages, with the expansion of cultivated demesnes and the growth of urban life and commerce, the vast deserted areas are diminished. Nonetheless, large forests remain, and the Hundred Year War, plague, peasant revolt and flight in the fourteenth and fifteenth centuries again desolate the countryside.[47]

Here, then, is a primal meaning of solitude in the medieval period: the solitude of the forest, dangerous with wild animals and robbers. A man alone in these solitudes risked his life. According to Randall Cotgrave's *Dictionarie*, "Homme seul est viande aux loups" (A man *alone* is meat for wolves).[48] Yet into these solitudes went the monk and the hermit, as they had since the spread of monasticism in Gaul in the fifth century. There they lived beyond the bounds of society, in the realm of the outlaw. In the *Moniage Guillaume*, William wanders into a large and solitary valley; for seven leagues around there is neither town nor human being, excepting isolated hermits who are periodically robbed and beaten by thieves. The hermit dwelling (Guidon's) which William approaches is protected by a surrounding hedge of thorns and a ditch, and the hermit is at first afraid to let William in. Thus the dangerous wilderness continues to be also the blessed retreat of the monastic ideal.[49]

The history of monasticism in the Middle Ages, however, is the history of its growing involvement with the "world." The cycle repeated itself again and again: small communities of laboring monks cleared forests and cultivated crops. As the monasteries became settled and rich with produce, more monks came to make it larger; serfs and tenants were engaged to work the growing domains that the monks could no longer work alone. The monasteries began to engage in trade and sometimes moneylending. Amassing tremendous wealth, they became centers of both business and culture, and consequently the monastic ideal of renunciation of the things of this world became corrupted. Medieval monks were often of noble birth; as landowners and merchants who commanded serfs, tenants, and craftsmen, the monks' primitive ideal of a classless society free of cupidity was abandoned. Far from being solitudes to which one retreated from the evils of society, monasteries in fact became centers of society themselves (especially in the tenth and eleventh centuries), breeding the very evils from which it had been the original monastic impulse to flee.[50]

Thus, although solitude continues to be associated to some extent

with the monk's life, the worldly and populous monasteries often are
no longer solitudes in the classic sense; now the hermit's life is the
truly solitary one. Indeed, in the eleventh century a number of ere-
mitical movements arose which returned to more austere, uncultivated
deserts and to the intermediate system of "lauras"—individual
hermits' cells grouped around a common center.[51]

The letters of Abelard and Heloise express most fully the tradition
behind the medieval concept of religious solitude and the crisis it
was undergoing. In this respect the first letter, written by Abelard to
a friend recounting his troubles, is most illuminating. Abelard gives
in detail Heloise's learned arguments against marriage. She draws an
explicit parallel between the classical philosophers who retreated from
an evil age (Seneca's letters to Lucilius are cited) and the early biblical
and monastic recluses (Jerome figures importantly). If the emphasis
is on the philosophers in this passage, it is on the monastic tradition
in the eighth letter, in which Abelard establishes a rule for Heloise's
nunnery. Here he launches into an *éloge* of solitude that passes in
review the entire history of monasticism, from the prophets and John
to the Eastern hermits and Church Fathers.

Comparing the true monastic solitude of earlier times with the
corruption of the ideal in the present, Abelard speaks in terms very
similar to the historical sources cited above:

It is surely by a machination of the clever temptor, our principal enemy,
that almost all of the old monasteries, which had at first been built in solitudes so as to avoid the commerce of men, later took in men when religious
zeal had cooled, gathered in droves of male and female servants, saw large
towns rise on sites chosen as retreats, and returned to their age, or better
still, drew their age to themselves. By plunging into a thousand troubles, by
binding themselves slavishly to the domination of spiritual and temporal
powers, in their desire to lead an idle life and to live off the product of
others' labor, the monks—that is, the solitaries—have lost both their name
and their character.[52]

Abelard therefore searches out a true solitude in which to settle and
is eventually followed by disciples. His disciples, living a simple life
in huts around a center (similar to the "laura" system), resemble
hermits, says Abelard, more than students.[53]

Abelard's students work the land and build a larger sanctuary for
their greater numbers; eventually the sanctuary is transformed into
a nunnery, of which Heloise becomes the abbess. During a short period,
the nuns live in poverty. Then "that solitude, once haunted only by
wild beasts and brigands," [54] becomes more opulent. Bishops and abbots
begin to seek out Heloise. Although the outcome is unsure, the nunnery seems to be advancing toward the common fate of "solitudes."

We have observed that the monasteries, especially in the tenth and eleventh centuries, became important centers of society. The country estate, which in imperial Rome functioned as an escape from the urban centers, experienced the same fate. With the advent of the Middle Ages, beginning in the Merovingian period, a well-known development occurred, which, as Arnold Hauser terms it, "removed the centre of gravity of social life from the towns to the country." [55] In the early feudal period, although it is now generally acknowledged that a pure form of closed household economy did not exist (trade never ceased entirely in the Middle Ages), nonetheless there is a tendency for the manor to function as a society unto itself, as far as possible producing for its own needs and not beyond them. Although the nobility visited the towns, and sometimes maintained townhouses, in general they lived on their domains.[56]

A system that has as its basic social unit the feudal manor, and in which urban life is still secondary, cannot feel the contrast—pleasant country estate versus evil city—upon which the theme of rural solitude is based. If the demesne is a society, it is not a solitude. Even with the rise of the court in the twelfth century, this equation remains valid. The courts themselves are the estates of local princes and powerful lords. Nobles move from estate to estate, to war, and back to their own demesne. The court is therefore neither associated with urban life nor with autocracy, as in classical Rome.

Thus although John of Salisbury and Gautier Map, early "pre-humanist" clerks at the royal courts of England and France in the late twelfth century,[57] write their *De Nugis curialium* (Frivolities of Courtiers), in which they fulminate against avarice, envy, flattery, and hypocrisy at court (largely influenced by classical sources), their critique had very little influence on other writers of their time. Moreover, they present no positive ideal in opposition to court life.

Only at the waning of the Middle Ages, in the latter part of the fourteenth and in the fifteenth centuries, does the theme of "le mépris de la Cour" (contempt for the Court) acquire any eminence, largely within a rather narrow pre-humanist circle. In the mid-1300s, Philippe de Vitry, Bishop of Meaux, wrote a short poem, "Le Dit de Franc Gontier," which influenced writers within the pre-humanist movement and without. It established a theme that by then corresponded to a growing disaffection with court life. The feudal system was in transformation: powerful princes had consolidated immense principalities and were struggling against the extension of royal power under the Valois. The royal court acquired greater importance and a new character: the feudal nobility increasingly became a dependent court aristocracy, existing side by side at court with bourgeois officials, who were often ennobled by the king.[58] Autocracy and a rising urban bourgeoisie were beginning to be linked to court life in a trend that only reached its conclusion in *ancien régime* society. The court poet Eustache Deschamps describes the atmosphere of the times in many of his poems:

> I well know the merchant's labors,
> The expenses of the great, and merciless finance,
> The ostentatious display of cardinals and clerks,
> The powerful position of kings and the suffering of nobles,
> The greed and heavy spending of judges . . .
> The common good is not loved at all;
> No one can trust another;
> Material gain is sought after, and not at all the person;
> The valiant man has nothing and the evil man is successful.[59]

The life of Franc Gontier provides the positive ideal to contrast with these evils of court and city life. He is a simple peasant, living with his dame Helaine, "Under green leaves, on soft grasses beside a chattering brook." [60] After a simple and healthy meal, Gontier goes into the forest to chop wood; as he chops, he piously thanks God for the security of his life. He does not know the luxury of princes, but he need not bend his knee to "tyrant" either. He knows neither ambition, cupidity, nor lechery, and his "joyous freedom" is compared with the slavery of the "court serf." Secure from the wheel of Fortune, independent of serflike obedience to the monarch—such are the pleasures of Gontier's life, "far away from business cares."

Thus in the late Middle Ages the negative theme of "mépris de la Cour" is linked with a positive pastoral ideal—as in the "procul negotiis" theme of Horace and Virgil. However, the pastoral ideal is not linked with the nobleman's estate; only when the seigneurial domain is no longer the center of real social activity can it become the location of the *ideal*, creating the theme of "la plaisante solitude" on the country estate. This development will take place in the sixteenth century. In the late Middle Ages the nobleman's estate is rather an anti-paradise. Another humanist, Pierre D'Ailly, composed a companion poem for "Gontier" that contrasts, point by point, Gontier's simple and virtuous life with the tyrant's life in his rich chateau:

> But this bag of excrement, stinking cemetery,
> Sepulchre of wine, with puffed body and swollen belly,
> For all his wealth has yet no gladness in him;
> For an overful stomach finds no pleasure in savor;
> Nor is he delighted by laughter, sport, song or dance.
> For he desires, covets and craves so many things

That he finds true satisfaction in nothing he has.
He wants to acquire either kingdom or empire . . .
He suffers grievous martyrdom through avarice,
He fears treason, he trusts no one.
His heart is cruel, swollen with pride and anger,
Gloomy, full of care and melancholy.[61]

The late Middle Ages does not distinguish estate life and court; they breed the same evils and cares. The only way out is imaginary: the dream of happy peasant simplicity.

We have investigated the vicissitudes of solitude outside society in the medieval period: solitude within society, on the other hand, is nearly impossible in the medieval context. The feudal economy and the highly stratified, compartmentalized social system allow the individual to exist only within a group. The word "individual" in the Middle Ages means "inseparable" from a group or whole. Each group in turn has its place in a "great chain of being" which defines its relationship with other groups and its place in the universe. More important, the relation of service in return for protection that binds the feudal lord to his vassals is of a radically different nature than the contractual link that binds an employer and a wage earner. As the historian Marc Bloch points out, although the tie between the lord and a vassal living with him and serving him in his manor (the *provendier*) is more intimate than that between a lord and his vassal to whom a fief has been given, both ties are essentially different from the salary relationship.[62] The solidarity that results from feudal loyalties, and the consequent lack of any sense of isolation, is perfectly reflected in the medieval epic. Lukács writes in *The Theory of the Novel:*

The hero of the epic is, strictly speaking, never an individual. It has always been considered an essential characteristic of the epic that its subject is not a personal destiny, but rather that of a community. Rightly so, since the closed and finished system of values defined by the epic cosmos creates too organic a whole for a part of it to so fully isolate itself, to so vigorously stand on its own, that it discovers itself as interiority and becomes a personality.[63]

Thus, in the *Chanson de Roland*, at the moment when Roland is most alone—as he is dying, after all his men have died before him, at Roncevaux—he is most gloriously one with "la douce France," with its chief and symbol, Charlemagne, with his men, his God, and all of Christendom. His men fight to protect France and, through her, all Christendom. Their "loyal compagnonnage" ends only in death, and in death they are promised paradise by the representative of God,

Archbishop Turpin, who fights at their side. Charlemagne and the French knights ride toward Roncevaux, praying God that they may arrive in time to fight side by side with Roland. Near the end Roland, alone with the dying Turpin, gathers all of his dead companions together in a row so that he may be with them for the last time. When Turpin dies, Roland remains with his sword Durendal, which he addresses tenderly. At his last moment Roland brings to mind again France, the men of his lineage, and Charlemagne, his lord. He weeps to leave them but then, feeling death coming, "He offered his right glove to God: Saint Gabriel took it from his hand . . . Roland is dead; God has his soul in Heaven." [64]

Roland's overzealous *prouesse* in refusing to blow the oliphant never becomes problematical enough to place in doubt the solidarities that bind him indissolubly to his men and his country. Indeed, his refusal is not an act of individual self-assertion; he fears that by calling for help he will lose renown and, *through him,* his lineage and France will lose renown. [65] Roland is tightly surrounded throughout the battle by the presence of what he belongs to, what he is fighting for, what he *represents*. His death is quite literally a passage from the protecting arms of his country, his family, and his lord, into the arms of the heavenly host; he passes directly from the feudal community into the heavenly community, offering his glove as a token of fidelity to his new lord.

With the rise of courtly society in the twelfth century, social solidarities and relationships are modified, but remain strong and clearly defined. The growing tendency to award fiefs to vassals, fiefs that gradually become hereditary, creates a new class of knights—a "petite noblesse" in an inferior position to the great lords and princes. It is largely from within this class that the new courtly ethic and the "amour lointain" of courtly love arise. [66] This sublimated love does not reject physical possession altogether, but affirms the power of spiritual union over physical chastity or separation. The relationship between the knight and his beloved liege-lady allows for no sentiment of solitude. It assures the triumph of spiritualized communion which no material circumstances can alter.

The lover often keeps his love secret even from the lady at first, but feels an intimate bond with her from the start. Le Chatelain de Coucy writes of one lady who does not yet know of his love:

> As soon as I saw her, I left my heart a hostage to her,
> And it has since stayed long with her.
> I never wish to take it away. [67]

Even in long periods of separation the lover feels united with his lady. Conon de Béthune, for example, writes this lament of a lover leaving on a Crusade:

> Alas! oh Love, how hard it will be
> For me to part from the best lady
> Who was ever loved or served.
> May God in his goodness bring me back to her
> As surely as I sorrow to leave her.
> Alas! What have I said? I am not leaving her:
> Although my body goes to serve our Lord,
> My heart remains entirely in her keeping.[68]

The Tristan and Iseut legend well illustrates this "étreinte des coeurs." Tristan is obliged to leave Iseut many times. He desires her, pines for her, yet is never really without her, for he has no other thought than their love. He sends Iseut the magic dog whose bell makes one forget all sufferings, but Iseut also refuses its comforts and throws the bell into the sea. She will continue to remember and suffer with Tristan. Tristan's love drives him to return again and again to Iseut, for the honeysuckle (*chevrefeuil*) torn from the hazel will die. When he does die, thinking only of her, Iseut must also die. By a sort of extension of the *chevrefeuil* imagery, after their death a briar grows from Tristan's grave, climbs over the chapel on either side of which they are buried, and takes root in Iseut's grave. Although it is cut several times, it grows back each time, and King Mark finally allows it to remain. Thus, love's union triumphs over obstacles: the lovers may be separated physically but not in the spirit, and their destiny—as Tristan puts it, "Ne vous sans moi, ne moi sans vous"—is definitively fulfilled in death.[69]

In the early and high Middle Ages, then, human links and solidarities are paramount. Only at the end of the medieval period, in the fourteenth and fifteenth centuries, do they begin to weaken as the feudal system falls into disorganization and disintegration. Side by side with the growth of a bourgeosie that will later replace the ruling nobility, a crisis develops within that nobility, particularly after the Hundred Years War. Peasants have fled the land, the land is impoverished, and nobles are obliged to lease under unfavorable conditions. Society is in transition and dislocation: there is a general sense of malaise and even despair which is reflected in many of Deschamps' poems.[70]

The new social type of which Villon is the most illustrious representative is a product of this period of upheaval. As Hauser describes him,

The *vagans* was a cleric or scholar who roamed about singing and reciting, a runaway priest or a student who had abandoned his studies—that is, a déclassé and a bohemian. He is a product of the same economic revolution, a symptom of the same social movement which had produced the town bourgeois and the professional knight, but he already shows important signs of the social restlessness of the modern intelligentsia . . . At bottom he is a victim of the upset social equilibrium, a transitional phenomenon typical of times when masses of people are abandoning the social groups to which they had formerly belonged.[71]

This lack of foundation in any established class—with its secure network of human relationships—accounts for the striking modernity of Villon's poetry. He is poor and rootless in the city, where increasingly money is the supreme ruler. As the research of Marcel Schwob and Pierre Champion has shown, Villon knew men connected with royal finance administration. He attempted to obtain gifts from the wealthy men he knew and was often refused. In the Grand Testament he satirizes many of the financiers. These financiers, who were also tax collectors, speculators, usurers, and wealthy merchants, were generally despised by the poor—with whom Villon was in contact during his errant life.[72]

As a poor urban poet Villon ridicules the pastoral ideal in "les Contrediz de Franc Gontier." He would rather live like a well-fed *chanoine* who drinks day and night and dallies with his mistress. The same poet, in "Le Lais," paints a vivid tableau of himself writing alone in his room in the Latin Quarter on a cold, windy night. He has no fire and writes with only a candle:

> Finally, while writing tonight,
> Alone and in good humor,
> Drawing up and composing these legacies,
> I heard the Sorbonne bell . . .[73]

He starts to pray, but his mind wanders: instead of the Virgin, "dame Memoire" sets the philosophical jargon of the *sorbonnard* running through his mind, which in turn sets in motion his sensations and Fantasy. When his mind clears, his ink is frozen and his candle has blown out. He falls asleep and cannot finish his legacy.

This extraordinarily concrete image of the poor poet working alone in his Parisian room, his mind filled with strange fantasies rather than pious prayers, is the first—and isolated [74]—example of a form of solitude which will be the very emblem of the nineteenth-century poet. But Villon lives in an end time, and before the poet will return again, rootless and alone, to the City, a new (albeit transitional) society must rise and fall: *l'ancien régime.*

2

L'Ancien régime:
Agreeable Wilderness,
Pleasant Solitude

I

The period from the Renaissance to the French Revolution corresponds in France to the early development of the capitalist mode of production. Although some scholars have attempted to locate the true origins of capitalism in the growth of towns and trade in the high and late Middle Ages,[1] Marx places the beginning of the "capitalist era" in the sixteenth century. He is followed in this dating not only by the Marxist economic historian Maurice Dobb, but also by the French historians of the *Annales* group: Henri Hauser and Henri Sée.[2]

In the sixteenth century, the merchant class that had been born in the towns of the later Middle Ages exercised an increasing control over the craftsman-producer; trade organizations controlled city governments and either escaped or limited the regulations of the craft guilds. Even more important, a privileged element arose within the craft guilds themselves. The master craftsmen became a more and more exclusive group by setting up increasingly high fees and requirements for entry into their ranks. They came to constitute a new class—nonworkers who were both manufacturers and merchants—and to create beneath them a class of wage laborers. According to Hauser, conflict between these workers and the new bourgeoisie was common from the reign of François I, and by the 1580s the powerlessness of the poor worker within the guild was complete. Thus by the late sixteenth century a source of profit and therefore of capital accumulation existed in the propertyless class of hired workers.[3]

Capital accumulation was also effected through an enormous increase in foreign trade and speculation; the medieval fairs had given way to international *bourses* based on credit. But still another method of accumulation existed for the bourgeoisie: the purchase of land. And, indeed, the owners of the land were often obliged to sell it. The crisis of the nobility in the late Middle Ages culminated in disaster in the sixteenth century, with the devaluation due to the influx of precious metals; the seigneur, living on a fixed income, was severely impoverished by the consequent rise of prices. He was obliged to sell his fief to the merchant, manufacturer–merchant, or royal administrator who wished to consolidate his new wealth in land. Many of these new landowners were ennobled in the process. This sort of land transfer seems to have accelerated in the last quarter of the sixteenth century.

The purchase of feudal lands by the bourgeoisie is of central importance in the transition from feudalism to capitalism, for it has the double result of consolidating bourgeois wealth and power, and completing the ruin of the old aristocracy. It is a crucial part of the process by which one ruling class supplants another. Thus not only is the bourgeois position strengthened, but the noble is obliged to remain as a poor *hobereau* on his land, often working it himself like a peasant, or to move to the royal court where he serves as the powerless minion of an increasingly autocratic monarchy. Many nobles who exercised their ancient military function in the wars of religion (the expenses of which contributed to their impoverishment) remained afterwards at the court. If they returned to their demesnes, it was as poor *gentilhommes campagnards*.

The growing importance of the royal court is matched by the growth of cities and a general movement of population from the countryside to urban centers. Again the center of gravity shifts—from the country and the rural demesne back to the court and city, in which industry is now organized on a higher level than at the close of antiquity.[4]

These major social transformations create a context for the reintroduction of the theme of solitude on the country estate. In French literature of the later sixteenth century the theme is adapted—often even directly imitated—from classical Roman literature. An "influence," however, can never in itself explain its adoption at a given moment nor the specific configuration it is given. A classical motif is adopted only when it corresponds to the needs of a new social situation. In sixteenth-century France, it is the shift of social gravity to an autocratic court and a reinvigorated city operating on a capitalist basis, with the division of the nobility into hobereau and courtier and the new bourgeois seigneur, which makes the classical theme of country solitude an "influence." The demesne, no longer the center of social activity, can become the location of the ideal.

The ideal is not of a single class, but of both the bourgeoisie and the nobility. In the evolution of culture the *ancien régime* is the period of transformation from an aristocratic, feudal vision of the world to the bourgeois vision of the nineteenth and twentieth centuries. The social phenomena connected with the ideal of country solitude are, as we have seen, a crucial part of the transitional process from one ruling class to another. Consequently the theme is of a cross-class nature. Both bourgeois and noble are employed by the monarch as court retainers and royal administrators; both the new bourgeois seigneur and the hobereau hold land. Moreover, the sixteenth century is the great period of class amalgamation: bourgeois are ennobled in greater numbers than ever before or after. Thus, as we shall see, the theme of solitude is expressed by a class spectrum from the *noblesse d'épée* to the ordinary bourgeois.

The classical influence upon sixteenth-century French literature is mediated first through several foreign sources. Already in the Italian Quattrocento the theme is important in the life and works of Petrarch. Established at the papal court in Avignon, Petrarch retired to a country house in the Vaucluse intermittently, between political missions, travels, and periods in Avignon. During the periods of public life and travel, Petrarch constantly yearned for the *solitaria vita* of the Vaucluse.[5]

The solitude of Vaucluse looks both backward and forward: backward to the farms of the classical Latin writers with which Petrarch consciously associates it [6] and forward to the mountainous, wild solitudes of Rousseau and the Romantics.[7] Vaucluse is in Haute Provence, at the foothills of the Alps, in an uneven terrain of crags and grottos, woods and valleys. In this retreat Petrarch is far from his beloved Laura in Avignon; yet she is always present to him in separation, as were the ladies of courtly lovers. In fact, the farther Petrarch is from Laura, the closer he is to her. As he wanders *solo y pensoso*, over mountains, woods, and open country, he holds continual conversation with Amor.[8]

Not only did Petrarch write often of his solitude in letters and poems; he also composed a Latin treatise on the life of solitude. *De Vita solitaria* is an apology for solitude and an encyclopedia of solitudes, both biblical-monastic and classical. Participating both in the receding medieval world view and the new Renaissance vision, it sets the two traditions of solitary life side by side, treating them as expressions of the same mode of existence opposed to that of the *dives*—the man who pursues wealth in cities. Indeed, while Petrarch enjoyed the humanistic pleasures of self-cultivation and poetry in his rustic retreat, his brother Gherardo chose the dominant medieval form of solitude; in 1342 he entered the Chartreuse de Montrieux. For Petrarch, these two forms of solitude are of the same essence.

A more contemporary influence on the French sixteenth century is the *Menosprecio de corte y alabanza de aldea* (1539; Contempt for the Court and Praise of the Village) by the Spanish bishop Antonio de Guevara. We find in the *Menosprecio* of Guevara, who was both an ecclesiastic and a nobleman, a blending of religious and humanist elements. But the classical Latin themes are predominant. One leaves the court to escape Fortune and the evils of ambition, avarice, hypocrisy, as did the Romans. But the world of court and city is even more evil now. Romans fled the age of iron to the country; now men must flee the "age of mud." [9]

The work is not simply an imitation of ancient writers. Guevara gives very concrete advice to those he might convince to take up country residence. They are advised not to accept a public position in their village, "because there is nothing so troublesome, nor so difficult for the mind to tolerate, as the burdensome charge of the common people." [10] He adds that this does not absolve the seigneur from helping and guiding the poor villager. Indeed, he offers seigneurial authority as an advantage that the powerless courtier does not enjoy: "Another privilege of village life is that the gentleman or bourgeois who lives there can be the greatest, or one of the greatest, in benevolence, honorable repute or authority . . . For men who have elevated thoughts but a low fortune, it would be better to live honored in a village than humbled and without favor at court." [11] This book is not addressed, then, only to the gentilhomme. The bourgeois is also invited to return to the land.

In this sixteenth-century version of the "mépris de la Cour," the positive ideal in opposition to court (and city) is no longer the peasant figure of Franc Gontier. It is the seigneur, often poor himself, but ruling the peasantry in his village and on his estate. The *Menosprecio* soon became a bible for Spanish gentlemen discontented with court life, and a literary model as well.[12]

Guevara's treatise was translated into French as early as 1542, in Lyon, at a time when the theme of the pleasures of rustic life was coming into vogue in France, and it seems to have had a direct influence upon Maurice Scève's eclogue, *Saulsaye* (1547). The appearance of the theme in the mid-sixteenth century corresponds to the revival of the classical eclogue and the motif of the Golden Age at the same time.[13] The three are often blended, as we may see in *Saulsaye*.

The full title of Scève's poem is *Saulsaye: eglogue de la vie solitaire.*
Two shepherds, Philerme (from Greek: lover of solitude) and Antire
(the contradictor), meet in a willow grove near Lyon and, in the final
section of the poem, they debate the merits of the solitary life. Philerme enunciates the classical protest against the cupidity, ambition,
and antagonism that reigns in cities. Antire responds by criticizing the
"idleness" of solitude and praising the virtuous life of acquisition:

But by pursuing gain one avoids the vice
Of idleness, from which many great evils result.
Moreover, for those who come to possess it
Through their own virtue, what they have acquired does them so much good
That they keep from commiting misdeeds for the sake of their honor.[14]

Later Antire adds that he who reaches "high degree" through acquisition is more respected than one who inherits it.[15] Antire, then, quite
clearly represents the new bourgeois ideology of striving after wealth
(an activity identified with virtue), opposed to the leisure of both
nobility and bourgeois who buy land and live as seigneurs. Philerme
responds with an *éloge* of the tranquility of country life and a long
passage on the delights of the shepherd's life, associated with that of
the seigneur ("Il est Seigneur des boys grans et espais").[16] Familiar
imagery also associates it with the Golden Age: the earth gives its
products to him unaided.

Here the shepherd is only a literary equivalent of the seigneur. This
seigneur flees city rather than court, and one of the qualities of the
shepherd is that he does not possess name or title.[17] The context of
the debate is entirely bourgeois in *Saulsaye:* should the wealthy Lyon-
nais leave city and business for the rustic pleasures of landowning?
Indeed, the aristocracy of the rich industrial and merchant city of Lyon
was principally made up of newly rich bourgeois rather than of nobles,
and Scève himself was from a wealthy and respected bourgeois
family.[18]

From the mid-century on, the theme of country solitude had an
increasing currency: in translations of Italian and Latin sources, in
prose and poetry, most notably of the Pléiade,[19] and in small collec-
tions specifically devoted to the theme, including poems (or excerpts)
by several authors.[20] Some of the writers were bourgeois or ennobled
bourgeois, many descended from feudal nobility. Often these praises
of country life offer not only an ideal for the seigneur but also an
ideological justification of the peasant's servitude; the peasant's happiness is made to depend precisely on his simple needs and lack of
ambition. If he aspired to a better life he would no longer be happy.[21]
In one poem, the hobereau is pictured hunting, gardening, overseeing

the work in the fields, and watching the woodcutter chop.[22] This last detail illustrates the relationship between pastoral and seigneurial solitude. The image remains the same while the social role shifts; Franc Gontier chops wood, while the rural seigneur watches it being chopped. The two roles can be blended, however; to the extent that the seigneur is poor and must do the physical labor himself, his life more and more resembles that of the peasant.

In these sixteenth-century works the theme of country solitude blends with the pastoral, as it had in Roman antiquity. Seigneurial solitude and peasant happiness are two sides of the same coin: the ideal of rustic life on the estate, which is a "Republic"[23] in itself and which dimly reflects the mythical community of the Golden Age. At about the same time, another writer, drawing upon Seneca, writes a philosophic meditation accenting the individualistic tendency of the theme: Michel de Montaigne.

Montaigne came from a family of Bordeaux merchants who bought the land of Montaigne at the end of the fifteenth century. His father held several high magisterial positions in Bordeaux, was ennobled in 1519, and became mayor of the city in 1554. In the same year Montaigne himself became a *conseiller* at the Cour des Aides de Perigueux and, in 1557, a member of the Parliament of Bordeaux. Thus the family was not only of the newly ennobled and landed bourgeoisie, but specifically of the *noblesse de robe*—nobility based on the purchase of office.

In 1570 Montaigne resigned from his public position and retired to his estate, where he soon began composition of the *Essais*. Chapter 39 of book one of the *Essais*, entitled "De la solitude," was composed largely between 1572 and 1574.[24] Following Seneca, Montaigne points out that the wise man can live alone in the crowd of city or court, but that he will choose country retreat: "It is not that the wise man cannot live anywhere content, yes, and alone in a palace crowd; but if he has the choice, says he, he will flee even the sight of a throng. He will endure it, if need be, but if it is up to him he will choose solitude."[25] The wise man can withdraw into himself when he is in society, and thus enjoy a certain solitude within society. This solitude—a temporary, voluntary, and tranquil withdrawal—is by no means similar to the modern form, which is a permanent, anguished awareness of the opacity of human consciousness, an inescapable, unwanted psychic isolation. Montaigne's wise man, on the other hand, is not unable to communicate with men in society; he simply chooses to "shut off" this communication on occasion so as to enjoy the richness of his own inner world. Moreover, such solitude is in fact easier to enjoy in retreat.

Even in retreat, however, the wise man must withdraw from the people and things upon which he might become dependent: family, servants, and property.

We should have wife, children, goods, and above all health, if we can; but we must not bind ourselves to them so strongly that our happiness depends on them. We must reserve a back shop all our own, entirely free, in which to establish our real liberty and our principal retreat and solitude. Here our ordinary conversation must be between us and ourselves, and so private that no outside association or communication can find a place; here we must talk and laugh as if without wife, without children, without possessions, without retinue and servants, so that, when the time comes to lose them, it will be nothing new to us to do without them . . . Let us not fear that in this solitude we shall stagnate in tedious idleness: "In solitude be to thyself a throng." TIBULLUS.[26]

Here then, is a radical rejection of "la vie commune"—life with others not only in society but in the society outside society: the estate.

In the society of others we do not live for ourselves. The soldier, scholar, courtier, and even the landowner, each responds to the desires and concerns of others.[27] We must learn to live an inner life that is entirely for ourselves. The implication of Montaigne's reflections on solitude is that the true life, in which we are not "alienated" from ourselves, is the solitary, inner life rather than life with others. This conception is the polar opposite of the Marxist interpretation of alienation which identifies alienation with solitude. For Montaigne, since one cannot realize oneself in "la vie commune," one must withdraw to do so. This radically individualistic trend of the theme will later became separated from country solitude altogether. For the Romantics, self-realization will consist in the cultivation of the poet's solitary soul within the bounds of the city, but aloof from it.

II

The poems of country solitude in the seventeenth century are often anthology pieces, and the theme is given its classic statement at the beginning of the century by the Marquis de Racan, in the well-known "Stances" (ca. 1618). The "Stances" are an invitation to retire to the country after a full life of public service—addressed to a gentilhomme friend who owns a neighboring demesne. The poet and his companion are like ships coming into a calm haven after a voyage on turbulent seas; they will find respite on their land from the "winds of favor" that agitate court life. The poet addresses his land in the last stanza:

Agreeable wilderness, abode of innocence
Where, far from vanities and splendor,
My repose begins and my tourment ends,
Valleys, rivers, rocks, pleasant solitude,
If you were at first witness to my disquietude,
Be witness henceforth to my contentment.[28]

Allusions to the Golden Age continue to occur—in the "Stances" and elsewhere, as in one of Guez de Balzac's letters (September 4, 1622), written from his *désert:* there remains in the innocent virtue of the village peasants "several grains of that gold of which the first centuries were made." [29] But for Balzac to achieve this state of innocence within himself, he must leave both village and manor to visit a secret spot known only to him:

I also sometimes go down into that valley, which is the most secret part of my wilderness (*désert*), and which until now was not known to anyone . . . If I pause ever so little there, it seems to me that I return to my first innocence. My desires, my fears and my hopes cease all of a sudden; all the movements of my soul abate and I have no passions whatsoever, or if I have any, I govern them like tamed beasts.[30]

Balzac enjoys a *double* retreat: the solitude of his estate, with the community of peasants and household, and within it, the further retreat to an uncultivated, wilder spot where he is alone with himself. This second solitude is the physical equivalent of Montaigne's retreat from his household into the "back shop" of his inner self.

In this early period of the century, another form of retreat is pictured by the baroque, or "grotesque," poets. In the ode "La Solitude" by Saint-Amant, the solitude is not a country estate at all, but the wild terrain of Belle-Ile on the coast of Brittany. Instead of a placid, rural demesne that calms disquietude if one settles there, Saint-Amant visits solitudes that "delight my disquietude" ("plaisent à mon inquietude").[31] The landscape is rugged: precipices, wild torrents, jagged shores, swamps, forests. The ode inspired several other poets of the period. Best known is Théophile de Viau's "La Solitude" (1621), in which the location of the solitude is a deep forest, cold, shadowy, and windy. The forest solitudes of the Middle Ages were feared and avoided rather than visited with delectation—an indication both of a changed attitude and of the growing domestication of forest areas.

The early seventeenth century, then, sees the expression of both the classic rural solitude and a wilder one—though still eccentric—in the "grotesque" poets Saint-Amant and Théophile.[32] At the same time, in opposition to the current of praise for rural life, a certain court literature develops (sometimes in the form of ballets and mascarades performed at court), which ridicules the figure and life of the country gentleman in favor of the refinement of court and salon life. It will continue into the later seventeenth and eighteenth centuries, a function of the continuing antagonism between court/city and country.[33] This literature provides the reverse image of the "mépris de la Cour."

The evolution toward absolute monarchy, which had begun at the end of the Middle Ages, of course culminates in the reign of Louis XIV. Already under Henri IV and Louis XIII a bureaucratic machinery had developed, which controlled not only the nobility, whose position had already been weakened in the sixteenth century, but also the upper bourgeoisie of the *robe*. This control was effected largely through the agency of the *intendants*, public inspectors who assured royal control of the apparatus of power throughout the provinces. At the same time, as we have already seen, the nobility was lured to court where, dependent on the good will of the monarch, it fell more and more under royal control. The monarchy's control over both classes reached its peak under Louis XIV.[34]

From 1670 the royal court was established at Versailles, a court more authoritarian than all previous French courts. Alongside Versailles, Paris dominated the provincial cities as a cultural center; together they constituted "La Cour et la Ville." Erich Auerbach, in his study of the sociological meaning of that expression, which became current in the second half of the century, shows that its two elements form a coherent whole, making up the literary public to which classical works were addressed. "La Cour" was made up largely of the nobles who had left their land to seek favor at court. "La Ville," on the other hand, referred specifically to the elite of the Parisian bourgeoisie.[35]

The noblesse de robe formed the "connecting link" between court nobility and urban *grande bourgeoisie*:

Spreading side by side with prosperity, humanism, and its ideal of *otium cum dignitate* also encouraged the flight of the bourgeois from their class . . . by now these *grands bourgeois* had become *honnêtes gens*, to whom it did not even occur to repair their fortunes by business activity—instead, they sought the help of the king or his entourage, more lucrative offices, pensions, sinecures. They had become totally parasitic. This phenomenon of mass flight from economic life shows us a new aspect of *la ville*, which accounts for what it had in common with *la cour*.[36]

Thus a relatively homogeneous literary public under Louis XIV consists largely of nobility and an increasingly important robe, both dependent on the monarchy and both owners of land to which they may retreat from "La Cour et la Ville"; this retreat is one aspect of the ideal of *otium cum dignitate*.

During the reign of Louis XIV the majority of writers belong to the intermediate class of the robe; a minority belongs to either the nobility or the merchant and manufacturing bourgeoisie.[37] In the preceding discussion of the theme of country solitude in sixteenth- and early seventeenth-century writers, the majority were of noble origin. Now we find expressions of the theme of retreat—and satire of "La Cour et la Ville"—in La Fontaine's *Fables*, in the *Epîtres* of Boileau, and in La Bruyère's *Caractères*.[38] All of these major authors of the period descend from and frequent the milieu of the robe. Consequently, although the theme cuts across classes throughout the ancien régime, the shift in class equilbrium in society at large is reflected in the changing class patterns of authorship.

The classical French writers, like their classical Roman counterparts, carefully distinguish rural retreat—either occasional or at the end of a career—from permanent, misanthropic withdrawal from society. The life of court and city, however, seems to have sometimes made this latter alternative alluring. The eleventh book of Fénelon's *Télémaque* (1699) recounts how King Idoménée is misled by an ambitious flatterer, his adviser Protésilas, to order the death of the virtuous officer Philoclès. When Philoclès is attacked, and learns that he is falsely accused of conspiracy against the state, he withdraws to the isle of Samos to live in solitude. There he lives like a hermit, in a cave, eating simple foods and reading to make himself a better man. When Idoménée's government is reformed by Mentor, an officer is sent to bring Philoclès back. He responds:

Do you see . . . this grotto, better suited for hiding wild beasts than for being inhabited by men? For so many years now I have tasted more sweetness and repose than in the gilded palaces of Crete. Men no longer deceive me; for I no longer see men, I no longer hear their talk, poisoned with flattery; I no longer need them; my hands, hardened by work, easily give me the simple nourishment that I require . . . But he [Protésilas] did me no harm; on the contrary, he did me the greatest good; he delivered me from the tumult and servitude of business; I owe to him my cherished solitude, and all the innocent pleasures I experience in it.[39]

But the envoy Hégésippe criticizes this irresponsible misanthropy: "Are you then, he said to him, insensitive to the pleasure of seeing again your kin and friends, who yearn for your return . . .? Is it permissible to give oneself over to a wild philosophy, to prefer oneself to the rest of the human race, and to prefer ones repose to the welfare of ones compatriots?" [40] When he learns that such is also the will of the gods, Philoclès dutifully returns home. He soon asks permission to retire to a solitude nearby where he is consulted daily by the king and Mentor. This is the proper solitude for an upright gentleman: a limited retreat analogous to that of the country estate.[41]

Only certain forms of religious solitude are complete and permanent. In seventeenth-century France, as in the late Roman empire, the more radical form of withdrawal from society is religious. We must appreciate the distance, for instance, between Pliny and Anthony, and between Boileau and the Solitaires of Port Royal. The nunnery of Port Royal, fallen at the close of the sixteenth century into the worldliness and corruption toward which monastic communities always tended, was reformed in the early seventeenth century by the young abbess Mère Angélique. Soon the nunnery also became a center of Jansenism under the influence of the abbot Saint Cyran. In 1637, Antoine Le Maître, the first of the Solitaires, retired to Port Royal and was followed by members of the Arnauld family as well as others such as Nicole and Pascal. This lay community of men was constituted largely from families of the robe. True solitude for the Jansenists means complete disengagement from the "world"; the world is totally evil, and the only alternative for the Christian is radical retreat from that society of the kind practiced by the Solitaires.[42]

Lucien Goldmann, in his sociological study of Pascal and Racine, seeks to demonstrate "the link between the economic and social situation of officers in the seventeenth century, at the same time attached and opposed to a particular form of State, absolute monarchy, which could not in any way satisfy them . . . and the tragic, Jansenist ideology of the *essential* vanity of the world and salvation in retreat and solitude." [43] But though it is true that the Jansenist vision in its specificity may be linked to the relation between robe and absolute monarchy, we have seen that retreats from society—including radical religious forms of retreat—took place long before the social situation analysed in detail by Goldmann. Some further explanation is necessary, therefore, to embrace the whole tradition of retreat from society.

On the basis of the evidence, one must reject an interpretation that would define the theme as the expression of one class—the nobility—which is dying, which therefore withdraws from social life and glorifies that withdrawal. The theme is expressed not only by the entrenched nobility, but by the robe and the urban bourgeoisie (as we shall see, the theme will be extended and transformed by Rousseau and the early Romantics). As the balance of social forces changes, and as these changes are reflected in the predominance of one class or another in the major authors of the period, the theme passes from one group to another and is altered by its particular class perspective; but a basic continuity makes the theme a cross-class phenomenon.

Why does such a continuity exist? Recalling the many manifestations of the theme, both in classical antiquity and ancien régime France, we might view the unifying principle of solitary retreat as a revolt against the conditions of a new social order—the early market economy, the beginnings of industrialism, and, in the sixteenth century, the full advent of capitalist organization. The theme is an expression of early revolt in the prehistory and early history of capitalism. Country retreat is defined in opposition to many aspects of the new order: trade, war, the autocratic court, even the early forms of urban ugliness and pollution.[44] But the essence of the critique does not lie in any one specific institution. It lies in the very nature of the new order. Country solitude is always a retreat from a society based on competition, antagonism, self-interest. Appearing under many guises, as ambition, avarice, flattery, hypocrisy, luxury, and the like, the underlying principle remains the same. In a society increasingly ruled by money, self-interest becomes a primary motive of human conduct.

Over against this society based on antagonism and competition, retreat is a search for lost community among men. It is often associated metaphorically with mythical, ideal communities—the Golden Age, the Kingdom of Heaven—where men live united. The estate is sometimes conceived as a community more perfect than the one left behind (the estate as a "royaume," "empire," or "république" which the seigneur rules beneficently), and the monastery in its purer manifestations is an attempt to create a fraternal community that does not know self-interest. Yet the theme of retreat to solitude is often informed with the ideology of the order it spurns; it is in many cases itself an expression of the new individualism. From Pliny and Seneca to Montaigne, the humanist tradition of country retreat conceives of rural solitude as a means to retreat into oneself. The new community is not exterior—the estate itself—but the interior "crowd" within oneself. The solitary is himself a community; he communes with his ideas and his readings. Likewise the hermit communes with God and men through private meditation, and even the monk's life is largely devoted to solitary meditation—his secondary retreat from monastery life.

Thus while the theme transcends the new social order in protesting the antagonism that rules human relations, it reflects at the same time the new bourgeois ideology of individualism. Ideal and ideology are joined in the paradox that community is sought in the individual. Conversely, in seeking retreat on the seigneurial estate, on the land that endures as money does not, the theme reflects the vision of the feudal aristocracy, even when expressed by a *robin* or bourgeois (who buys land and wishes to live a noble style of life). The noble or the bourgeois ideological element is given more or less weight in different texts.[45]

I have suggested that solitary retreat is an escape from the competition and self-interest inherent in capitalism. But these forces are precisely the agents of social fragmentation, which in the introductory pages of this study are identified as the root cause of solitude *within* society. Does solitude in society exist then already in the ancien régime? Georg Lukács in *The Theory of the Novel* considers solitude to be part of the vision of the novel, from its beginnings in *Don Quixote*. In this study, which precedes his adoption of a Marxist perspective, Lukács defines as "closed civilisations" the worlds that produce Greek tragedy and the feudal epic; in these literatures men are united in a network of fixed social and religious relationships. Only with the advent of the novel does the individual face the world as a separate, solitary unit:

Thus this first great novel of world literature stands at the beginning of the era in which the God of Christendom begins to abandon the world; in which man becomes solitary and is able to find meaning and substance only in his own soul, which is nowhere at home; in which the world, set free from its paradoxical anchorage in a "beyond" that is also present, is abandoned to the immanence of his own meaninglessness.[46]

To this affirmation by the pre-Marxist Lukács, we might counterpose his later statement in *History and Class Consciousness* concerning reification: "Commodity fetishism is a *specific* problem of our age, the age of modern capitalism . . . The distinction between a society where this form is dominant, permeating every expression of life, and a society where it only makes an episodic appearance is essentially one of quality." [47] Solitude, alienation, and reification are aspects of the same indissoluble whole. Thus Lukács' comment applies equally to the phenomenon of solitude in society. Although the *basic causes* of solitude in society are already in existence in ancien régime France—the early developments of capitalism discussed above and the concomitant rationalism and individualism that accompany the rise of the bourgeoisie—nonetheless these forces are not yet dominant, and they do not yet inform all aspects of human life in that period.

Although men in the new order to a large extent already act as separate, isolated individuals, the social structure of this transitional period still contains many solidarities carried over from the old feudal order. The new social and economic forms have not made the quantitative advance that culminates in a qualitative change. Consequently, they have not yet created a conscious awareness of solitude in society.

We might say, however, that there does exist a partial and implicit awareness of solitude in society—a solitude that is still only episodic. The word *isolé*, borrowed in the sixteenth century from the Italian word meaning "like an island" and first used as an architectural term,[48] became a *mot à la mode* [49] under Louis XIV; it was applied to men who are not tied to others by bonds of family, love, and such. Thus La Bruyère writes of the courtier: "[He] has no retinue; he is without obligations and human bonds; he may be surrounded by relatives and other human beings, but they are not essential to him; he is detached from everything and, as it were, isolated (*isolé*)." [50] The word does not yet have its modern meaning, however, which includes the consciousness of one's own solitude. It is still close to its geographical and architectural meanings of separateness and disconnection.

In "A Moral Essay, Preferring Solitude to Publick Employment," also written in the latter part of the seventeenth century, the Scotsman Sir George Mackenzie develops the paradox that there is more society in solitude than in courts and other high places:

But albeit Society were to be valued at the Rate imagined, yet solitary Persons enjoy more the Sweets of Society, than great Men do: For in all Addresses to these, the Addressers consider only what is fit for their private Interest; and little else is added, besides the dropping of a flattering Expression or two: And when any disinterested Subject is fallen upon with them, it is spoke to with so much Constraint, and the Speakers are so hemm'd in by Discretion and Respect, that the Discourse is manag'd with much Disadvantage.[51]

Although the principal matter of the essay is a traditional praise of country retreat and self-cultivation, inspired largely by Seneca, this passage suggests a paradox that is implicit in the theme: one flees *from* the solitude of conflicting interests in society *to* the solitude of community in rural retreat. This paradox is not fully developed, however, and it is not generalized. The passage does not directly associate solitude and society, and it refers only to the constrained conversation between princes and other "great Men" and their followers. Indeed, the paradox cannot be given full expression, since the mixed, transitional nature of society has not yet created a consciousness of the isolation of the individual in society.

These considerations suggest the far limits of awareness of solitude in society in the ancien régime. The Pascalian vision of *deus abscon-ditus* represents the far limits of metaphysical solitude for this period. Already in the seventeenth century not only the human community but also the religious community of God and man are beginning to break down; rationalism is corroding the medieval world view in the initial phase of a religious crisis that will culminate in the late nineteenth and twentieth centuries. Lucien Goldmann points out that Pascal comes at the Cartesian turning point in the development of rationalism.[52] For the tragic, Jansenist consciousness, God is now hidden, both ever present and ever absent, and the world is blind to him altogether. Since the tragic consciousness requires certainty, Goldmann concludes, the tragic vision includes the solitude of man: "But the absolute demand for theoretical and practical certainty also implies a second consequence: the *solitude* of man between a blind world and a hidden and mute God. For between tragic man—who accepts only the univocal and the absolute—and the contradictory, ambiguous world, no dialogue is ever under any circumstances possible."[53]

Indeed, in a meditation on the "Mystère de Jesus," Pascal portrays—almost two centuries before Romanticism—the solitude of Jesus in Gethsemane, abandoned by his sleeping disciples. Yet while in this passage Jesus is alone on earth, among uncomprehending men, he is not separated from heaven. Only God knows of his suffering, and Jesus prays to him: "Jesus, seeing all of his friends asleep and all his enemies vigilant, gives himself entirely to his Father."[54] And Pascal himself knew the presence of God; he writes in the "Mémorial," in the throes of a mystical experience, "Certainty. Certainty. Feeling. Peace . . . Forgetfulness of the world and of everything, except God."[55] Thus Pascal's hidden God must not be confused with the religious crisis of the death of God and the consequent solitude of man in an indifferent and absurd universe. This crisis occurs only in the nineteenth century after having been prepared by the deistic and atheistic theories of the *philosophes*, and the further progress of rationalism and the sciences. For Pascal, God is always *both* absent and present to man.

III

After the economic depression of the seventeenth century, marked by periodic famines and epidemics, the eighteenth century experiences prosperity and industrial expansion. From about 1730 an increasing agricultural prosperity was accompanied by industrial growth, further developed by the introduction, later in the century, of newly invented machines from England. This industrial development ensured the increasing dominance both of the bourgeois class and of urban society. During the Regency that followed the death of Louis XIV, the royal court was moved from Versailles to Paris, and the center of cultural life shifted entirely from the court to Parisian salons and cafés.

The bourgeoisie now dominated cultural life; both the writers and the wealthy financiers whose patronage they sought came from that class. And the larger reading public (writers began to attempt to support themselves by the sale of their writings) was constituted principally of the middle class. With the dissolution of the autocratic court, a freer and more audacious intellectual and social life became possible for a largely bourgeois intelligentsia.[56]

Although nobles and rentiers continue to live on their estates either permanently or for part of the year,[57] the praise of country solitude is not an important theme in the eighteenth century as it was in the seventeenth. The dominant attitude toward solitude is elaborated in the *Encyclopédie*—a product of the bourgeois intelligentsia at the center of cultural life. The author of the article on *le solitaire* comments:

> It seems to me that in our tranquil era a truly robust virtue is one that walks firmly through obstacles, and not one that flees them. Of what merit is that weak-complexioned wisdom that cannot tolerate the open air, nor live among men without contracting the contagion of their vices, and that fears leaving an idle solitude so as to escape corruption? . . . A *solitary* is, in regard to the rest of mankind, like an inanimate being; his prayers and his contemplative life, which no one sees, have no influence on society, which has more need of examples of virtue before its eyes than in the forests.[58]

Likewise in the articles on *la solitude* and *le philosophe*, the author warns against total religious or philosophical retreat, while adding that the Christian philosopher may better himself by occasional retreat. The emphasis is on the danger of misanthropic or "fanatical" religious solitude, and on the pleasures of society, rather than upon the benefits of occasional retirement. The conception of solitude—as a retreat from society—remains the same, but the attitude has noticeably changed. For the *philosophes*, man is above all a social being. Thus he must not only not withdraw himself to a solitude where he is unable to exercise this social being, but he also must not stand aloof within society.

The *Encyclopédie* includes an article on the word *isoler*. After giving its architectural meaning as primary, the *encyclopédiste* adds:

An isolated man is free and independent; he is dependent on nothing else. One saves oneself much affliction, but one also deprives oneself of many pleasures by *isolating oneself (s'isolant)*. Is there more to be won than lost? I really don't know. But experience has taught me that there are many circumstances in which the *isolated (isolé)* man becomes useless to himself and others; if danger presses upon him, no one knows him, no one is interested in him, nor reaches a hand out to him. He has neglected everyone, so he cannot solicit aid in a moment of need.[59]

This commentary indicates several things: that the separate, independent individual continues to be a current conception; that the man who is *isolé* is not isolated in the modern sense, but only independent; and that the philosophes consider this aloof independence to be antisocial and therefore reprehensible.

In the eighteenth century not only is the traditional solitude of retreat deemphasized and even frowned upon, but the new solitude within society that will infect modern times—the failure of communication—is unimaginable. Robert Mauzi, in a study of the idea of happiness in the eighteenth century, makes this clear:

In fact, never was man less conceived as a solitary being. Never did man think less in terms of the particular vocation of the individual soul, or in terms of that difficult problem that the philosophers have since called the *communication of consciousnesses*. For the eighteenth century, man's aptitude for deciphering his fellow men, for revealing himself to them, goes without saying. The mystery of the individual is not recognized. No one can desire solitude, unless he is a "misanthrope," that is, a monster, or a "vaporish man," that is, a madman. The essence of man is to be a sociable animal. Man alone becomes a living chimera, or he is taken for a *méchant* —which was Rousseau's mishap.[60]

The conception is just the opposite from Montaigne's: if man's essential being is in social communication, then he is "alienated" from himself, and he does not really exist at all, when he withdraws from society. Criticizing the solitude of retreat,[61] and not yet conscious of solitude within society, the eighteenth-century bourgeois writer does not develop any thematics of solitude.

Nor do we yet find in the French novel, in which often an individual hero encounters all levels of society in his travels and adventures, any real consciousness of solitude. Gil Blas, for instance, is an isolated individual on the road, but he does not experience his rootless wanderings in society as solitude. It is rather in the English novel (capitalism developed earlier and more completely in England than in France) that we encounter both the most advanced awareness of solitude in society and the greatest bourgeois optimism. *Robinson Crusoe* (1719), as Ian Watt has suggested, must be interpreted as an allegory of the triumphant and cheerful solitude of the individual in capitalist society.[62]

Particularly interesting is the first chapter of Defoe's sequel, *Serious Reflections of Robinson Crusoe* (1720): "Of Solitude." The bulk of the essay is given over to an argument against solitary retreat for the Christian (a point of view shared by the encyclopedists). Rather than retire to a monastery or a hermitage, the Christian should retire into himself. With the proper mental retirement, one can be alone in the midst of men and business. This is a theme already familiar to us in Seneca and Montaigne, but here Defoe carries it further. Whereas for the two humanists inner retreat is easier in a country solitude, for Defoe the opposite is true; solitary meditation is easier in society than in an austere solitude where one is obliged constantly to provide for one's material needs. Thus Crusoe is more alone as he writes his reflections in London than he was on his island.[63]

But there is an ambiguity in Defoe's notion of solitude within society. Speaking of life on a desert island, Crusoe says: "Sometimes I have as much wondered why it should be any grievance or affliction, seeing upon the whole view of the stage of life which we act upon in this world it seems to me that life in general is, or ought to be, but one universal act of solitude." [64] The ambiguity lies between "is" and "ought to be." The main body of the essay argues that the life of the meditative Christian in society *ought to be* a solitude, but one important passage suggests that man *is* necessarily alone in society:

All reflection is carried home, and our dear self is, in one respect, the end of living. Hence man may be properly said to be alone in the midst of the crowds and hurry of men and business. All the reflections which he makes are to himself; all that is pleasant he embraces for himself; all that is irksome and grievous is tasted but by his own palate.

What are the sorrows of other men to us, and what their joy? Something we may be touched indeed with by the power of sympathy, and a secret turn of the affections; but all the solid reflection is directed to ourselves. Our meditations are all solitude in perfection; our passions are all exercised in retirement; we love, we hate, we covet, we enjoy, all in privacy and solitude. All that we communicate of those things to any other is but for their assistance in the pursuit of our desires; the end is at home; the enjoyment, the contemplation, is all solitude and retirement; it is for ourselves we enjoy, and for ourselves we suffer.[65]

This passage generalizes, as none of the passages previously cited do, the necessary solitude of the egocentric individual in society. We communicate only our own desires, so that others may help us achieve them; the roots of solitude are in self-interest. Such a conception (episodic though it still is) contrasts sharply with the encyclopedists' view of solitude as misanthropic retreat opposed to the uncomplicated pleasure of social relations.

In France the turning point between the ancien régime and the modern era for the theme of solitude (as for much else besides) comes with Rousseau. In his two *Discours* (1750, 1753), Rousseau carries the classic critique of hypocrisy, flattery, ambition, and the like, to a higher level of consciousness. He writes in the *Discours sur les sciences et les arts:*

Before art had moulded our behavior, and taught our passions to speak an artificial language, our morals were rude but natural; and the different ways in which we behaved proclaimed at the first glance the difference of our dispositions. Human nature was not at bottom better then than now; but men found their security in the ease with which they could see through one another . . . In our day, now that more subtle study and a more refined taste have reduced the art of pleasing to a system, there prevails in modern manners a servile and deceptive conformity . . . We no longer dare seem what we really are . . . Thus we never know with whom we have to deal . . . What a train of vices must attend this uncertainty! Sincere friendship, real esteem, and perfect confidence are banished from among men.[66]

In the *Discours sur l'origine de l'inégalité parmi les hommes* we learn the cause of this evil:

On the other hand, free and independent as men were before, they were now, in consequence of a multiplicity of new wants, brought into subjection, as it were, to all nature, and particularly to one another; and each became in some degree a slave even in becoming the master of other men: if rich, they stood in need of the services of others; if poor, of their assistance; and even a middle condition did not enable them to do without one another. Man must now, therefore, have been perpetually employed in getting others to interest themselves in his lot, and in making them, apparently at least, if not really, find their advantage in promoting his own . . . Insatiable ambition, the thirst of raising their respective fortunes, not so much from real want as from the desire to surpass others, inspired secret jealousy, which is the more dangerous, as it puts on the mask of benevolence, to carry its point with greater security. In a word, there arose rivalry and competition on the one hand, and conflicting interests on the other, together with a secret desire on both of profiting at the expense of others. All these evils were the first effects of property, and the inseparable attendants of growing inequality.[67]

In society based on property, then, men are masters, slaves, and enemies to one another; to realize their self-interest they must manipulate other men, through either force or guile. Relations based on antagonism and deception are false relations, which do not allow men to know each other. Here Rousseau clearly points to the relationship between capitalism and solitude in society, although he identifies the social malady described with the advent of property—a notion that is left vague but that would at any rate antedate the advent of capitalism. It is no coincidence that Rousseau, one of the principal precursors of nineteenth-century socialism and Marxism, should also discover the solitude in society which was implicit in the ancien régime period. In his novel *La Nouvelle Héloïse* (1761) this solitude appears for the first time in French literature, although still episodically.

Most of the novel's action takes place outside the city, but at the end of Part Two (letters 13–27) Saint-Preux writes to Julie from Paris. He first experiences Paris as a desert solitude:

I enter this vast desert of people with a secret dread. This chaos only offers me a frightful solitude in which a dismal silence reigns. My soul in the crowd attempts to pour itself out, but everywhere finds itself closed in. "I am never less alone than when I am alone," said an ancient author; for my part, I am only alone in the crowd, where I can give myself neither to you nor to others. My heart would like to speak but it feels that it is not being listened to at all.[68]

Saint-Preux goes on to satirize the evils that were associated with property in the *Discours sur l'origine de l'inégalité*. He concludes the same letter: "Judge for yourself if I am right to call this crowd a desert, and to be frightened by a solitude in which I find only a vain semblance of feelings and of truth . . . So far I have seen many masks, but when will I see faces of men?"[69]

Further on Saint-Preux makes it clear that he is not analyzing Paris and Parisians, but the City and inhabitants of any big city.[70] Saint-Preux feels himself becoming corrupted by the enveloping atmosphere of the city, and is delighted at night to return to his lodging and retreat into himself. This solitary existence of Saint-Preux in Paris prefigures the solitude of the urban poet of the nineteenth century. But the solitude of rural retreat remains the dominant theme in *Héloïse*. While expressing the theme in its traditional form, Rousseau also extends, or "radicalizes" it.

As I have pointed out, most of the action takes place outside the city. The estate of Clarens, where Julie settles with her noble husband Wolmar, is a well-ordered community ruled by a beneficent seigneur. The goodness of Wolmar and Julie makes harmonious relations possible between masters and servants, while strictly maintaining the social hierarchy.[71] Within this traditional rural solitude, there are two "secondary" solitudes of the type illustrated in one of Balzac's letters. Julie walks in a hidden orchard that has been artfully planted so as to give the impression of a wild, natural solitude. She calls it her "Elysée." On the other side of the manor is an orchard that is in fact wild, where the lovers once walked. The wild orchard is the solitude of nature and passions (Saint-Preux), whereas the planted orchard is the solitude of nature and reason (Wolmar).

Beyond the estate lies the wild nature of the mountains. Before Julie's marriage to Wolmar, Saint-Preux had written her describing the mountain country and the simple, uncorrupted peasants of Le Valais. He had afterward returned to another solitude on the other side of the lake from where Julie was living, to be nearer to her. These solitudes are located in a wild Swiss landscape of mountains, boulders, and rushing torrents. They are associated with Saint-Preux's passion and the melancholy of the lovers' suffering, while the country estate is the domain of Wolmar, to whom Julie is joined in a *mariage de convenance*.

Thus Rousseau introduces in *Héloïse* a new solitude that has hardly ever been sought before [72]—the wild solitudes that in the Middle Ages men avoided in fear of robbers and beasts. They now become the environment in which a harmony is established with the agitated and melancholy soul of the Romantic poet or lover. Although appearing only momentarily, like the solitude of Paris, the mountain solitude of Saint-Preux is an important radicalization of the retreat theme; the urban bourgeois now retreats beyond the rural estate (which as land is noble in origin) to a place that is the polar opposite of the civilized city. Such is the "romantic" solitude of the Isle de Saint Pierre and the exotic solitude of Bernardin's *Paul et Virginie* (1787).[73]

Although Rousseau is highly original in introducing a new thematics of solitude (indeed, with Rousseau for the first time solitude becomes an obsessive, central concern; words relating to solitude are repeated constantly, and the theme colors his entire work), nonetheless he is a product of the eighteenth century as well. As Robert Mauzi has shown, in the little-known "Lettres sur la vertu et le bonheur" Rousseau asserts that man's natural state and greatest happiness are in society rather than in solitary retreat. Rousseau writes, for instance: "If man lived isolated he would have few advantages over the other animals. It is in mutual frequentation that his most sublime faculties develop and the excellence of his nature is revealed. While thinking only of providing for his needs, he acquires, through the commerce of his fellows, the feelings that should make him happy and the knowledge that should enlighten him." [74] These lines could just as well have been written by an encyclopedist.

Mauzi rightly points to an ambivalence in Rousseau's thought, which is the result of his transitional situation between the eighteenth century and the modern era: "If sociability leads to transparency and the union of souls, it is certain that it expresses all of man and contains his happiness. But if it volatizes into the vanity of appearance, it only reflects a distorted man, separated from himself, unhappy. Depending on whether Rousseau is envisaging the first or the second term of the alternative, he opts for sociability or solitude." [75]

The synthesis of these two poles of thought—poles beyond which the ancien régime does not go, illustrated by Montaigne on the one hand and the encyclopedists on the other—will produce the dialectic, Marxist interpretation. For Marxist interpretation, *both* terms of the antithesis are true: man is a social being, and he is alienated from that social being in the present society. From this understanding follows the necessity of changing society to allow the human being to realize his happiness in society. In the pre-Revolutionary period this intellectual step is impossible, for the idea of radical social transformation is unimaginable. For Rousseau it is therefore one or the other, not both: either man realizes his being in society, as manifested in *present* society, or he is alienated in society and must retreat from it. For the dialectic of solitude, and for the full-fledged crisis of solitude in society, we must await the nineteenth century and the advent of advanced industrial capitalism.

3

Modern Times

I

Although it was not until the 1830s that the Industrial Revolution gained real amplitude in France, the period from the French Revolution to 1830 saw the beginnings of full-scale industrialization. Under the Empire and Restoration, factories multiplied and grew, and technical innovations greatly increased productivity. The industrial cities expanded rapidly and, with them, the power of the bourgeoisie—especially the new industrialists. Most of these trends had already been set in motion in the ancien régime, but their sudden acceleration in the early nineteenth century transformed a quantitative evolution into a qualitative change.[1]

The Romantic movement, which developed in conjunction with the advent of mature capitalism and touched virtually all European countries, came to fruition in the early years of the nineteenth century in Germany and England; in France, on the other hand, a full-fledged movement occurred only in the 1820s. In Germany there were strong Romantic strains already in the "Sturm und Drang" movement, in Schiller and in the early Goethe. Goethe's *Sorrows of Werther* (1774), which portrays a solitary young commoner largely alienated from social life, was as important an influence in Europe as Rousseau's *La Nouvelle Héloïse*.[2] Indeed, the Romantic attitude toward life, and the figure of the isolated genius in particular, is by virtue of its peculiar history a feature of German culture in general.

Following the Thirty Years' War in the seventeenth century, German economic, social, and political development was severely retarded; Germany never developed a strong commercial bourgeoisie and remained divided into semifeudal principalities. The German intelligentsia had little or no influence on political and social life, and was not nurtured by a centralized court or an educated bourgeois public. Sometimes referred to by Marx and Engels as "die deutsche Misère," this poverty in the realm of concrete life makes the German intellectual a solitary and renders his thought abstract and idealized.

According to Madame de Staël, who played a major role in introducing German culture in France, the Germans "seek in heaven the space that their narrow destiny refuses them on earth. They delight in the ideal because there is nothing in the present state of things that speaks to their imagination." For her the German is a solitary, and "the solitary man needs an intimate feeling to take the place of the external movement that he lacks." De Staël defines as German traits later associated with Romanticism in general and claims that Rousseau, Bernardin de Saint-Pierre, Chateaubriand, and others are, even if unconsciously, "of the German school." [3] Thus what occurs in nineteenth-century Romanticism is a generalization to European culture of a tendency already present in Germany: the sense of lonely homelessness of the cultivated elite in society becomes a more and more general experience. At the same time, there is an intensification and modification of the experience in Germany; German Romanticism presents us with a "neue Einsamkeit," far more complete, unwanted, and painful than previously. [4]

In England, where a Romantic movement develops parallel to the German in the first decades of the nineteenth century, we may notice the tension between two contradictory poles of the Romantic vision that will continue—in different forms and with different weight given to the poles in each case—throughout Romanticism and its aftermath. With "Byronism," after about 1815 as important an influence on European Romanticism as that exercised by Rousseau and Goethe, the isolation of the "superior man" becomes aggressive and contemptuous; the Byronic hero despises the philistine society in which he lives shut up within himself, giving to others by his manner and actions only intimations of the inner life that lies beneath. The Wordsworthian ideal for the poet, on the other hand, provides a striking contrast: although possessed of "more lively sensibility . . . and a more comprehensive soul, than are supposed to be common among mankind," the poet is "a man speaking to men," "singing a song in which all human beings join with him," "carrying everywhere with him relationship and love . . . the poet binds together by passion and knowledge the vast empire of human society, as it is spread over the

whole earth, and over all time." [5] The two poles represented by the
Byronic hero and the Wordsworthian poet—proud isolation versus
the attempt to reestablish global human community, to speak for
and to the common man—often uneasily coexist within individual
Romantic works and authors, as for example in De Staël, who at the
same time glorifies the superior man and enunciates a moral duty of
solidarity through "pity" with all mankind.

Romanticism is similarly politically and socially ambivalent, in different countries and at different moments either reactionary or progressive, aristocratic or bourgeois. In France it is at first, following the
Revolution, an aristocratic and reactionary émigré literature, but the
later Romantic movement is increasingly bourgeois in character.[6] In all
of its manifestations, however, the Romantic vision is to be distinguished from the dialectical Marxist stance. Marxism affirms both
that man is a communitarian being and that he is alienated from
community in modern society; it claims that the socioeconomic basis
must be and is in fact in the process of being transformed to establish
community on a higher level. The Romantics, on the other hand,
continue to vacillate between the two poles of affirmation of community and affirmation of isolation as Rousseau had done, though the
affirmation of community tends to lose ground progressively as the
century advances. Often the Romantic affirmation of community takes
place purely in the realm of the spirit—as a quasi-mystical communion
with the "people" or a return in imagination to the past. And when
the Romantics attempt to act toward the end of recreating fraternity
among men, it is as prophet-leaders bringing their vision to the
masses, an idealistic and elitist dream that is dashed in the real course
of events.

By far the most influential text for the sentiment of solitude in early
French Romanticism is Chateaubriand's *René* (1802). Here solitude
is present in many forms. René, like Saint-Preux, finds himself unadapted to social life and alone among other men: "I soon found
myself more isolated in my own country than I had been in a foreign
land. I wanted to throw myself for some time into a world that meant
nothing to me and that didn't understand me." [7] Unable to find an
outlet for his soul's outpourings in a society that does not recognize
profound feeling, he retires to a suburb to live without friend or
parent: "Unknown to all, I mingled with the crowd: a vast desert of
men!" [8] In *René*, then, we find the elitism of the sensitive soul, solitary
in its grandeur, repulsed by the philistine masses and living aloof
within society. This form of solitude in society will be characteristic
of Romanticism and much of the literature of the nineteenth century.

The imagery of this solitude, it should be noted, is adapted from the ancient forms of solitude. For the Greeks, solitude was the condition of exile from the *polis;* René, and the modern, Romantic sensibility, is "exiled" within his own city. Likewise, where in ancient literature solitude was a *literal* desert or wilderness, now society itself is described as a desert. Thus the concrete realities of exile and wilderness which were the solitudes outside society of the ancient period become in the modern era *metaphors* for the poet's solitude in society.[9]

Soon René tires of his retired life in the city; he retreats to a country solitude, which does not, however, bring him tranquility. On the contrary, since it provides him with no sufficient object for his infinite yearnings, he experiences only a troubling mixture of turbulence and ennui. He therefore seeks a more radical retreat, of the kind that had already enticed Bernardin de Saint-Pierre: the exotic wilderness of the colonies, in this case the Louisiana Territory, where he joins an Indian tribe and takes an Indian wife. But he is driven even from the primitive Indian civilization to spend entire days alone in the woods, abandoning his wife. There his soul still gains no rest. At the end of René's story, the missionary Souël judges severely both his Romantic elitism and his retreat to the deserts of America. This admonition however, had little effect on the readers of *René;* as Chateaubriand himself later admitted, the reading public responded to the tormented personality of René and not to a strict moral lesson reminiscent of the attitude toward misanthropic retreat that was current during the ancien régime.

Senancour's *Oberman* (1804) shares the *mal du siècle* of René—a malady defined by Chateaubriand in the *Génie du christianisme,* as the troubled melancholy caused by passions without any object, in a solitary soul.[10] Although Senancour's family belonged to the *petite noblesse,* Oberman's malaise begins with his refusal of the new world of business and industry. He hopes that his father will come to understand, "that it is not enough that a position the object of which is self-interest and contentious strife, be regarded as an honest one, because one acquires through it, without stealing, an income of thirty or forty thousand pounds; and that I could not, after all, give up being a man to become a businessman." [11] Faced with the prospect of making a career for himself in society, "I examined myself and I rapidly considered all that surrounded me; I asked other men if they felt as I did; I asked things if they were to my inclination; and I saw that there was no harmony between myself and society, or between my needs and the things that society has produced." [12]

In modern society, Oberman is like a deaf man in the midst of a crowd: "I am alone. My heart's forces are not being communicated at all; they react within the heart, they wait: here I am in society, wandering, solitary in the midst of a crowd that means nothing to me; like a man who long ago was struck by accidental deafness." [13] From this experience, Oberman concludes that man's real life is within himself, that the influences upon it from outside are secondary to the inner life itself; he lives separated from the objective world around him, in the world of his own autonomous imagination.

This mal du siècle, which closely resembles René's lonely torment, drives Oberman also to retreat. He is not satisfied by the solitude of the country outside Paris, where he cannot ignore the misery of the peasant villages he encounters on his walks. Like Saint-Preux, he must retreat farther from society's ills, to the mountainous region of the Valais in Switzerland.

But Oberman is unable to attain happiness in his alpine chateau any more than in the city. He yearns for a communion of souls in an ideal marriage or a perfect friendship with a person of superior sensibility like himself. He realizes that communion with nature cannot replace this human communion as it sometimes had for Rousseau. He asks of Nature: "What would you be to man if you did not speak to him of other men? Nature would be mute if men no longer existed . . . Felt nature exists only in human relations." [14] His disenchantment grows, and he ends by resigning himself to living out his days with no perfect human entente, and increasingly indifferent to the natural beauties that once inspired him.

Solitude at the beginning of the century, then, develops Rousseau's theme of the inadaptation of the sensitive soul to society and his retreat to the wilds of nature—with the difference that this retreat no longer brings peace. For the poet now always brings his malaise with him into his solitude, as only the unphilosophic of the Roman landowners brought their envy and ambition with them to their estate. Now inquiétude is part of the mood of solitary retreat, in harmony with the desolate and rugged natural surroundings.

In the early 1820s, under the Restoration, the first works of the Romantics themselves begin to appear. Lamartine's Méditations (1820) departs only in tone from the pre-Romantic thematics of solitude. Generally speaking, Lamartine's retreat to nature is more positive and less tempestuous than that of Chateaubriand and Senancour. His solitude is rolling countryside as well as jagged peaks. In the countryside he experiences the repose that René and Oberman did not find. [15]

Solitude not only brings repose but also allows the soul to expand toward the infinite. Alone in nature, Lamartine is able to rediscover the God whom modern rationalism has seriously placed in doubt. Part of the reason for the continued torment of René and Oberman in solitary retreat is their lack of communion with God in nature. René's troubled solitude is contrasted with the tranquil missionary retreat of the Père Souël, and of the Père Aubry in *Atala*. But Lamartine is able to converse with God:

The fire of ardent piety that our mother had lit and fanned incessantly with her breath in our imagination as children, sometimes seemed to be extinguished by the winds of our era, and the rain of passion's tears: solitude always lit it again. As soon as there was no one between my thoughts and myself, God revealed himself and I conversed, so to speak, with him.[16]

Lamartine senses a divine presence in nature, then, which Senancour's Oberman did not. Nature is empty and dead for Lamartine only once, just after the death of a beloved woman, in the first poem of the collection, "L'Isolement":

> What are they doing, these valleys, mansions, cottages,
> Vain objects whose charm has vanished for me?
> Rivers, rocks, forests, solitudes so dear,
> You lack a single being, and all is depopulated! [17]

Here the death of the loved one leaves an emptiness in the soul of the poet and consequently in the solitudes he contemplates, for they are always in harmony with his state of mind. Conversely, in "Souvenir," written many months later, the emptiness has given way to a melancholy memory, and so the lover's human presence is felt everywhere in Nature by the poet:

> It is you whom I hear, whom I see
> In the wilderness, in the cloud:
> The wave reflects your image,
> The breeze carries your voice to me.[18]

In his commentary on "L'Isolement," Lamartine speaks of his burning desire to try his poem on "the heart of a few sensitive men. As for the public, I didn't think of them, or I hoped for nothing from them." [19] And, in "La Charité," he claims that his purpose in writing is not to be famous in the eye of the public:

> It is, rather, to reverberate, in the night of mystery,
> For the echoless soul of a poor solitary
> Who hears only a distant sound on earth,
> And to slip my voice into his heart's crevices.[20]

Here Lamartine enunciates a new definition of the function of poetry. The poet, as a member of the small elite of sensitive souls, attempts with his poems to establish contact with other elite souls isolated from society. He scorns the larger public that reflects the debased values of society.

Thus already under the Restoration, the growth of publishing and advent of a mass bourgeois reading public is creating a gulf between writer and general public. The bourgeoisie of the growing industries is more and more despised by the sensitive and creative young, from its own ranks as well as from the nobility. With the fall of Napoleon, heroism and idealism can no longer be lived out on the battlefield, and many young men turn to writing. There is a rise in number of writers, and a concomitant elevation of the conception of the artist.[21] He is not entirely separated from society and the public, however, and will not be throughout the course of Social Romanticism in the first half of the century. Alfred de Vigny's "Moïse" (1822), for instance, projects another conception of the poet's role which provides some link with the larger public. Moses is a symbol of the man of genius; he is a prophet leading by divine inspiration, communicating his visions to the people. Yet he is nonetheless isolated from the people; he pays for his glorious role of leadership with solitude. Adulated, but not loved as a human being by his flock, he complains to God on the mountain: "I have walked ahead of all the rest, sad and lonely in my glory," and "Alas! Lord, I am powerful and solitary,/Let me go to sleep in the earth's embrace." [22]

While both are elevated conceptions, Vigny's definition of the artist's function as prophet-leader differs from Lamartine's correspondence of solitary souls. Both are elite conceptions, but the former still allows for a communication from on high with the public, whereas the latter allows only for communication within the elite of the sensibility. These two conceptions will exist side by side during the first half of the century, until the social role of the artist-prophet is largely eliminated after 1848.

There is some agreement among historians and economists that in Western Europe, and in France in particular, 1830 marks the point of "take-off" [23] for the industrial economy of modern capitalism. In 1830 the period of class conflict between bourgeoisie and proletariat has begun. The bourgeoisie under the July Monarchy is for the first time in full political power; the nobility no longer has any power in public affairs. The proletariat becomes aware for the first time of its existence as a class separate from and dominated by the ruling bourgeoisie. A working-class movement begins to take form, and the first developments in socialist theory appear. Not only does class antagonism split society down the middle, but the cutthroat competition among men and businesses for profits creates a general atmosphere of antagonism and insecurity. The reifying agency of money is now all-powerful in every aspect of life.[24]

In the 1830s the Romantic movement, after the struggles of the preceding decade, emerges victorious as the dominant artistic trend of the time. It emerges also out of its early association with aristocratic reaction, as fully middle-class and liberal in its politics. Not only are more of its representatives of bourgeois origin than before, but the aristocratic writers turn to liberal politics and express bourgeois themes in their creations. As Hauser points out, in spite of its aristocratic origins Romanticism was a middle-class movement; the Romantics addressed a middle-class public while despising it at the same time.[25]

The Romantic poet of the 1830s and 1840s is cut off from his public and his class because they debase all other values to the value of money; he lives in the general atmosphere of competition between individuals no longer bound by other social ties, and concretely experiences the individualistic, competitive system as a free agent in the publishing market.[26] In this context, he feels a loneliness in society which we can trace back to Rousseau but which now becomes more permanent and desperate. Rousseau's retreat from society to wild nature, reenacted by Chateaubriand, Senancour, and Lamartine, gives way to a new, ambiguous form of withdrawal. The poet does not flee beyond the bounds of society; he retreats instead to his solitary study within the city.

We can trace these changes in the works of Vigny after 1830. *Stello* (1832) marks Vigny's disenchantment with the politics of reaction. No longer legitimist, but despising the newly formed bourgeois monarchy, he retires from the political arena altogether. In his historical novel *Cinq-Mars* (1826), the Romantic hero was a young nobleman who destroyed himself in the desperate struggle against Richelieu and his policy of weakening the nobility. In *Stello* a young poet living in the solitude of his room suffers from crises of despair and considers devoting himself to a political cause or writing a treatise on government. The Docteur Noir tells him three stories (one of which is Vigny's first version of the Chatterton story) about poets mistreated and misunderstood under various political regimes, as a remedy for his urge to political involvement. The poet must not affiliate himself with a sociopolitical group and express its cause in his writings. Instead, "Alone and Free, Accomplish your Mission. Follow the conditions of your being, free from the influence of all Associations, no matter how attractive. For Solitude is the only source of inspiration. Solitude is holy. All Associations suffer from the vices of the convent." [27] Thus the poet must be not a monk, but a hermit. Yet he is a secular hermit, and his hermitage is in the desert of the city (here is another example of the figurative transposition of earlier forms of solitude).

After the propagandistic *Cinq-Mars*, then, Vigny turns in *Stello* to the concept of *l'art pour l'art*. Instead of leading the People, the Poet can only hope to communicate with those of the "Republic of Literature" who will read and appreciate his art. "The Republic of letters is the only one whose citizens are truly free, for it is composed of isolated thinkers, often unknown even to each other." [28]

With *Chatterton* (1836), the image of the poet alone in bourgeois society is complete. Chatterton is a young *roturier*, tragically isolated from his own class, which now dominates an inhuman social system. His landlord John Bell represents the industrial bourgeoisie and enunciates their ideology of exploitation. The version of the story in *Stello* gives only a passing reference to Bell; the real villain is the Mayor, representing the government that fails to aid the poet. In *Chatterton*, on the other hand, the emphasis shifts to John Bell and therefore to the economic system. At the beginning of the play, after brutally dismissing an injured worker Bell brags that he worked hard to become a factory owner, and now has the right of domination and profit:

Let each person act in that way, and he will become as rich as I. The machines diminish your salary, but they increase mine; I am very sorry for you, but very pleased for myself. If the machines belonged to you I would think it quite right that what they produce belong to you; but I bought the machines with the money that I earned with my own hands; do likewise, be industrious, and most especially, be thrifty.[29]

In this apology for capitalism, Bell unwittingly stresses an important aspect of its inhumanity: each man's fortune is built on others' misery; each man is against all others as an enemy in the struggle for wealth.

Not only is the poet Chatterton alone in face of the bourgeois John Bell and the official representative of the government, the Lord-Mayor, who refuses to support him unless he takes a position of some public usefulness, but he is also isolated from his aristocratic acquaintances. Their drunken debauchery and insolence reveal their insensitivity to the poet. For Vigny the nobility is in decadence, and the true elite is now the aristocracy of poetic genius. The only human bonds possible for Chatterton, then, are with the sensitive few who understand him— with the Quaker in the Bell household, and especially with Kitty Bell.

But these ties cannot save him. He has sold his soul on the market by contracting debts with the intention of selling a manuscript before the debts come due: "I have showed disrespect for my immortal soul, I have hired it out by the hour and sold it—I am the one at fault, I

deserve whatever comes of it." [30] He cannot produce inspiration at a
given time and in given quantities; he refuses to fabricate something
that is not an inspired creation, and so he is unable to meet the dead-
line. In despair Chatterton destroys his poetry and commits suicide, a
victim of the contradiction between his poetic soul and the society
into which he is born.

It seems clear from the above account that we must reject the
interpretation of *Chatterton* given by Jean-Paul Sartre. Concerning
the young Flaubert's infatuation with Vigny's hero, Sartre writes:
"But he naively imagines that this young commoner, miserable and
sublime, can represent all *poètes maudits*. This is not true to the work:
Chatterton can only be Vigny himself. His solitude, his natural nobility
in fact only symbolizes the magnanimity and the solitude of the fallen
nobility." [31] According to Sartre, Chatterton's final destruction symbolizes the ruin of the landed nobility in face of the triumphant bourgeoisie. Yet Chatterton *does* represent the *poète maudit*, misunderstood
by both bourgeois and nobility. His solitude is no longer the solitude
of the estate, but rather the solitude of the urban poet's lonely room.
The conception of the poet we find in *Chatterton* will be repeated by
most of the bourgeois poets later in the century; it will in fact come
to constitute one of the dominant images of the modern, bourgeois
poet.

Vigny himself, however, lived as a solitary not only in Paris but also
at his country manor. "La Maison du berger" (1844) in *Les Destinées*,
calls upon an idealized woman, Eva, to join the poet in a *solitude à
deux* in his country retreat. There they can escape the industrial city,
although the city is already extending itself into the countryside by
means of the railroad—which Vigny severely criticizes as being an
ugly and dangerous instrument created solely for profit making. On
his estate the poet is far from the vulgar profane, but he must be with
a beloved woman for nature to come alive for him. Going further
even than Senancour, Vigny pictures a Nature cold and hostile to
Man unless humanized by the projection of the Woman into it:

> Eva, I will love all things in creation,
> I will contemplate them in your dreamy eyes . . .
> Come and place your unblemished hand on my tortured heart,
> Never leave me alone with Nature
> For I know it too well not to fear it. [32]

As René Canat suggests in his study of Romantic and Parnassian
forms of solitude, the Romantics sought intimacy and communion
with three exalted beings: Nature, Woman, and God. [33] Throughout
the course of Romanticism communication of each kind underwent a

crisis. The Woman still holds a last hope of human consolation and intimacy in "La Maison du berger." She also transmits to the poet the cry of suffering humanity in the cities; listening to this cry in solitude, through her compassion, the poet can reflect and gather his forces to return to offer the people his leadership (Vigny never entirely abandoned his sense of social mission).[34]

Nature, on the other hand, is no longer a consoling presence in itself. And in another poem of *Les Destinées*—"Le Mont des oliviers," written between 1839 and 1843—we can observe the related crisis of communication with God. We have seen how in "Moïse" Vigny transforms (and, from the point of view of historical accuracy, distorts) the Biblical leader Moses into a symbol of the solitary Romantic poet. The account of Jesus' night in Gethsemane in "Le Mont des oliviers" undergoes a similar mutation. Jesus becomes another symbol of the Poet who wishes to teach his people the mysteries of the universe. Unlike Moses, however, he cannot make contact with God.

Jesus calls his Father in heaven, but the skies remain dark and no answer comes. In anguish he seeks the human comradeship of the sleeping disciples: "He shrinks back, he comes down, he cries out in fright:/Couldn't you have prayed and stayed awake with me?" (I, 17–18). In the second section of the poem he addresses God, begging to be allowed to live; he has spoken only the word "fraternity" to the suffering human race, but wishes to continue his mission by answering for them the questions of life. He asks the answers to these questions, but again the sky remains dark. Isolated between the dark sky and the dark earth—"The Earth without light, without star and dawn,/ And without the soul's light, as it still remains" (III, 9–10) [35]—Jesus sees only the torch of the approaching traitor Judas.

This version of Jesus' agony, which differs greatly from the texts in the synoptic gospels—texts that affirm Jesus' faith in the divine and angelic presences about him—indicates the enormous difference of consciousness between the ancient and modern periods. Solitude among men, and metaphysical solitude in a universe without God, have completely transformed the meaning of the ancient, religious documents. Vigny's version also differs from Pascal's, in the "Mystère de Jésus"; in the latter text Jesus is alone among men who are blind to the divine, but he is a divine figure himself, maintaining a close relationship with God. In Vigny's poem Jesus becomes the human poet for whom neither heaven nor earth offer any communion.

After 1830, as Romanticism triumphed, the modern realist novel, or the fictional mode sometimes termed "critical realism," had its beginnings. As Ernst Fischer points out, the one grew out of the other:

"Romanticism and realism are by no means mutually exclusive opposites; Romanticism is, rather, an early phase of critical realism. The attitude has not fundamentally changed, only the method has become different, colder, more 'objective,' more distant." [36] The fundamental attitude of revolt against the new industrial capitalism and the ruling bourgeoisie remains the same, though the structure of the revolt changes. Consequently the solitude of the hero and his relation to society, although similar, are modified subtly.

The hero of the novels of Balzac and Stendhal is isolated from society because he is exceptionally talented, intelligent, sensitive in a world that does not recognize him. Yet he does not have the stature of the Romantic "genius," and he does not remain entirely aloof within society. He is alienated from society but always attempting to assimilate himself into it, and partially corrupting himself in the process. Caught between the purity of his ideals and the temptation of success in a bourgeois society, he is an "unheroic" hero: "Too bourgeois to be heroic, too lonely and sensitive to be bourgeois, the contradictory unheroic hero is a tragic misfit in modern society." [37]

Balzac, in spite of his understanding of the inhuman mechanisms at work in the society of the July Monarchy, was also aware of its dynamism and creativity. Paul Lafargue, contrasting in 1891 that later period with Balzac's era, writes:

In Balzac's time . . . the colossal concentration of capital that characterizes our period was only in its beginnings in France . . . The life struggle was not demoralizing; it did not degrade man, but developed in him certain qualities: courage, tenacity, intelligence, vigilance and foresight, an ordered mind, etc. Balzac observed and consequently described men who struggled one against another, having recourse only to their own powers, physical or spiritual.[38]

Balzac has a fascination and enthusiasm for these positive aspects of modern society which the disdainful and aloof Romantics lack.

The unheroic hero thrusts himself into the competitive race of society in an attempt to win what it offers: wealth, luxury, fame. In the process society passes its contagion to the young hero. He is obsessed with the desire for money; he can conceive of love only in the guise of luxury—in courtesans and society women. This is a major theme of La Peau de chagrin, in which the young artist Raphaël is destroyed slowly, his life shrinking away like the "fatal skin" in the maelstrom of Paris. His affairs with the wealthy, cynical, and spiritually sterile Foedora completes his corruption by society:

The contagious leprosy of Foedora's vanity had taken hold of me at last. I probed my soul, and found it cankered and rotten. I bore the marks of the devil's claw upon my forehead. It was impossible to me thenceforward to do without the incessant agitation of a life fraught with danger at every moment, or to dispense with the execrable refinements of luxury. If I had possessed millions, I should still have gambled, reveled, and racketed about. I wished never to be alone with myself, and I must have false friends and courtesans, wine and good cheer to distract me. The ties that attach a man to family life had been permanently broken in me.[39]

The hero, however, is at least initially homeless and poor in Paris. And like the Romantic hero, he withdraws to a solitary room, a *mansarde* where he devotes himself to Science or Art. Thus Raphaël is happy, "at the thought of living on bread and milk, like a hermit in the Thebaïd, while I plunged into the world of books and ideas, and so reached a lofty sphere beyond the tumult of Paris." [40] Balzac comments on the dangerous loneliness of this existence—an existence common to many young men: "How much young power starves and pines away in a garret for want of a friend, for lack of a woman's consolation, in the midst of millions of fellow-creatures, in the presence of a listless crowd that is burdened by its wealth!" [41]

Similarly Lucien de Rubempré lives for a time in a garret and experiences the life of the *bohème parisienne*. This life is a product of the new social situation of the writer in the nineteenth century. As publishing expands, it becomes more difficult for a young unknown writer to achieve the recognition that would allow him to earn a living, and a marginal bohème appears consisting of such unknowns. While living this marginal existence, Lucien joins a closely knit and idealistic cénacle—the circle of friends around Daniel d'Arthez. This milieu is united in a fraternity of shared ideas and feelings that contrast with the false friendships and conflicting interests in society at large.[42] Accompanying the image of the young poet as hermit in his garret, then, there exists the complementary image of the poet as monk, living in the community of a cénacle. Although Lucien will reject this life to throw himself into journalism and the scramble for wealth and pleasure, D'Arthez and his friends remain pure in their studious solitude.

For the unheroic hero, solitude within the city and in the retreat of mansarde or cénacle replaces the solitudes of the country and of wild nature, as it had for the Romantic poet during the same period. In Balzac and Stendhal there is a tendency to undercut the traditional themes of solitary retreat from society. In *La Peau de chagrin* Raphaël, near death, leaves Paris for a mountainous retreat in Auvergne. After several days, furious at the curiosity and pity of the peasants, he returns to Paris, where he dies.

The first chapter of the second book of *Le Rouge et le noir* is entitled ironically "The Pleasures of Country Life," with the epigraph from Horace: "O rus quando ego to aspiciam!" In this chapter a philosopher is returning to Paris from a country solitude where his repose has been continually bothered by the machinations of village politics. He concludes: "I'm leaving that inferno of hypocrisy and chicanery. I'm going to seek solitude and rustic peace in the only place where they exist in France: in a fifth-floor apartment overlooking the Champs-Elysées." [43] And Julien Sorel himself, although his happiest moments occur in a grotto in the mountains—away from all society, both provincial and Parisian—nonetheless dreams there of Paris and the Parisian beauty he will someday love.[44]

The *province* of Balzac and Stendhal is part of modern society and shares its vices. The Saumur of M. Grandet, the Angoulême of the Père Sechard, and the Verrières of M. de Rênal and Valenod contain in microcosm the same cruel system ruled by money. On the other hand, the fascination of the realists with the workings of modern society involved a love of the big city.

Indeed, in opposition to the lesser movement (temporary or permanent) of nobility and grande bourgeoisie to their country demesnes, which nourished the ideal of country solitude in ancien régime poetry, the growth of industrial cities in the eighteenth and nineteenth centuries produced an enormous movement of population from rural areas to the towns. This movement is reflected in the structure of the novel. From Marivaux's *Paysan parvenu* and the works of Restif de la Bretonne, to *Le Rouge et le noir*, *Illusions perdues*, and Flaubert's *Education sentimentale*, the novel is often the story of a young provincial, petty bourgeois or peasant, leaving the country to seek his fortune in Paris.

There may remain in these young men a nostalgia for the family bonds that gave security and community in their provincial homes. Thus Lucien de Rubempré, in a low moment, thinks of the family he left behind: "Lucien walked along the boulevards, dazed with grief, looking at the carriages and the passers-by, feeling himself diminished and alone in this crowd that swirled about, whipped up by the thousand interests of Parisian life. Looking back in his mind to the banks of the Charante, he thirsted for the joys of the family." [45]

Yet there is no turning back: the general movement of history is not only from the country to the city, but also toward the industrialization of the country itself. Marx wrote of the great periods of Western history:

Ancient classical history is the history of cities, but cities based on land-ownership and agriculture . . . the Middle Ages (Germanic period) starts with the countryside as the locus of history, whose further development then proceeds through the opposition of town and country; modern (history) is the urbanisation of the countryside, not, as among the ancients, the ruralisation of the city.[46]

Although the full-scale industrialization and modernization of the countryside occurred only in the second half of the century, closely connected with the development of the railroads, the process was already beginning in the 1830s and 1840s. It had occasioned Vigny's protest in "La Maison du berger," and it troubled George Sand, who writes in the appendix to *La Mare au diable* (1846) that the Touraine is fast becoming civilized, and that her native Berry is one of the last outposts of traditional rural life: "For alas, it is all disappearing . . . Still another year or two perhaps, and then the railroads will throw their bridges across our deep valleys, carrying away, with the speed of lightning, our ancient traditions and marvelous legends."[47] Sand's pastoral novels paint a nostalgic and thoroughly idealized picture of the patriarchal peasant family and community which will soon be corrupted by the advance of industrial civilization.

The realist novel of the 1830s and 1840s, then, is the novel of modern, industrial society, from which there is no escape. This society ruled by money reifies and fragments human relationships. And yet we do not encounter in Balzac a vision of universal, tragic isolation as we will in Flaubert and later in the twentieth-century novel. The Romantic vision is still part of Balzac's interpretation of the world. While the Balzacian hero is isolated from society, communication is still possible between souls who are not yet entirely deadened by society. Beside Father Grandet's incomprehension there is the "admirable entente de coeur" between Mme. Grandet and Eugénie, and between Eugénie and Charles before he leaves for the Indies.[48] Beside the false friendships of the journalists in *Illusions perdues*, there are the true friendships of D'Arthez' circle, and beside *l'amour mondain*, the true love of David Séchard and Eve.

Indeed, while the unheroic hero is succeeding in his conquest of society, while he is famous, wealthy, and sought after by society's women, in short while he is most integrated in bourgeois society, he is no longer aware of solitude. In Balzac it is the failures and the not-yet-arrived in society who feel alone. It is also the others who are marginal in modern society: the *célibataires* (the old maid and the priest, as in *Le Curé de Tours*), the old men (Goriot), and the poor relatives.[49] For solitude to penetrate throughout society, so that the social composite is nothing more than an aggregate of lonely monads, modern industrial capitalism must undergo important changes.

II

After the initial take-off period of the 1830s and 1840s, during the Second Empire industrial capitalism makes its great "economic leap forward."[50] The railroads now spread a network of lines all over France and its new overseas territories. There is a further sharp rise in the number and size of cities, and a tremendous increase in production as science becomes more and more closely allied with industry in the search for technological innovations. The Second Empire is the classic period of liberal economy, of laissez-faire competition at its full intensity, and now capitalism makes its full impact felt on all details of daily life.[51]

The Second Empire, following the 1848 Revolution and its brutal repression, is also a period of heightened class antagonisms. For the first time an armed proletariat has fought a ruling bourgeoisie whose interest lies in quelling worker revolts by whatever means necessary. The bourgeoisie has become an entrenched ruling class defending its now-complete domination.[52] The liberalism of the Social Romantics is no longer possible; disgusted by their own class but unwilling to espouse the cause of the workers' movement, most writers now retreat from engagement in society far more radically than they had before. They are further pressed to this retreat by an almost total separation between the philistine entertainment enjoyed by the mass bourgeois reading public and their attempts at serious creation, which are appreciated by only a small public of connoisseurs.[53]

The theory of *l'art pour l'art* comes to the fore. Art no longer has the glorious social function of inspired leadership which it had for the Social Romantics; now it is written for its own sake. The creation of beautiful forms is seen as an end in itself. The Parnassians in some cases attempt to render these forms "impersonal," thereby denying also the function of expressivity to poetry. In these cases the poet no longer wishes to communicate his emotions, his inner state, to the "sensitive few."

Leconte de Lisle writes in one poem ("Bhagavat," in *Poèmes antiques*) of three Indian brahmans who meditate by the Ganges:

> But the Brahmans, mute, burdened with long life,
> Immersed in superhuman inactivity,
> Buried alive in their austere dreams,
> And solitary inhabitants of the River's reeds,
> Weary of the vain noise of man and cities,
> Drew their pleasures from an unknown world.[54]

Yet the brahmans are still plagued by passions in their solitary contemplation. They are told by the river goddess Ganga to go to the
dwelling of Bhagavat on the mountain, and there they attain, through
a vision of him, the perfect, infinite state of passionlessness. The aim
of Leconte de Lisle's poetry is to achieve this impassivity by replacing
the vulgar *frisson lyrique* of the Romantics with the calm beauty of
polished, poetic forms. A Fourier socialist from 1845 until the failure
of the 1848 Revolution, Leconte de Lisle's disillusionment expresses
itself in a violent and bitter withdrawal that seeks to tranquilize itself
in art for art's sake.

Leconte de Lisle's cold solitude is not thawed by even the hope of
communication with God; the progress of the positive sciences and
biblical exegesis caused in him a religious crisis more severe than
Vigny had undergone. The historical approach to religion was beginning to make headway; religions were now being seen as human
constructs that are created and eventually die. Beginning with an
intense hatred of this succession of jealous and tyrannical gods created
by men, Leconte de Lisle comes eventually to feel a melancholy at
the dying of the gods and to reproach mankind for letting them die.
But he never recognizes the hope that a real God might exist in whom
he would find meaning and solace.[55]

The Parnassian poet of the Second Empire is totally isolated in
society, rather than partially so like the Social Romantic and the unheroic hero. Several of the best-known poems of Baudelaire (who
was associated although not fully identified with the Parnassian movement) have the poet's isolation as their subject.[56] "L'Albatros" portrays
the Poet in the image of a bird who flies high and does not fear the
tempest, but who is taken captive by men on their ship (society)
because he has followed it too closely. On the ship he is ungainly
because he is made for flights of genius and not for pedestrian activities. He is ridiculed by the men and cruelly tortured by them. A
comparison with one of Hugo's images for the Poet is revealing. For
Hugo he is alone at the prow of the ship as he guides it: "Progress is
his goal, the good is his compass;/As the pilot, he stands isolated at
the bow of the ship." [57] For Baudelaire, on the other hand, the Poet
has nothing to do with the direction of the ship. He is rather a captive
on it, an exile from his true country, which is the azure of the
imagination.

Indeed, the poet retreats from society now principally through the
agency of the imagination. In Baudelaire the voyages are *voyages
imaginaires*, and the moments of relief from society come in *paradis
artificiels*. Baudelaire is the first French poet of the modern city, and

he remains within it. To escape from it he returns at night to his room. "One a.m." (*Le Spleen de Paris*) begins:

Alone at last! There is no sound but the rattle of a few belated and weary cabs. For a few hours I shall have the privilege of silence, if not of rest. At last the tyranny of the human face has vanished, and I shall suffer only by myself . . . First of all, let me turn the key twice in the lock. I have the notion that this turning of the key will increase my solitude and strengthen the barricades that, for the moment, separate me from the world. Horrible life! Horrible city! [58]

In his room the poet attempts to escape the reality he has left outside through dreaming, which is often stimulated by alcohol or drugs. In these dreams he conjures up an ideal world. In "La Chambre double," as the poet dreams his room is transformed into a paradisiacal place of harmony and calm, filled with odors of exotic perfume. The poet is aware that here Time no longer carries him toward death; he has achieved a moment of eternity is his perfect delight. Then someone from the outside knocks on the door; the spell is broken, and he sees his room as it really is: "Horror, my memory returns—my memory! Yes, this hovel, this dwelling of everlasting dreariness, is really mine. Mine, this silly furniture, dusty and dilapidated; the hearth without flame or live coal, and befouled with spittle; the gloomy windows where the rain has traced furrows in the grime." [59] The poet finds himself again in his mansarde, the "mansarde réelle" that Champfleury described in *Chien-Caillou* (1847) in contrast to the idealized, literary mansarde. Retreat to a real study is no longer a satisfactory escape, as it was, for instance, in Musset's "La Nuit d'octobre"; [60] the study must become a paradise. And with the brutal return to his real room the poet is tempted by the only permanent escape: suicide.

While this despair of the poet utterly alienated from his society, dreaming and suffering in his room, is still the principal image of solitude, there is also a growing awareness of the problem of communication for human beings in general; the failure of human communication condemns men to a *solitude morale*. As René Canat defines it, this solitude

is the painful certainty that each individual is, as it were, walled up in his Self, and that everything that exists is impenetrable for him. This solitude is therefore entirely different from the momentary feelings of isolation that men of all times might have experienced, and that suppose on the contrary belief in intimacies that are abruptly broken by circumstances. [61]

Already in the first half of the nineteenth century there were in French literature occasional moments of awareness of this common fate of modern man. Musset's Fantasio (1834), the young Romantic bourgeois of Munich, has a momentary glimpse of it. He complains to his friend Spark:

If I could only get out of my own skin for an hour or two! If I could be that man who is going by! . . . I'm sure that man has a thousand ideas in his head that are entirely foreign to me; his essence is peculiar to himself. Alas! all the things that men say to each other resemble one another; the ideas they exchange are almost always the same in all their conversations; but within each of these isolated bodies, what nooks and crannies, what secret compartments! It is an entire world that each person carries within himself, an unknown world that is born and dies in silence! What solitudes all of these human bodies are! [62]

Here is a fully elaborated conception of the failure of language to convey the complexities of each individual's thoughts and feelings, and of the existence of a complete world, unknown and unique, within each individual. Yet Fantasio is principally concerned about getting out of his own skin, escaping the ennui of the dissatisfied Romantic soul in bourgeois Munich. His momentary ruminations about human beings in general grow out of his particular desires, and in fact the only solitude embodied in the characters throughout the play is Fantasio's own.

Among the Parnassian poets the feeling of universal moral solitude is more widely and fully experienced, although still not a major preoccupation. I have already mentioned the death of the gods in Leconte de Lisle and the absence of nature as a form of retreat and solace in Baudelaire. When the third of the trio in which the Romantics sought communion and intimacy—the woman—also fails to fulfill this function, not only is the poet left more completely alone than his Romantic counterpart, but he is also led to meditate on the nature of human love in more general terms.

In another of the prose poems of Le Spleen de Paris, "Les Yeux des pauvres," Baudelaire writes of his disillusionment upon discovering the difference between his mistress' feelings and his own in response to the same spectacle. They had wanted to share all their thoughts: "We had promised each other that all our thoughts would be in common and that our two souls henceforth would be but a single one;—a dream that is in no way original, after all, unless it is that, having been dreamed by all men, it has been realized by none." [63] Sitting in a café, they see a family in rags standing in front of them looking with wide, fascinated eyes into the café. Baudelaire is touched and even a bit ashamed; he turns to his mistress to read the same thoughts in her eyes, but she complains that the poor family is unbearable and asks that they be sent away. Baudelaire concludes: "It is that difficult to understand one another, my beloved angel, and to such a degree thought is uncommunicable, even between people who love each other." [64]

Sully Prudhomme's collection of poems, *Les Solitudes* (1869), gives us the fullest elaboration of the theme of universal solitude in the poetry of this period. The title is the same as the Spanish Baroque poet Gongora's *Las Soledades*. And yet the change in kind of these plural solitudes is highly significant. Gongora's solitudes are the various aspects of wild nature: shores, mountains, fields, and so forth, whereas Sully Prudhomme enumerates the varieties of solitude in modern society, from early childhood in school, to the lonely agony of the dying man. On the other hand, the plural of Sully Prudhomme's title contrasts with the singular of D'Arlincourt's Romantic novel, *Le Solitaire* (1821).[65] D'Arlincourt portrays, in an historical setting, the solitude of the lone, suffering Romantic soul, while Sully Prudhomme portrays the many solitudes beside the Romantic's.

Some of the poems in *Les Solitudes* do reiterate the familiar theme of the superior soul isolated from the vulgar crowd ("Damnation," "La Mer," "Le Peuple s'amuse"); others portray the "marginal" solitudes we noticed in Balzac ("Première solitude," "Un Exil," "La Laide"). Yet "L'Une d'elles" is the portrait of a rich society lady who is still secretly unhappy: she too feels alone, and she dies without having experienced either romantic or maternal love. Although many of the poems express the melancholy of unhappy love, in "Ne nous plaignons pas" the poet recognizes that an even more terrible solitude is the passionless habit and familiarity of married couples.

Indeed, Sully Prudhomme generalizes the failure of communication between individuals in society. The subject of "Les Caresses" is the impossibility, for parents and children, friends and lovers, to achieve union of spirit through physical embraces:

> Caresses are but uneasy raptures,
> Fruitless attempts of poor love, that tries
> The impossible task of uniting souls through bodies.
> You are separate and alone like the dead,
> You unfortunate living beings tormented by the kiss! [66]

In "La Voie lactée" the poet compares men to stars, which seem close together to the earth-bound observer but are in fact far apart. Finally, in the "Dernière solitude," the problem is summed up in the failure of language and gesture:

> In this huge mascarade show of the living,
> No one speaks as he wishes or walks as he likes;

Made to reveal, the word only disguises,
And the face is no more than a mask with studied features.[67]

The vision of universal human solitude in society which Sully
Prudhomme creates, by the juxtaposition of individual solitudes in
the plural entity of his collection, is first fully integrated into a novelistic world in the works of Gustave Flaubert. In the 1850s and 1860s,
this vision is not yet suffused throughout the climate of culture; the
earlier form of solitude in society—the alienation of the superior
soul—is still the dominant image. Just as Rousseau created the type of
the isolated Romantic hero several decades before it became part of
the cultural climate, Flaubert is a precursor of the twentieth century
in his creation of a world of solitary monads—the first full elaboration
in novelistic terms of the occasional generalizing statements that preceded it. It is the modernity of his vision that has stimulated the
recent intense interest and enthusiasm in Flaubert's works.

It is significant that the word *solitude* (as well as *isolement*) is not
included in Flaubert's "Dictionnaire des idées reçues" when it was one
of the most common Romantic clichés (others of which are found
there). Solitude was not a *lieu commun* for Flaubert, but a terrible
reality. In his *Oeuvres de jeunesse* (before *Madame Bovary*), solitude
is experienced in its purely Romantic form [68]—which, as I have already
suggested in opposition to Sartre's point of view, is a typically bourgeois alienation. It is the first manifestation of an inherent contradiction in bourgeois society; in an unprecedented development, the most
talented, sensitive, and intelligent of the ruling-class young find themselves in disharmony with, and obliged to revolt bitterly against,
their own class. This first stage precedes the deepening of the contradiction to its full proportions: bourgeois society, by its very nature,
creates the misery of solitude *throughout* its own ruling class.

With the first of the novels of his maturity, *Madame Bovary* (1857),
Flaubert's new ironic perspective begins to undermine the Romantic
hero. The poetic soul, far from being glorified in its alienation from
society, is now seen as hopelessly and absurdly divorced from reality.
This is the fate of Emma Bovary in the provincial society of Yonville,
which partakes of society at large, ruled by the same petty ambitions,
cruelties,' and stupidity. As in Balzac, the country is no longer a
solitude of retreat; although Flaubert himself retired definitively after
his attack in 1843 to his country estate Croisset, the estate does not
play any role in his novels. Emma, the daughter of a *paysan enrichi*,
is not sensitive to the beauties of nature on the farm, for she knows
them as a peasant rather than as a seigneur. It is the wilder, Romantic

solitudes that make Emma dream, the far-away, exotic landscape of *Paul et Virginie*.[69]

Finding herself in the midst of bourgeois society through her marriage with Charles, with no possibility of realizing the Romantic union of souls for which she yearns, she turns in desperation to two men whom she imagines to stand outside this society: the clerk Léon and the supposed aristocrat Rodolphe, who lives nearby on his estate. Her Romantic passion, however, has blinded her pitifully: Léon and Rodolphe are as much a part of bourgeois society as the others. Emma transforms them in her imagination into the Romantic Heroes of her readings, just as Léon at first transforms her into the Romantic Woman.

She never comprehends their real personalities, and they do not understand her. In the end the petty bourgeois in Léon shows itself: after an adventure that is in danger of becoming too complicated, he decides it is time to "be serious" and leaves Emma for Paris to seek his fortune. Rodolphe, on the other hand, the anonymous chevalier of her dreams, soon reveals his true nature; cynical and debauched, he does not believe in love and coldly seduces Emma for his own sexual pleasure. Rodolphe does not understand the strength and sincerity of Emma's passion, and underlying his misunderstanding is the inadequacy of language to express the uniqueness of each individual's sentiments:

He was unable to see, this man so full of experience, the variety of feelings hidden within the same expressions. Since libertine or venal lips had murmured similar phrases, he only faintly believed in the candor of Emma's . . . as though the abundance of one's soul did not sometimes overflow with empty metaphors, since no one ever has been able to give the exact measure of his needs, his concepts, or his sorrows. The human tongue is like a cracked cauldron on which we beat out tunes to set a bear dancing when we would make the stars weep with our melodies.[70]

One aspect of *Madame Bovary*, then, is a demystification of the once-glorious Romantic solitude. Yet far more original is the portrayal of a society that is radically fragmented: solitude is no longer the privilege of the sensitive few, but the misery of the whole. All the inhabitants of Yonville are separated from one another by what was for Flaubert the essence of bourgeois society, *la bêtise*—an insensitive egoism that blinds them to the character and problems of others, and their philistine tendency to reduce all experience to the physical level. Nothing can be comprehended which cannot be translated into terms of goods, money, or physical comfort. This form of stupidity creates the tragicomic incomprehension of the priest Bournisien when Emma attempts in desperation to unburden her anguish to this "doctor of souls." In spite of his function, the priest is unable to believe that human needs go beyond material comforts. He protests: " 'It seems to me that when one has firing and food . . . for, after all . . .' 'My God! My God!' she sighed. 'Do you feel unwell?' he asked, approaching her anxiously. 'It is indigestion, no doubt?' " [71]

From the well-meaning but simple-minded doctor Charles and the mindless fonctionnaire Binet, to the egotistical, vain, and ambitious apothecary Homais and the ruthless merchant Lheureux: each member of the Yonville community is shut off in his self, although each has adapted himself to solitude as Emma has not.[72] In addition to this fragmentation within the bourgeois community, there are class divisions that are concretized in the description of the Comices Agricoles. The bourgeois notables sit on the reviewing stand, while below them the peasants and servants watch, with the animals standing off behind. After the speeches, and after the award by the "bourgeois épanouis" of a medal to the servant Catherine Leroux, for fifty-four years of service which have reduced her to the level of the animals she has cared for, the oppression recommences: "Now that the speeches had been read, everything fell back into place again, and everything into the old grooves; the masters bullied the servants, the servants beat the animals." [73] The Comices illustrates in a single scene both the hypocrisy and the reality of Yonville society.

In L'Education sentimentale (1869), the scope of the novel widens from a provincial town to all of contemporary French society. Frédéric Moreau is an "unheroic" hero—a young provincial bourgeois of exalted sensibility, but weak-willed and mediocre, who allows himself to be paralyzed and degraded by the Parisian society he attempts to conquer. Like Emma Bovary, Frédéric's loves are based on illusions, Romantic literary images or symbols which do not correspond to the reality of the loved person. His great love, Mme. Arnoux, is simply the woman upon whom he superimposes his mental image of the Romantic Woman: "A woman's face had always shone on the horizon of his imagination, so that, seeing her for the first time, he had immediately recognized her." [74] Yet unlike Emma, Frédéric never manages to force a confrontation between reality and his dream. His passion for Mme. Arnoux is experienced only on the level of dream.

Frédéric's other loves are as illusory as this primary one. As Victor Brombert has pointed out, they are never loved for themselves, but serve as profaned substitutes or "mattresses" for Mme. Arnoux, with whom he never consummates his passion.[75] Beyond this, they function only as symbols of abstract entities: Rosanette as the fresh immodesty of Nature, Mme. Dambreuse as the wealth and sophistication of High Society. Whenever Frédéric penetrates beyond these veils, he is disgusted or bored with the person he finds. Corrupted by the characteristic vices of Parisian society, Frédéric snobbishly disdains Louise Roque—the simple girl who waits in her garden back home in provincial Nogent—until he finds it necessary to court her for her money and property.

Although friendship was for Flaubert relatively more satisfying than love, the friendship of Frédéric and his old schoolmate Deslauriers is experienced only in the future and the imperfect tenses. In their exalted youth they share dreams of their future life; reconciled again in old age, they share pitiful memories of the past. But in their maturity the basic differences in their temperaments, and the latent class hostility between the poor son of a *huissier* and the well-to-do bourgeois, draw them further and further apart. The slow dissolution of their friendship culminates in Deslaurier's betrayal of Frédéric: he attempts to seduce Mme. Arnoux, and marries Louise Roque.

All the nihilism of *L'Education* is summarized in the episode from their youth which the two old friends recall at the end of the novel. For exalted adolescents the brothel of "La Turque" has the attraction of mystery and poetry. The young Frédéric enters with a bouquet, like a fiancé; but the spectacle of the prostitutes frightens him, and he runs away. Nonetheless, as the two friends comment in the deadly phrase that terminates the novel: "That was the best time we ever had!" For then they were pure in their Romantic idealism, and Frédéric's innocence could still refuse a sordid reality. Now Frédéric and Deslauriers have passed through the bordello of society, and although they have remained unproductively alienated from it, they have also been irremediably corrupted by it.

This degraded society, like the society of Yonville but on a far wider and more inclusive scale, is an agglomeration of solitary and hostile monads. Each of the principal groups around which social relations revolve in the novel is in reality profoundly disunified. The group of students which meets in Frédéric's room to discuss politics (just before the 1848 Revolution), although superficially united by revolutionary ardor, is in fact a hodge-podge of different class backgrounds, and frustrated ambitions hide behind revolutionism in many cases. The artistic reunions at Arnoux's Art Industriel (where art itself is degraded to a commercial enterprise), and the world of intrigue at Rosanette's gatherings, are characterized by egoism, vanity, and cruel betrayal. Most inhuman of all, in the salon of M. and Mme. Dambreuse, where the haute bourgeoisie meets, human relations exist only insofar as they advance business interests. The *néant* of these relations is nowhere better symbolized than in the scene of M. Dambreuse's funeral. His "friends" do not even force themselves to make hypocritical gestures of grief. And, the ceremony terminated, "the funeral carriages took the men of affairs back to their business; the ceremony had not been too long; and this was matter for congratulation." [76]

Where Flaubert has already created during the Second Empire a new vision of solitude throughout modern society, the nineteenth-century form of elite solitude reaches its most extreme form in the Symbolists and Decadents of the 1880s and 1890s, and will continue into the early twentieth century. Proust's conception of artistic solitude, for example, descends directly from the Symbolists. At the end of the century, retreat from the contagion of society is, following Baudelaire, entirely artificial and imaginary; the reaction against Rousseau's solitudes of Nature reaches its point of culmination. Des Esseintes, the hero of Huysmans' *A Rebours* (1884), sells his ancestral chateau to buy a small house in the suburbs of Paris, where he closes himself in to enjoy the most elaborate refinements of a decadent aestheticism. Instead of retreating to the hermit's austere, natural desert, he seeks a comfortable, aesthetic equivalent: "Already he was dreaming of a refined Thebaïd, a desert hermitage combined with modern comfort, an ark on dry land and nicely warmed, whither he could fly for refuge from the incessant deluge of human folly." [77] Rather than sleep in a true hermit's cell, Des Esseintes decorates a comfortable bedroom to give the illusion of a hard, stone cell.

The nobility is pictured in its final agony. Both Des Esseintes and Villiers de l'Isle-Adam's *Axël* (1890) are the last childless members of aristocratic families which will die with them. Unconditionally despising the bourgeois world around them, they ultimately negate life itself. Axël tells Sara: "Live? The servants will do that for us," [78] and the two lovers commit suicide, knowing that reality can never live up to their dreams. Similarly, Mallarmé's Hérodiade tells her nurse: "I love the horror of being a virgin"; she loves the perfect solitude of her "useless flesh." [79]

Only in pure art, utterly separate from life, can the superior soul continue to live. And through this art a communication may be established, not of living sentiment but of aesthetic delectation, between the new, smaller elite of connoisseurs. Des Esseintes writes of the *poème en prose:* "The novel, thus conceived, thus condensed in a page or two, would become a communion, an interchange of thought between a magic-working author and an ideal reader, a mental collaboration by consent between half a score persons of superior intellect scattered up and down the world, a delectable feast for epicures and appreciable by them only." [80] To assure this isolation of the poet from all but a few connoisseurs (now the poet's alienation is sought rather than lamented), intentional obscurity and difficulty are cultivated, as in the new *trobar clus* of Mallarmé.

A sense of metaphysical anguish and solitude is also acute in the Symbolists and Decadents. Axël abandons the "occult world," aware of the relativity Science has imposed on all doctrines and unable to make direct contact with the divine energy.[81] Des Esseintes is unable to believe in a Catholicism that loses its magic in the banality and materialism of the bourgeois world. At the end of the novel, leaving his suburban house for Paris on his doctor's orders (his aestheticizing solitude, instead of bringing him relief, has only worsened his nervous sickness), Des Esseintes prays: "Lord, take pity on the Christian who doubts, on the sceptic who would fain believe, on the galley-slave of life who puts out to sea alone, in the darkness of night, beneath a firmament illumined no longer by the consoling beacon-fires of the ancient hope." [82] Huysmans himself was to turn to a mystical Catholicism a decade later, to escape this dilemma.

Thus the intellectual elite exists in a more and more inhuman isolation. Its retreat from modern, bourgeois society takes the most extreme forms: the retreat within the city of decadent, life-refusing aestheticism (in the aesthete's hermetically closed room), or of a bohemia farther outside the limits of bourgeois society than ever before, as well as the real departure for exotic, primitive lands, more than ever removed from Western civilization. These are the solutions of Mallarmé and Verlaine, on the one hand, and of Rimbaud, who gives up poetry for adventure in Africa, on the other. They will continue to be major forms of retreat for the artistic elite into the early twentieth century.[83]

III

In these last years of the nineteenth century, a basic transformation of the mature capitalist system was beginning to take place—a transformation that was to have a determining influence on the artistic vision of solitude in society. In brief, competitive capitalism was tending toward monopoly capitalism. Although there were isolated cases of monopolist concentration before 1860, they were exceptional. In the late 1860s and the 1870s, at the same time that free competition reached its height, the process of concentration began; but its take-off period came during the extended depression and crises which, by limiting competition, aided its development, from the mid-1870s into the 1890s. The monopoly form only became dominant at the beginning of the twentieth century.[84]

Monopolist concentration involves the elimination or absorption of small competitors and the creation of large economic entities—societies of stockholders, controlled by a managerial board, funded by increasingly wealthy and powerful banks, engaging in extensive foreign investment (often in the newly annexed colonies), and limiting competition with other large enterprises by means of agreements. It is characterized by the formation of a managerial and financial oligarchy, by a growing, hierarchical bureaucracy of business functionaries, and by an increasingly numerous rentier class living off stockholdings.[85]

So a quantitative evolution over the last decades of the nineteenth century becomes a qualitative change. In monopoly capitalism the individual entrepreneur is replaced by an immense corporate organization. The new system effects "an institutionalization of the capitalist function." [86] The system is increasingly impersonal; the individual has less power to control his own destiny within it and is less able to comprehend its workings. The periodic crises that shake it are now entirely determined by its own mysterious inner laws (the mid-century economic crisis was the last to be set off by agricultural failure, which had largely determined economic patterns previously [87]). In 1891 Lafargue summarized the change:

In our time, the life struggle has taken on another character, becoming harsher and more accentuated as capitalist civilization has developed. The struggle between individuals has been replaced by the struggle of economic organisms (banks, factories, mines, gigantic stores). The strength and intelligence of the individual disappear before their irresistible force, blind like a force of nature . . . The past character of the life struggle has changed, and with that change human nature has been modified; it has become baser, more paltry.[88]

This change in the status of the individual in monopoly capitalism alters the nature of the individual's solitude. Two parallel passages from André Gorz's La Morale de l'histoire will serve as models of two experiences of solitude within society. In reference to the competitive phase of capitalism, Gorz writes:

In the heroic period of capitalism the goal of individuals was to "rise" in a social hierarchy that was largely open and characterized by its mobility. The competitive economy was essentially an economy of penury; and the individual could win, by his tenacity at work and his ability, the means to develop and satisfy higher needs than others'. His success, won upon and against all the rest, was solitary; it was synonymous with a degree of individualization and autonomy not allowed the common man. The rich man decided his needs himself, by *distinguishing* himself. His wealth was the totality of opportunities that he took away from the rest; "man" was "man alone," proud, combative, and disdainful.[89]

In twentieth-century society, on the other hand, the individual no longer has this power to distinguish himself; his needs and actions are determined by the organization. He becomes progressively alienated from himself, and consequently from others within the group:

The arbiter of success is the opinion of *others*, and this opinion is unimpeachable because its subject is an *absence*; it is the soft voice of insinuation, the voice of *no one*. It defines for you the social proof of success; it persuades you that you will be a reject and a failure if you ignore its advice. And if following this advice does not bring you happiness, be careful not to admit it; you would be viewed as a traitor; you would give proof of your inadaptation; the community would expel you. Fear reigns, and fraud; individuals hide their actual reality, their solitude and misery, so as to appear what they are not: successful and happy Others.[90]

The alienated and solitary men of the lonely crowd, described here by Gorz, have their origin in the decline of the individual in monopoly capitalism. The difference between the two solitudes is a structural one: the exceptional, elite individual, solitary in his distinction from the mass, as opposed to a sum of individuals living solitary, side by side within an organization and within society as a whole. In the nineteenth century, although bitterly opposed to each other, both the Romantic poet and the entrepreneur are elite individuals corresponding to the heightened individualism of that period. As the individual's role diminishes, the distinction between elite and mass weakens. The way is paved for the generalized acceptance of a new vision of universal solitude among all human beings.

Consequently, although we have noted isolated examples of this new vision before the 1880s (for universal solitude is a latent contradiction of capitalism itself, not just of its last phase), only in the last decades of the nineteenth century and the first decade of the twentieth, in coordination with the evolution of monopoly capital, does it permeate the cultural climate and definitively supersede the earlier conception. These developments correspond also to the great religious crisis: in the triumph of positivism, in the influence of Renan and his *Histoire des origines du christianisme* (1863–1881), and in Nietzsche's epochal declaration of the death of God. The new vision of solitude will possess a far more intense metaphysical dimension than the one it replaces.

René Canat wrote his study of solitude at the turn of the century (completed in 1903, published in 1904) and justifies his choice of subject in a significant way: "Of all the motifs of sadness that the nineteenth century has known, it seems to me that mental solitude (*la Solitude morale*) has been the most acute, 'that mental solitude,' says M. Bourget, 'in which so many persons live today that one can truly say that it is the fate, not of such and such an individual, but of modern man himself.' " [91] And indeed the theme of universal solitude is expressed by most of the writers of the late nineteenth century. A common denominator of Maupassant's short stories and novels—which cover a period from 1880 to 1891—is the lack of communication in love (often expressed in the antagonism of the sexes and the bestiality of the relation between man and woman) and the solitude in which all men always live.[92] The theme is taken up by Anatole France and is a principal subject of minor writers of the time: Paul Margueritte, Marcel Prévost, Edmond Haraucourt.[93]

But the structural changes from an elite conception of solitude to a universalized one is best illustrated in Paul Valéry's *Monsieur Teste* (1896) and Henri Barbusse's *L'Enfer*, a decade later (1908). Teste lives in a world entirely ruled by money. He tells the narrator: "Gold is, as it were, the mind (*esprit*) of society." [94] In this world each individual is separated by an unbreachable wall from others and yet, as M. Teste says, "*They* are eaten by others." [95] Teste consequently establishes a superiority over others by a voluntary solitude of withdrawal in his room and a complete refusal to allow his inner, intellectual life to be in any way determined by the prejudices, common sentiments, and so on, which come to us from others.

Still this superiority is not one of opposition, but of degree. Teste carries the inhumanity of capitalist society to its extreme. Far from being alienated like the Romantic soul, Teste is "an isolated system in which the infinite does not figure at all." [96] He takes the bourgeois obsession with facts, figures, and rationality to its ultimate degree, rejecting all feeling and insisting that he who cannot prove with facts and logic is his enemy. He considers himself and others as *things*, and with perfect logic insists on calling his wife by the word representing what he wants of her, sometimes simply *Etre* or *Chose*.

Thus the "incommunicable genius" of Teste, whose wife calls him a "mystic without God," is the demonic genius of the system itself expressed in pure form. Others, he says, are his caricature and his model. And indeed he is that very characteristic social being of the early monopoly period, the rentier: "he lived on mediocre weekly operations at the Stock Exchange." [97] Teste's elitism is an attempt to redeem himself by living his solitude and reification as an independent, superior individual rather than as a member of the lonely crowd;

in doing this he becomes a monster rather than a hero—a monster who, as Valéry admitted, could never exist.[98]

In Barbusse's novel, the element of elitism is abandoned altogether. The narrator is, like many unheroic heroes of the nineteenth century, a petty bourgeois who has just arrived in Paris from the provinces. Yet unlike them, he comes only to take a minor job in a bank, not to conquer society. During the entire novel he remains isolated in a drab hotel room. Unlike the poet retreating to his mansarde, however, the narrator remains there so as to observe other persons. He is able to see into the adjoining room through a hole in the wall, and the scenes that take place there under his gaze symbolize the realities of life in general. The principal scene is the meeting of an adulterous couple who realize that in spite of their sexual relations they are alone. The man of the couple teaches the narrator an important truth. He tells the woman: "I perceived that each person is a world." [99] The narrator develops an idealist philosophical line of thought from this idea: "I cannot accord to the world any other reality than that of my imagination. I believe in myself and I am alone, since I cannot get out of my self . . . What could prove to me that beyond my thought, the boundaries of which I cannot pass, the world has an existence separate from me?" [100] If one's consciousness is a solipsistic world, one cannot die, he concludes, although this is not enough to end his obsession with death.

Thus the narrator looks in upon the spectacle of others to discover the human condition he shares. When he leaves his room to go out among the anonymous pensionnaires of the hotel and into the urban crowd, his solitude is that of the ordinary man:

I start out. I come and go in the midst of a naked reality. I am not a man of strangeness and exception. I desire, I cry and call out—and I recognize myself everywhere. I reconstitute with everyone else the truth spelled out in the room I spied on, the truth which is this: I am alone, and I want what I don't have and what I no longer have! One lives on this need, and one dies of it too.[101]

The narrator, then, is part of the lonely crowd—not simply because of his mediocrity but because, as he realizes, all the people he brushes against have the same frustrated desire for an infinite, timeless communion with others. The superior soul no longer stands above the vulgar crowd in his thirst after the infinite; Everyman now suffers daily the same fate.

Moreover, ordinary men are fully and painfully aware of their frustration and solitude. The people who pass through the room next door are as conscious of their solitude as the narrator; the world is hell for them as well as for him. Also in Edouard Estaunié's collection of short stories, *Solitudes* (1922), the ordinary people who experience solitude within their social relationships suffer acutely from their isolation, although they are not always aware that they suffer a common fate. This awareness of the ordinary man marks a progression from the early manifestations of the theme of universal solitude. In Sully Prudhomme's *Solitudes*, in Baudelaire and Flaubert, there still exists a differentiation of consciousness between the more sensitive protagonist and the "others" who simply undergo their isolation unconsciously, like the inhabitants of Yonville in *Madame Bovary*. Only Emma is fully aware of her own solitude, and only Flaubert is aware of that of the others.

The weakening of the elitist conception of solitude (it does not disappear entirely) is reflected also in the idea of art's function. Romain Rolland's Jean Christophe (1904–1912) refuses to write music for a tiny elite that cultivates its difference from ordinary existence. He hopes that the small number of young men who will first appreciate his music will grow larger and larger: "So, according with the unvaried rhythm of the universe, there was formed about him the little family of genius, grouped about him, giving him food and taking it from him, which grows little by little, and in the end becomes one great collective soul, of which he is the central fire." [102] Rolland, in his afterword, "Aux amis de Jean Christophe," speaks of the wide circle of "friends," known and unknown, he has wished to reach through the person of Jean Christophe, who expresses for them the collective soul. And Jules Romains, in his preface to *Les Hommes de bonne volonté* (1932), tells the reader: "I also want . . . to speak for everyone and to be heard by the greatest number possible. An effort like the one I am undertaking calls for the vastest human communion, an immense camaraderie." [103]

The problem of solitude is now posed as a collective problem, and the solutions attempted will be collective. Especially in the period of the *entre-deux-guerres*, the writer will attempt to win his own escape from the condition of solitude, with that of others, in the reconstitution of human and metaphysical communities. Proust's solution to collective solitude in society is, as we shall see, still an individual one: the Symbolists' aestheticism. Only after World War One do many writers turn to collective solutions, but two important writers of the late nineteenth and early twentieth century already point the way. Zola not only portrays the huge collective entities that rule monopoly capitalist society, but also the collectivity that struggles against them: the People. Indeed, we might say that the hero of the epic *Rougon-Macquart* (1871–1893) is the people as a whole, as a vital revolutionary force.

At the other end of the political spectrum, in the mid-1890s Maurice Barrès turned from the individualistic "culte du moi" of his earlier writings to the nationalism that characterizes his works in the twentieth century.

During the entre-deux-guerres these two directions will become important cultural trends. To the Right, flight from solitude will be sought in nationalism, which unifies Frenchmen in the land and in tradition, in Catholicism, which not only restores contact with God but brings men together in the order of the Church, and finally in fascism, in which the individual abandons his identity to the State. Observing the growth of the nationalist movement before World War One, Romain Rolland is already aware of this aspect of its appeal. Jean Christophe's young friend Georges represents a new generation nourished on Barrès, Maurras, and the growing Action Française:

However, he did not understand his old friend's ideas. He used to wonder how Christophe could bear his soul's solitude, and dispense with being bound to any artistic, political, or religious party, or any group of men. He used to ask him: "Don't you ever want to take refuge in a camp of some sort?" . . . "One must take root" (s'enraciner), said Georges, proudly echoing one of the pontiffs of the time.[104]

To the Left, on the other hand, the solution to human isolation will be sought not in a reactionary attempt to return to an earlier state of social and religious integration, but in the militant effort to move beyond the present capitalist order—to a socialist society in which men will work and live in concert rather than in institutionalized conflict. In the solidarity of struggle to achieve this goal, men are already united in a common effort. After World War Two, with the defeat of fascism, the failure of revolution in the advanced Western countries, and the stabilization of capitalism, a new and deeper pessimism will set in. An inescapable solitude will dehumanize men on all levels of their being. At the beginning of the twentieth century, then, the evolution I have attempted to trace is completed. Solitude has been transformed from a place outside society to a universal state of mind within society, and an aristocratic, feudal vision of the world has given way to a wholly bourgeois vision. The new vision, which is at the same time anti-bourgeois since it reveals an explosive contradiction in bourgeois society, will penetrate the literature of the twentieth century in all of its aspects: not only in its function and ideology, but in its themes, structure, and techniques.

PART TWO

Solitude in the Twentieth-Century French Novel

4

❧

Du côté de chez Swann:
The Unknowable Other

I

The first part of my study required a cursory examination of many
literary texts. The second part, on the contrary, consists principally
of detailed analyses of five exemplary texts. Each is first situated
within the author's work as a whole, and in relation to other authors.
I wish to examine the *total* expressions—not only in overt theme and
idea but in characterization, literary structures, techniques, and style—
of the problem of solitude in specific texts, and to relate those expressions to broader socioeconomic development.

The first of my texts—*Du côté de chez Swann*—was chosen for
several reasons. As the first section of the original trilogy that was
to comprise *A la recherche du temps perdu*, it is the only one published
before the war, in 1913. The other two original sections—*Le Côté de
Guermantes* and *Le Temps retrouvé*—were progressively expanded
during and after the war, until Proust's death in 1922, while the 1913
edition of *Du côté de chez Swann* remained entirely unchanged.[1]
Swann is therefore in the strictest sense a prewar novel. By placing
it first among the important twentieth-century novels of solitude in
society, I may further contradict the notion that the anguish of solitude
has its roots in the moral crises of the world wars. As I have attempted
to demonstrate, the new vision is first expressed in Flaubert and
becomes generalized at the end of the nineteenth century with the
rise of monopoly capitalism.

Moreover, *Du côté de chez Swann* is, as critics soon recognized,[2] a microcosm of Proust's whole work. Proust introduces into it almost all of the major themes and techniques of the complete *A la recherche*; thus we may study the Proustian vision in a text of manageable size. A single exception relating to the study of solitude in *Swann* is the absence of a critique of friendship (to parallel the critique of love). The narrator's new-found friendship with Saint-Loup in *A l'ombre des jeunes filles en fleurs* is the occasion for introduction of the theme, which is later elaborated in *Le Temps retrouvé*.[3]

Proust's major themes are already present in his first fictional works. *Les Plaisirs et les jours,* a collection of short pieces written for literary revues principally over the period 1891–1893, and *Jean Santeuil,* an early version of *A la recherche* written in the second half of the 1890s, contain many of the themes (although not yet the techniques) that will be more fully orchestrated in *A la recherche.* In *Les Plaisirs et les jours* we encounter the opposition between a profound, fulfilling life of solitary retreat and a superficial, sterile life in high society ("Violante ou la Mondanité"); [4] the subjectivity of love and impossibility of true communication in love ("Mélancolique villégiature de Mme de Breyves" and "Rêve"); jealousy, the hidden life of the loved one, and lying ("La Fin de la jalousie"); the nostalgia for perfect possession of the mother and the desecration of the mother ("La Confession d'une jeune fille"). Thus the basic motifs of Proust's mature vision exist already in his work of the 1890s,[5] precisely during the period in which the new awareness of universal solitude is becoming widespread in literature.

Proust's career corresponds exactly with the period of transition from one capitalism to another, and from one vision of the world to another. The period from 1830 to the beginning of the twentieth century, from Balzac and Stendhal to Proust, is one of cultural continuity. Arnold Hauser has called Proust the "last great impressionist and aesthetic hedonist," [6] and Edmund Wilson has pointed out his relation to the Symbolist movement. Proust also, in his work and his life, glorifies the function of art and the necessary retreat of the artist from society to his solitary room, in which he may establish contact with himself and others.

Yet if Proust comes at the end of one era, he stands at the beginning of another. His novel is the first full expression of the "modern subjectivism" which Hauser defines as the conception "that we possess only a deformed version of reality and that we are imprisoned in the subjective forms of our thinking." [7] Hauser rightly traces the literary roots of this subjectivism back to Flaubert and Emma Bovary, and its philosophical roots go back much further. The philosophic trend of "Idealism"—which places in doubt the reality and form of the world external to the subject, and emphasizes the ways in which the vision of the subject shapes the world it contemplates—extends from Descartes through Berkeley and Kant, to philosophers whose influence on Proust was more direct: Schopenhauer and Bergson.[8] Yet as a German critic of Proust, H. R. Jauss, asserts, in the domain of literature Proust's subjectivism goes beyond Flaubert's. For Proust there no longer exists a single external reality common to all, but rather a multiplicity of individual worlds that are cut off from one another.[9]

Proust's is the first of the great twentieth-century novels that are products of a universally fragmented society, that reflect and protest the failure of community and communication. Virtually every modern author is touched by the anguish of fragmentation, and that anguish is at the center of the novels discussed here. In this context, with Proust's relation to both the nineteenth- and twentieth-century thematics of solitude in mind, one must reject any interpretation of his vision of human isolation as a product of his own peculiar psychic makeup, a distortion of the world through his personal mental and physical "sicknesses." Such is Edmund Wilson's conclusion in his chapter on Proust in *Axel's Castle*: Proust's syndrome of dependence on mother, failure of relations with women, and impossible demands made upon friends determines his "dismay at the apparent impossibility of making connections with other human beings." [10] Although the specific configuration and content of this vision are certainly conditioned by Proust's peculiar circumstances and psychic makeup, the vision itself reaches far beyond his individual life, and through the highly individualized expression of his novel, he gives voice to the contradictions of a whole society and economy.

The relation, of course, is not direct. The characters of Proust's world—both grand bourgeois and noble—have no productive relation to the functioning of society; with the exception of the few characters who practice a liberal profession, they live off their family fortunes or stock-market investments (Swann, for example), and the only working-class characters who figure importantly are domestics in their service. Like Valéry Larbaud's traveling millionaire Barnabooth (*A. O. Barnabooth* was also published in 1913), Proust's characters seem entirely shut off from the struggles of the larger society, although they live in a parasitic relation to it. Proust writes in *Pastiches et mélanges* of reading the newspaper:

that abominable and voluptuous act called *reading the newspaper*, thanks to which all the calamities and cataclysms of the universe during the last twenty-four hours—the battles that cost the life of fifty thousand men, the crimes, strikes, bankruptcies, fires, imprisonments, suicides, divorces, the cruel emotions of stateman and actor—are transmuted for our personal use, for us, who are not concerned (*intéressés*), into a morning feast, and combine excellently, in a particularly tonic and stimulating way, with the ingestion—so much to be recommended—of several swallows of café au lait.[11]

Yet, without knowing it, Proust was *intéressé*; the forces at work in the ambiant society, which seem so distant and indifferent to him as he reads their surface, daily expression in the morning paper, profoundly molded the structure and meaning of his novelistic world.

II

At the beginning of the Combray section of *Du côté de chez Swann* (48–49), [12] the narrator Marcel tells us that the village of his childhood exists in such a deep recess of his memory, and is imbued for him with colors so different from his present existence, that it seems an inaccessible, supernatural "Au-delà." Indeed, one of the two contradictory meanings of Combray in the novel is the rural paradise lost, in which community may still be enjoyed and from which Marcel is expelled in adult life. This image of unity has its center in the relationship between Marcel and his mother and grandmother, but extends beyond it to the entire family group and all of Combray.

Marcel's mother and grandmother are both portrayed as supremely loving, utterly selfless, humble, sweet, and good. On the night that Swann comes to visit, and the child Marcel stays awake to kiss his mother, she calms him by reading one of the *romans champêtres* of George Sand, which had been chosen for him by the grandmother. The grandmother feels that they will develop Marcel's sensitivity to artistic excellence while preserving his innocence of evil. The tone of these novels perfectly suits the moral sensibility of the mother who reads them (12, 39–42). The mother and grandmother are for Marcel living expressions of the rural innocence and goodness of Sand's novels of nostalgia for an anti-industrial paradise of simple peasant folk; as such they stand at the center of Marcel's first world—the rural village community of Combray—as the principles of ultimate good.

Marcel, a hypersensitive child, yearns to prolong infinitely the perfect unity with the mother which newborn infants enjoy, but which must inevitably be broken as the child grows. For the newborn baby the world is one: mother and child make an unbroken whole. Marcel experiences the anguish of partial separation from his mother already within the "paradise" of Combray. He finds himself no longer perfectly one with her, but rather an "I" detached from his mother's "I" and set free in a world of "others." One of his characteristic fears is of strange rooms—his own room in Combray transformed by the magic lantern and, later, hotel rooms. Familiar rooms, he tells us, are filled with "mon moi" (10). They are friendly and secure, for when he is in them he is not faced with "otherness," with the world beyond the bounds of his self.

On the night of Swann's visit, after Marcel has sent a note to his mother asking her to come, the diningroom where she is eating suddenly loses its fearful "otherness":

For that forbidden and unfriendly dining-room, where but a moment ago the ice itself—with burned nuts in it—and the finger bowls seemed to me to be concealing pleasures that were mischievous and of a mortal sadness because Mamma was tasting of them and I was far away, had opened its doors to me and, like a ripe fruit which bursts through its skin, was going to pour out into my intoxicated heart the gushing sweetness of Mamma's attention while she was reading what I had written. Now I was no longer separated from her; the barriers were down; an exquisite thread was binding us. (M 41)

The space in which his mother enjoys the company of others is hostile because it is filled with other selves. This hostility is dissipated when Marcel's letter entirely occupies the mother's consciousness with his own *moi*, filling the room again with his presence.

But the moment in which unity with the mother is most perfectly, though temporarily, regained, is the goodnight kiss. If the mother is the principle of ultimate love and good, the kiss is the sacrament of communion with her: "she bent her loving face down over my bed, and held it out to me like a Host, for an act of Communion in which my lips might drink deeply the sense of her real presence, and with it the power to sleep" (M 17). Yet the communion of the kiss is each time lost and must be perpetually regained. Marcel would like to keep his mother with him all night, but realizes that his desire "ran too much counter to general requirements and to the wishes of others" (M 59). Thus his anguish of separation must repeat itself each night, and this same anguish will in fact continue throughout his life (37). He will search for, and never find again, "that untroubled peace which no mistress, in later years, has ever been able to give me, since one has doubts of them at the moment when one believes in them, and never can possess their hearts as I used to receive, in her kiss, the heart of my mother, complete, without scruple or reservation, unburdened by any liability save to myself" (M 265).

Beyond the narrator's relationship with his mother, the larger family—including grandparents, aunts, and uncles—is at least in one of its aspects a secure, unified community for the young boy. In the evening, as the family sits in the garden together around an iron table, the sound of the bell on the gate announces the intrusion of an outsider into their midst. The grandmother goes to see who it is: "And there we would all stay, hanging on the words which would fall from my grandmother's lips when she brought us back her report of the enemy" (M 18–19).

The family group is bound together by the rituals of their daily life, familiar only to them. Every Saturday, for instance, Françoise goes in the afternoon to the market in a nearby village, and the family has lunch an hour earlier than in the rest of the week:

The return of this asymetrical Saturday was one of those petty occurrences, intramural, localised, almost civic, which, in uneventful lives and stable orders of society, create a kind of national unity, and become the favourite theme for conversation, for pleasantries, for anecdotes which can be embroidered as the narrator pleases; it would have provided a nucleus, ready-made, for a legendary cycle, if any of us had had the epic mind. (M 155–156)

The family is brought together in a bond compared to those of the closed, medieval society which produced the national epics. It is a continual source of astonishment or amusement for members of the family that outsiders or *barbares*, as the family calls them, are not "in" on this change in routine (111). The metaphor the family uses is significant: barbarians were for Greek society all aliens, men of strange cultures living outside its bounds.

But the society of Combray as a whole is also closed against the outside. For those who live in it, Combray is thoroughly known in its houses, shops, and walks, and in its inhabitants. Tante Léonie, in bed by the upstairs window, is upset and curious when she occasionally sees someone pass whom she does not know, "since at Combray a person whom one 'didn't know at all' was as incredible a being as any mythological deity" (M 79). She ruthlessly presses an investigation until this mythological creature is again reduced to the proportions of the known. The nearby town of Méséglise is already in the domain of the alien unknown, and on Sundays when natives of Méséglise come to walk in Combray, Léonie does not know them and can only identify them as "people who must have come over from Méséglise" (M 191). The narrator takes walks "du côté de Méséglise," but the town itself remains throughout his childhood "as inaccessible as the horizon" (M 191).

Thus Combray as a whole marks the outer bounds of the paradise of unity for the young Marcel. Combray stands in sharp contrast with the urban world, huge, mysterious and anonymous, in which the narrator will later find himself, a lone "I" in the midst of others.[18]

Combray is, however, a false paradise. Just as the primordial unity with the mother is in fact already broken for the young Marcel, so too the community of Combray, and even the more intimate one of the family circle, contain all the elements of fragmentation—cruelty, deception, mystery—which will divide the society Marcel comes to know later. The most elementary of the divisions cuts Combray in half: the two *côtés*, or walks that Marcel and his family habitually take, never both on the same day. The "côté de Méséglise" and the "côté de Guermantes" are "unaware of each other's existence, in the sealed vessels—between which there could be no communication—of separate afternoons" (M 193). The two walks in different directions represent spatially a class distinction—between the bourgeois who live on the Méséglise walk—Swann, Legrandin, and Vinteuil—and the noble Guermantes on the other. Like the walks themselves, this class separation seems at first absolute to Marcel, and one of the major themes of *A la recherche* as a whole is his discovery of their joining.

Indeed, Marcel's family does not realize for a long time that Swann, who comes from a solid bourgeois family, has a social life in the aristocracy as a member of the Jockey Club. He, like many other Proustian characters, has a hidden, other life. In different milieux he is a different person altogether: "Certainly the Swann who was a familiar figure in all the clubs of those days differed hugely from the Swann created in my great-aunt's mind" (M 25). The aunt "creates" Swann by constructing an image based only on what ideas she has of him: "None of us can be said to constitute a material whole, which is identical for everyone, and need only be turned up like a page in an account-book or the record of a will; our social personality is created by the thoughts of other people" (M 25). The great-aunt's construction of Swann's social personality lacks a whole section of his life—in high society—which remains hidden from her.

But even the part of Swann's life known to Marcel's family—his quiet, bourgeois existence in Combray with his wife and child, his regular visits to the family—is obscure. The family is reduced to hypothesize whether he is unhappy with his wife (whom they never see, since she is not of "good society"), whether he loves her, and whether she lives, as rumor has it, with M. de Charlus (34). Very characteristically here, Proust introduces in passing a character who will slowly reveal aspects of his life and personality later on in *A la recherche*. For the moment, Charlus' "social personality" for the narrator's family is limited to his suspected liaison with Swann's wife; in "Un Amour de Swann" we learn that between Charlus and Odette,

"Swann knew . . . nothing untoward could ever happen" (M 454), but only at the beginning of *Sodome et Gomorrhe* do we discover his homosexuality and begin to be introduced to a whole hidden area of his life. By such contrasts between the first appearances of characters and their later manifestations, Proust translates into the structure of his novel a conception of human beings as revealing, like the tips of icebergs, only a small and sometimes deceptive part of their total being at any one time to any given observer.

Swann's life and feelings are all the more obscure since he has the habit of hiding his real feelings under irony and a concern with factual details (98). In fact, as we learn later in "Un Amour de Swann," his *vie mondaine* has rendered him superficial; he hides his inner self not only from others but from himself. Never asking himself important questions, never pursuing an idea or feeling profoundly within himself (210), he is an "inauthentic" person separated from his true self.

In addition to Swann, his wife, and Charlus, the momentary appearance of Gilberte opens a new, tantalizing, and anguishing field of the unknown to Marcel. Before he sees her, Marcel already invests her unexplored existence with the prestige of the equally unknown existences of Swann himself and Bergotte, the writer whom Marcel admires and the Swanns know personally. By association with Bergotte's writing, Marcel dreams of Gilberte in front of a Gothic cathedral (100). Thus Marcel's image of Gilberte and his feeling for her from the very start have nothing to do with herself; she is his purely subjective creature, colored by literary association as Swann's image of Odette is formed by association with a painting. When Marcel sees Gilberte for the first time in Swann's park, he senses "that unknown world of her existence, into which I should never penetrate" (M 203). Yet later when he plays with her every day in the Champs-Elysées, and is familiar with much of her daily routine, he does not really know her any more than at the start.

Legrandin, another Combray bourgeois, has like Swann a hidden life with the aristocracy; more than discreetly unmentioned, it is frankly contradicted by his attitude in the company of the narrator and his family. His base *arrivisme* and snobbery are hidden by hypocrisy; he deceives Marcel's family, and even himself, with his tirades against snobbery (129). His mental states are entirely closed off. He has two different social personalities, and each is unaware of the other's existence.

Legrandin's secret life is revealed to the narrator through chance encounters at times when Legrandin would have preferred not to have met Marcel and his family. The secret life of the Vinteuil family, on the other hand, is revealed by a characteristic Proustian device: Marcel sees a revelatory scene through the window of their house at Montjouvain (on the Méséglise way). In fact this voyeurism occurs twice. The first time (113), Marcel learns from what he sees that Vinteuil would like to play his music for others, but is so fearful of seeming vain and egotistical that he refuses himself the pleasure at the last minute. He so succeeds in hiding his work from those in Combray who know him that Swann, who some years before heard and admired the sonata of a great modern composer named Vinteuil, naturally assumes that the composer is a relative of Vinteuil, not Vinteuil himself (149, 214). Marcel's discovery merely reveals that something further is being hidden; only much later do we realize that the great composer and the piano teacher who lives at Montjouvain are one and the same.

The second scene of voyeurism reveals, in contrast to Vinteuil's self-sacrifice that conceals a great work of art, an act of sadism that foreshadows many further revelations of sadism and masochism (usually associated with sexual inversion) in *A la recherche*.[14] Vinteuil is aware at the end of his life of rumors in the village that his daughter is having lesbian relations with an older friend. This cruel *médisance* is, according to the narrator, the real cause of his death. The narrator learns the truth of the matter only after Vinteuil's death. Hidden in the same spot on a hill facing the Vinteuil's livingroom window, Marcel sees Mlle. Vinteuil, in the beginning of sexual play with her older friend, take pleasure in allowing her friend to insult and finally spit on a photograph of her father. The narrator tells us that it is probably this scene which later formed his idea of sadism (159). But he makes it clear that Mlle. Vinteuil's cruelty, although she gives it a more dramatic, symbolic form, is only the cruelty hidden in all men: "Perhaps she would not have thought of wickedness as a state so rare, so abnormal, so exotic . . . had she been able to distinguish in herself, as in all her fellow-men and women, that indifference to the sufferings which they cause which, whatever name else be given it, is the one true, terrible and lasting form of cruelty" (M 236–237). Cruelty is revealed not only in the daughter but also in the villagers who destroy Vinteuil, indifferent to his suffering.

Marcel, then, in his experiences "du côté de chez Swann," among the bourgeois of Combray, discovers only "others" who conceal a greater part of their lives, sometimes by deception. They conceal their profound being even from themselves, and hence also from him. What they sometimes reveal is either another level of inauthenticity or a basic cruelty that is at the root of men's relations with one another.

Moreover, some are irremediably "other" for Marcel by the nature of his subjective relation to them; he creates an image of them which originates more in his imagination than in them.

The "côté de Guermantes," the milieu of the nobility, is largely unexplored by the narrator in the first part of *A la recherche*. He does not have the occasion to investigate the otherness of the aristocracy, for in the family walks they never reach the source of the Vivonne River, where the Guermantes have their estate. Now he is only able to "create" them from his imagination, as he does Gilberte. Here the aesthetic prism through which he sees them is the tapestry and stained-glass windows that depict their medieval ancestors in the church of Combray, and his own magic lantern, which also shows one of their forebears, Geneviève de Brabant.

When he actually sees Mme. de Guermantes once in the church, Marcel is at first terribly disappointed: she has a large nose, with a blemish on a corner of it, and a red face. Her physical type and dress in no way distinguish her from the bourgeois of Combray. Immediately, however, his imagination operates to transform and ennoble her physiognomy. Then when she looks at Marcel, "avec bonté" (178), he immediately loves her. Although the psychic mechanisms that make Marcel fall in love with Gilberte (her look of disdain causes him to love her) and with Mme. de Guermantes are opposite, they are both equally unrelated to the objects of his love themselves.

In the society of Combray, then, the young Marcel in quest of perfect unity discovers only the world of others with its radical separations and hostilities, and what is more, he discovers it within the more intimate "society" of his family. For society at large has made inroads in the family, as surely as it has in Combray. Although at times the solidarity of the family closed to the outside gives him comfort, Marcel revolts against Françoise's ritualistic sense of the sacredness of blood ties; after the death of his aunt, he enrages Françoise by insisting that he is sad at her death because she was at bottom a good woman, but not because she was his aunt (154).

Marcel's family circle exhibits all the characteristic relationships of otherness that he finds beyond its bounds. He witnesses the cruelty of his great-aunt toward his grandmother (12), and later discovers the parallel brutality and cruelty of Françoise toward the chicken she beheads and the kitchen maid she persecutes. These acts are normally hidden from Marcel, who sees Françoise's "front" in the diningroom and only occasionally has glimpses of her other life in the kitchen and backyard (121–124). Tante Léonie pursues Françoise with suspicions that she steals (117); and she gives money to her weekly visitor

Eulalie to assure that she will continue coming (106–107), much as Swann will "buy" Odette's presence in "Un Amour de Swann."

Marcel sometimes makes discoveries about people within the family as a hidden observer. He overhears his aunt recount a nightmare that reveals her fear of being forced to leave her comfortable reclusion, when he enters her room while she is sleeping and remains there unnoticed (109–110). When he visits his uncle, wishing to gain access to the mysterious world of actresses which Adolphe frequents in another existence from the one Marcel knows, the situation is slightly modified. Marcel does not observe Adolphe from a hidden vantage point, but arrives on a day when he does not habitually come, thus breaking into a hidden sector of his uncle's life. All he discovers is another mystery, however; "la dame en rose" remains an enigma to him, and only much later will he learn that she, Odette, and Mme. Swann are the same person.

If Combray and Marcel's family already contain all the elements of otherness and fragmentation which divide society at large, there are also in the Combray section of *Swann* images of retreat from this microcosm of society. Tante Léonie withdraws only at the end of life, after the death of her husband, to "first Combray, then her house in Combray, then her bedroom, and finally her bed" (M 68), like most old people (only earlier than most) who slowly retreat from life as they near death. She lives a largely solitary life in her upstairs room, playing both hands of her card games and both sides of her imaginary conversations with Françoise (117). Her relation to the life going on outside her room is that of a spectator: she watches endlessly all that passes her window. The narrator and Proust himself, as adults, will come to resemble Léonie, retreating to a closed sick room and bed (which is also where they write), passive spectators of life beyond their room. Indeed, the young Marcel's conception of the theater, before he has actually seen one, suggests the relation to life of a man both physically withdrawn as a passive spectator and isolated by the unique nature of personal vision: "I almost believed that each of the spectators looked, as into a stereoscope, upon a stage and scenery which existed for himself alone, though closely resembling the thousand other spectacles presented to the rest of the audience individually" (M 102).

Marcel has in fact already begun his retreat from the ambient society of his childhood. We have seen how cruelty is one of the marks of otherness that characterizes the society of Combray and even of the narrator's family circle. Marcel's characteristic response to the cruelty of his great-aunt to his grandmother is flight: "I did what all we grown men do when face to face with suffering and injustice; I preferred not to see them; I ran to the top of the house to cry by myself in a little room beside the schoolroom and beneath the roof, which smelt of orrisroot" (M 16). Here the narrator explicitly relates this withdrawal to similar situations in adult life, and attempts to justify his retreat by claiming that it is a general rule of human conduct. His retreat in this circumstance is the bathroom, "which was for a long time my place of refuge, doubtless because it was the only room whose door I was allowed to lock, whenever my occupation was such as required an inviolable solitude; reading or dreaming, secret tears or paroxysms of desire" (M 16). In this room he experiences his first sexual pleasure in masturbation (for he never finds the imagined peasant girl he desires)—the *péché solitaire* which is the equivalent, in the domain of the erotic, of Tante Léonie's card games with herself.

The young boy also retires regularly to his own room after lunch. With the shutters closed, the impression on his senses of the summer day outside is diminished, and he thereby experiences it passively, at a distance and through the mediation of imagination (83). Here also Marcel reads, an occupation that, in contrast to his promenades in the immediate reality of the physical world and society outside his room, will put him in touch with his "real" deeper self, and will offer him the only possible communication with other men.

III

Although the second of the three parts of *Du côté de chez Swann*—entitled "Un Amour de Swann"—appears superficially to be an entirely discrete narrative (centered on a love affair of Swann's which occurred before the birth of Marcel), there are nonetheless very precise relationships linking the two. On the evening when Marcel waits for his mother's goodnight kiss, Swann is the stranger from outside the family who keeps her at the table; yet, as the narrator comments, he found out later that "a similar anguish had been the bane of his life for many years, and no one perhaps could have understood my feelings at that moment so well as himself" (M 42). The Swann who causes Marcel's suffering has himself experienced the torment of knowing that a loved one is in "some place of enjoyment where oneself is not" (M 42), in a hostile room filled with "otherness," through his relation with Odette recounted in "Un Amour de Swann." With Marcel, however, this anguish has entered his life before the adult love relation: "it must drift, awaiting Love's coming, vague and free, without precise attachment, at the disposal of one sentiment today, or another tomorrow, of filial piety or affection for a comrade" (M 42).

Thus Swann's love is an extension into adult life of Marcel's anguish in the world of "others" and his quest for lost unity. Swann's love, depicted in microscopic psychological detail, will allow us to examine more deeply the relation of the subject to the "other" in Proust's world. Similarly, the portrait of society in "Un Amour de Swann" is only a broadening of the Combray portrait into Parisian society. The two côtés are represented in the bourgeois salon of the Verdurins and the single soirée of Mme. de Sainte-Euverte, where we are introduced for the first time to the aristocracy that only existed as legend in the Combray section. The basic mechanisms that animate this Parisian society, we will discover, are the same as those of Combray.

The transition from an exploration of the narrator's own childhood to an incident in another man's life which occurred before the narrator's birth must nonetheless be explained. The narrator tells us at the end of the Combray section that he recently has spent his sleepless nights recalling not only his childhood days that the tea and madeleine have brought back to him in their original *parfum*, but also a memory not his own; further on he explains that Swann's love was recounted to him by a third person.

Here then is an explanation, but certainly an inadequate one, for the shift that takes place in the second part from the consciousness of Marcel to that of Swann. As a general rule in *A la recherche*, and in the Combray section in particular, the point of view is that of first-person narrator. The world is experienced through his subjectivity— or more precisely through the alternation of the consciousness of the younger Marcel who lives the remembered experience and the consciousness of the older Marcel as he writes down the memory. This technique, in contrast to the point of view of the omniscient author widely employed in earlier fiction, translates into the form of the novel Proust's awareness of each man's solitude, his inability to know others: "We exist alone. Man is the being that cannot come out of himself, that only knows others in himself" (III, 450).

The explanation given attempts to explain how Marcel came to know Swann's love in such detail and depth, but it is manifestly inadequate in the terms of Proust's own conception of the impossibility of knowing another person. How could the third person who recounted the story to Marcel have entered so completely into the consciousness of Swann, to follow every nuance of his feelings and thoughts? The inadequacy of the overt explanation simply reinforces our contention that Swann's love is an extension of the narrator's own mental states into adulthood. Although the character changes, we continue to experience the novelistic world through a single, isolated consciousness, and one whose experience of the "other" continues and deepens that of the young Marcel. Although the restriction of point of view to a single consciousness is not followed with perfect consistency in "Un Amour de Swann" (especially in the social scenes), it is nonetheless the dominant technique that informs the whole with Swann's vision.

Related to this technique of the isolated point of view is a stylistic trait that recurs often in Proust: a series of hypotheses about the motives, feelings, or thoughts of a character presented in an "either . . . or . . . or" structure. The series is usually linked by the "soit . . . soit" locution, but also often by alternative forms such as "peut-être . . . peut-être" and "ou . . . ou . . . ou." If the novelistic world with its characters is viewed exclusively from the vantage point of a single consciousness that has no omniscient knowledge of the thoughts and emotions of the persons around him, then the narrator can often only formulate hypotheses as to why a character acted in a certain way, made a certain expression or gesture. The interior of the "other" is obscure, and the narrative consciousness can never be positively sure that any given determinant of behavior is the right one. He can only guess that one of several possibilities might be accurate.[15]

Thus in the Combray section, in which even members of the family are "others" for Marcel, the hypothesis construction is often used to describe Marcel's uncertainty as to the meaning of their behavior. For example, when one of the two maiden aunts has attempted in a most enigmatic way to show her thanks to Swann for a gift, Marcel watches the expression of the other aunt:

En même temps ma tante Flora qui avait compris que cette phrase était le remerciement de Céline pour le vin d'Asti, regardait également Swann avec un air mêlé de congratulation et d'ironie, soit simplement pour souligner le trait d'esprit de sa soeur, soit qu'elle enviât Swann de l'avoir inspiré, soit qu'elle ne pût s'empêcher de se moquer de lui parce qu'elle le croyait sur la sellette. (25)

In "Un Amour de Swann" the hypothesis constructions are used often in relation to Odette, who is frustratingly enigmatic for Swann (for example, 233, 242, 319, 320), but also in relation to other characters: Brichot (251) and Forcheville (276–277) in the Verdurin salon and the Guermantes at Mme. de Saint-Euverte's soirée (329, 339).

In the case of Swann himself, the situation is more complicated. I have already pointed out that in "Un Amour de Swann" the narrator places himself within the consciousness of Swann and describes it in the finest detail. Thus when Swann hears the *petite phrase* of the Vinteuil sonata at the Verdurin salon, the narrator notes: "Or quand le pianiste eut joué, Swann fut plus aimable encore avec lui qu'avec les autres personnes qui se trouvaient là. Voici pourquoi: . . ." (208). He continues to analyze in great depth the impressions that the musical phrase had made upon Swann when he first heard it the year before. The "Voici pourquoi" locution, a frequent Balzacian *tournure*, is the exact opposite of the hypothesis. The narrator has access to the total contents of Swann's consciousness, and "Voici pourquoi" is introductory to his laying them unambiguously before the reader.

But there is inconsistency in Proust's narrative technique in the Swann section. While in general the contents of Swann's consciousness are revealed to us as if the narrator had complete access to it, in some passages Swann is treated like an "other," and the narrator employs hypothesis constructions in relation to Swann's mental states (for example, 223, 232, 233, 267). Swann becomes momentarily a mysterious being like any of the other characters the narrator confronts.

I might add that elsewhere the narrator employs (although far less often than the hypothesis) a related form, the additive series. In this construction he lists a number of complementary motives or feelings behind one act, thus affirming rather than hypothesizing something about the character (the grandmother, 11; Swann, 269; Mme. de Guermantes, 333, 340). By stressing the dense complexity of human feeling, however, the narrator reinforces the reader's sense of the obscurity of these characters. As Jack Murray notes, this is in fact the effect of the Proustian style of character description in general: "A screen of explanatory language intervenes between the reader and the character under observation, growing more opaque until that enigmatic surface—otherness—leaves him overwhelmed by an uncanny sense of isolation before the character. The character gradually retreats into a darkness where the reader may not follow."[16]

In Marcel's first relationships with Gilberte and Mme. de Guermantes, we saw how from the very start (from before he had even seen them) the young boy creates in his imagination a personage that in no way corresponds to the real person herself. In Swann's love for the coquette Odette de Crécy we may follow the workings of this psychological mechanism beyond its first stages through an entire adult love relationship; for the discontinuity between the images projected by the subjective self, and their objects in the world, is not a phenomenon limited to naive childhood fantasy. For Proust it has the status of a general law of human relations.[17]

From the beginning Swann is indifferent to, even repulsed by, Odette's physical traits. At the end of his liaison with her he will regret having wasted time on a woman "who was not in my style"

(M 549). He must therefore transform her displeasing physical type in his mind to correspond to his new feeling for her. Like Marcel, Swann beautifies the ugliness of people around him with aesthetic images. He sees a resemblance between Odette and Botticelli's painting of Jethro's daughter in the Sistine Chapel (225), and in the traits of his society friends he sees resemblances with faces in other paintings of the Renaissance masters, thus giving to his superficial, frivolous relations in high society a significance they do not possess in themselves (222–223).

Swann not only transforms Odette's physical features, but also her entire personality. Since she also manufactures an illusory image of his personality, the *rapprochement des coeurs* which seems to unite them is itself illusory. Odette imagines Swann as an awesome savant and an elite soul; yet her conception of intellectuality and sensitivity is based only on the lip service people give to them. She does not really understand the workings of Swann's sensitivity, and she does not realize—partly due to his deception, partly to her ignorance—that he is an intellectual dilettante who abandoned his work on Ver Meer years ago (his experience of love for her inspires him to take it up again). At first Swann is for her an ideal being whose mind she is unable to fathom; later, while still ignorant of the contents and mechanism of his mind, she is principally interested in making it "reasonable," molding it to her own specifications.

Swann, conversely, convinces himself that Odette is intelligent and appreciates art as he does. We slowly come to learn, however, that she is unintelligent, uneducated, and even superstitious, has a vulgar aesthetic taste and knows nothing about art. Far from being able to follow his theories, to which she doesn't listen, she has not even heard of Ver Meer, the painter whose work Swann is studying. When he occasionally realizes the discrepancy between his sophistication and taste and hers, he attempts to close the gap by imitating her attitudes and opinions. Yet Swann is never able to make his tastes, feelings, and thoughts correspond with hers (nor with those of the Verdurins, who are for him a sort of extension of Odette), and except for inklings of her vulgarity and stupidity, he knows next to nothing of the rest of her personality: " 'She?'—he tried to ask himself what that meant; for love resembles death . . . in making us probe further, in the fear that its substance will escape our grasp, the mystery of personality" (308).

Swann asks himself this question late in the progression of their love, as it nears its end; in its early stages, however, rather than attempting to explore the mystery of her personality, he has been occupied solely with tactics and calculations which have the negative purpose of keeping her from losing interest in him and seeing other men. Thus he refuses to see Odette before dinner, on the theory that if he seems to have other pleasures that he prefers to her company, she will desire him all the more; and he sees her home from the Verdurins' so that she will leave with no one else (218–219).

Swann's tactics are sometimes aimed at reviving his own feeling for the imagined Odette when the real one seems to be in danger of boring him:

Feeling that, since Odette had had every facility for seeing him, she seemed no longer to have very much to say to him when they did meet, he was afraid lest the manner—at once trivial, monotonous, and seemingly unalterable—which she now adopted when they were together should ultimately destroy in him that romantic hope, that a day might come when she would make avowal of her passion . . . he wrote, suddenly, a letter full of hinted discoveries and feigned indignation . . . and he hoped that, when the fear of losing him clutched at her heart, it would force from her words such as he had never yet heard her utter. (M 323–324)

From the beginning Swann's relation with Odette is marked by deception and cruelty, for it is only by seeming other than he is, and thereby making her suffer, that he feels he can secure her affection and keep his own alive. In the later evolution of the love relation, the *rapport de force*—domination and suffering—is reversed. Swann becomes jealous, and the power to hurt passes to Odette. The change occurs when the "otherness" of Odette suddenly confronts Swann. He has previously been comfortably assured that Odette has no hidden life with others after she leaves the Verdurin soirées, because he accompanies her home. But on the evening when he arrives late at the Verdurin's and finds her gone, the mystery of another existence not filled with his "moi" rises before him. He must discover where she is and what she is doing. A search through the *grands boulevards* ensues, where he finally locates her. But the idea of an unknown and hostile Odette has been planted in Swann's mind. He is jealous, and jealousy places him totally under her domination.

He has never really enjoyed being with Odette—he was irritated by the idea of seeing her on the very night he became jealous—but now he attempts desperately to see her often, to procure for himself the negative pleasure of calming his jealousy. By multiplying the times when his own "moi" fills her apartment and her life, Swann is able to calm his suffering momentarily. He suspects that Odette's pleasure in seeing him is not very great either, and that she only shows regret for having missed a chance to see him because she knows how much he enjoys seeing her (238, 280). Yet we have seen that Swann in fact does not enjoy the visits. Thus neither partner takes pleasure in the other's presence; yet both are condemned to seek it.

Since Swann's love is not based on Odette's real self, but on a self-generated image in his imagination, her presence has nothing to do with his love, can only disrupt it. Sometimes when he is not with her, "while he changed his clothes, he would be wondering, all the time, about Odette, and in this way was never alone, for the constant thought of Odette gave to the moments in which he was separated from her the same peculiar charm as to those in which she was at his side" (M 387–388). The sentiment that physical distance cannot separate the lover from his loved one is a theme of medieval courtly poetry. Yet in Proust it is emptied of its content: if the image of the loved one does not correspond to her real self, then the feeling of unity with the loved one, both in her presence and in separation, is rendered illusory. Although Swann feels for a moment that he is not alone, in the Proustian perspective he is *always* alone.[18]

If the real Odette is utterly indifferent to Swann, the pleasure and significance of sexual relations cannot be very great either. On the night when Swann for the first time has sexual relations with Odette (the same night he becomes jealous), the narrator abruptly cuts off the scene in the carriage, which has been described in some detail, at the point where Swann is holding Odette's head in the second before he kisses her. He holds her head away for a moment as if reluctant to bring his dream in contact with her physical reality (232–233). The kiss itself, the emotions Swann feels as he kisses her and "the act of physical possession (in which, paradoxically, the possessor possesses nothing)" (M 336), are skipped as altogether unimportant. The real pleasure in the event for Swann is not the sexual possession itself, but the difficulty of attaining it, the tactics of arranging the flowers on her bosom.

Although the sexual act does not provide it, real possession of the loved one is what Swann seeks (231). He desires a total and undivided relation in which the entire being of the loved one is known to him and devoted to him (as Marcel's mother once was to him). This lost relationship can only be regained through domination: "a painful longing to secure the absolute mastery of even the tiniest particles of her heart" (M 390). When Swann's psychological tactics of domination fail, and he finds himself on the defensive, he must resort to the most literal forms of possession. Thus Swann at one point takes Odette away from Paris and his rival, Forcheville. In their hotel in the south of France, however, Swann still fears that all the men around desire Odette, and he attempts to keep her away from their company (283–284). Later, when he suspects her of lesbian relations, he realizes that this form of possession is impossible, that he cannot guard Odette against all possible frequentation of women (364). Marcel, further on in *A la recherche,* will not resign himself to this impossibility, and attempts to possess Albertine as a chattel. Thus the *prisonnière* theme is foreshadowed here. Holding Albertine captive to him will be a distorted and degraded form of the primordial unity that Marcel vainly seeks in the world of others.

Yet Swann does not seek possession principally in the direct chattel form, but indirectly through the controlling medium of money. As he previously attempted to procure tenderness from her by simulating anger and coldness, now he sends her gifts, especially jewels, to stimulate her gratitude, "to elicit from her fresh particles of her intimate feelings, which she had never yet revealed" (384). More important than these gifts, he provides her with a monthly allowance by which he measures out his love and buys affection in return (268).

Swann realizes that his relation to Odette corresponds to the situation of the *femme entretenue,* and he probably (a "hypothesis") would not have been distressed "to discover that Odette's love for him was based on a foundation more lasting than mere affection, or any attractive qualities which she might have found in him; on a sound, commercial interest" (M 384). Indeed, it is intimated later that Odette may be considering marriage out of interest (354), which will throw a doubtful light on their marriage when we discover (in the last pages of *Du côté de chez Swann*) that she does become Mme. Swann. Here Swann reproduces, out of the same fear and insecurity in his contact with others which caused him earlier to use deception and tactics, the bourgeois relationship to others that Marcel noted in his parents (93). Swann uses the elements of social position and money to cement his tie with Odette. The femme entretenue, like the prisonnière, is a grotesque realization, degraded by the values of the ambiant society, of the lost unity Marcel seeks.

Swann, like Marcel, has a desperate need to possess and to dominate the entirety of the other's existence, and is obsessed with fears of a mysterious life hidden from him. Odette's entire past, and those hours of the day in the present when he never sees her, are areas of menacing unknown (239, 307). These deep waters—"Il surnageait pourtant à cet inconnu certaines occupations" (318)—are hidden by a surface of *mensonge.* Swann attempts to uncover Odette's lies or silences by all means possible: he interrogates friends and acquaintances, he opens letters, and once he even employs a detective agency. Yet the method of discovery that haunts him, and of which the others are merely extensions, is the same voyeurism that revealed something of Tante Léonie and the Vinteuils to Marcel.

Unlike Marcel, who witnesses the scenes at the Vinteuil house through windows opened for him, Swann returns one night after bidding Odette goodnight to find her window lighted but shuttered. With the possibility of opening the window and revealing the two persons he hears within, Swann feels a renewed sense of dominance over Odette: "now that Odette's other life . . . was within his grasp, before his eyes, in the full glare of the lamp-light, caught and kept there, an unwitting prisoner, in that room into which, when he would, he might force his way to surprise and seize it" (M 393). Odette's other life and her hostile room, both inhabited by some other "moi" than his own, can be broken into, filled again with himself, and placed under his domination.

Yet when he does knock on the window, he discovers nothing: two old men answer his call, since Swann's predisposition for revelation has made him mistake their lighted house for Odette's. This disappointment is representative of all Swann's attempts at discovery. Just as Marcel only uncovered further mysteries, Swann seeks the truth of Odette's life as one peels an onion. Each discovery only reveals a deeper layer of mystery to penetrate.

Near the end of their relation, Swann begins to suspect Odette of Lesbian relations as well as heterosexual ones, and although she admits to having had several such encounters (363), he cannot discover the extent and significance of them. She recounts one instance, however, which occurred at an early period in their love, on an evening they had spent together with the Verdurins in the Bois de Boulogne:

Never had he supposed it to have been so recent an affair, hidden from his eyes that had been too innocent to discern it, not in a past which he had never known, but in evenings which he so well remembered, which he had lived through with Odette, of which he had supposed himself to have such an intimate, such an exhaustive knowledge, and which now assumed, retrospectively, an aspect of cunning and deceit and cruelty. In the midst of them parted, suddenly, a gaping chasm, that moment on the Island in the Bois de Boulogne. (M 256)

Thus even the part of Odette's life which Swann thinks he knows and possesses entirely—evenings she has spent with him—are suddenly undermined by the hostile presence of her other life. With this discovery the last conceivable link between them dissolves. Odette becomes now a total stranger, entirely "other."

In the social worlds of the Verdurin salon and the soirée of Mme. de Saint-Euverte, Swann also finds himself in the realm of estrangement and antagonism. At the very beginning of "Un Amour de Swann," however, the Verdurin salon is presented to us in the images of social solidarity and religious communion. It is a *noyau, groupe,* or *clan* to which its members must give absolute allegiance. They must believe a Credo and are called the *fidèles,* like members of a church (188). The group must compete with other communities for its members' total participation—with other salons and, significantly, with the family and provincial community of the Combray type. Before holidays such as Christmas, New Year, or Easter, Mme. Verdurin lives in fear that her fidèles will abandon her to return to their provincial homes for family reunions (190). Like the communities of family and town in the Combray section, but more completely because it lacks the saving graces of maternal love and provincial stability, the Verdurin salon is a false community.

Like Combray, the salon's seeming unity is undermined by médisance, cruelty, and betrayal. This is most clearly illustrated in the related cases of Saniette and Swann. Good, simple, and timid, the elderly Saniette is treated with contempt by the other fidèles (203). When Forcheville violently insults Saniette, Swann surprises a look of complicity in Odette's eyes: "her eyes had sparkled with a malicious smile of congratulation upon his audacity, of ironical pity for the poor wretch who had been its victim; she had darted at him a look of complicity in the crime" (M 398–399).[19]

When Swann begins to fall into disrepute with the Verdurins because he is not enthusiastic enough in his fidelity, he first is the target of médisance and finally is betrayed by the Verdurins, who invite Odette to lunch with Forcheville, excluding Swann (263). Later they arrange one night in the Bois for Odette to return in their carriage with Forcheville. After this "execution" of Swann, Mme Verdurin exclaims: " 'No, but, don't you see, the filthy creature . . .' using unconsciously, and perhaps in satisfaction of the same obscure need to justify herself— like Françoise at Combray when the chicken refused to die—the very words which the last convulsions of an inoffensive animal in its death agony wring from the peasant who is engaged in taking its life" (411). Afterward Swann wonders whether Odette, hidden from him in the other carriage, had the same look of complicity in cruelty with Forcheville as on the night of Saniette's abasement (300).

Forcheville, the executioner of Saniette and Swann, who has great success in the Verdurin milieu and with Odette, illustrates the stupidity of the salon (251). As in Flaubert, social discourse is fragmented by *la bêtise,* incomprehension of and insensitivity to the concerns and ideas of others, and the *lieu commun* that replaces true exchange (200–201, 213). The fidèles do not really understand or enjoy the Vinteuil sonata and the works of the painter. These works are unfamiliar expressions of the profound self, and the fidèles live in the inauthentic, surface region of pose and deception. M. and Mme. Verdurin, whose laughter has become entirely humorless and ritualized, "resembled two masks in a theatre, each representing Comedy, but in a different way" (M 378).

Forcheville also exemplifies the way in which the social personality of the fidèles is defined by its relation with others, molded by others' reactions. Forcheville and others tailor their feelings and ideas to achieve approval. Their personality has no substance; it exists only as the constant readjustment of surface needed to create a favorable image that will allow them to be successfully integrated into the inauthentic collectivity. When the painter uses a slightly off-color word, Forcheville directs "a sweeping glance round the table to see whether it was 'all right' before he allowed his lips to curve in a prudish and conciliatory smile" (255). Similarly, Dr. Cottard is obliged to reverse precipitously his evaluation of Swann when he discovers in conversation with Mme. Verdurin that Swann is in disfavor (289).

The unity of the Verdurin salon, then, is an inauthentic one. The society of the fidèles is in fact made up of isolated individuals unknown to each other and to themselves, and whose relations are determined, as everywhere in the Proustian world, by egoism and cruelty.[20] The same mechanisms are at work in the aristocratic salon of Mme. de Saint-Euverte. The guests exhibit the same stupidity and insensitivity to the feelings of others. Although the Vinteuil phrase is so great, comments the narrator, that it might communicate its emotion to those at the party with a pariculariy musical bent, the aristocrats still do not recognize profound emotion when they encounter it in life, for they are only concerned with "la vie positive": social position and wealth (344, 348–349).

The evening is dominated by the highest example of aristocratic culture, Mme. de Guermantes (her title is the Princesse des Laumes at the time)—the same figure of whom Marcel could only dream at a distance in Combray. Yet her brilliance is due largely to her wit—the "esprit des Guermantes"—which is based almost exclusively on cutting médisance and on expressions of personal vanity (337, 339–340). She is indifferent to and incapable of understanding the concerns of others, even of a close friend like Swann. In fact the friendship of Oriane and Swann is superficial: "Swann and the princess had the same way of looking at the little things of life . . . On important matters, [they] had not an idea in common" (M 492). On the evening of Mme. de Saint-Euverte's party, Swann is suffering so acutely from jealousy over Odette that he attempts to communicate some of his feeling to Oriane. Just as he begins to stutter out his unhappiness, she interrupts him with social banter about someone she has just seen in the room; she has not even been listening (342–343).

This scene already prefigures the far more atrocious egoism and indifference to others of Oriane and her husband Basin at the close of *Le Côté de Guermantes*. When Swann announces that his doctors tell him he could die from one day to the next, they are more concerned about Oriane's having shoes to match her dress than about his impending death. They hurry off to their dinner party assuring Swann that he is perfectly healthy (II, 595–597). The goodness and love of the narrator's mother are not to be found in the aristocracy any more than in the bourgeoisie.

IV

Mme. de Guermantes was only a mysterious name to the Marcel of Combray; in "Un Amour de Swann," knowing her as an old friend does not bring Swann any closer to her. In the last, short section of *Du côté de chez Swann*—"Noms de pays: le nom"—Marcel becomes friends with the same Gilberte who was only a name and a hazy image, once seen in Combray. And she remains as distant from him in their friendship as she had before he knew her. Swann has the same basic relation to Mme. de Guermantes that he has with the bourgeois Verdurin (the narrator in Combray was shocked to see no physical difference between her and the bourgeois of the town); now Marcel repeats with Gilberte the relation of Swann with Odette.

The part of Gilberte's day when she is not playing with Marcel in the Champs-Elysées, and the days when she does not come at all, are for Marcel an anguishing *inconnu* (395, 406). Like Swann with Odette, Marcel takes no pleasure in being with Gilberte; for the real Gilberte with whom he plays is not the same as the imagined Gilberte he loves (400–401). He is only in contact with the beloved Gilberte when he is alone in his room at home, where the *moi profond* of his imagination has created her.

In the last pages of *Du côté de chez Swann* we are brought back to the narrator at the moment he is composing his book; he lives enclosed for months at a time in his "chambre fermée" (422). At the end of his life as at the beginning, the only solution to the failure of communication in a world of others lies in retreat; rather than the characteristic response to solitude of later twentieth-century authors—in collective action or affiliation—Proust and his narrator continue to choose the nineteenth-century withdrawal to the artist's room. In the solitude of his room the artist is in touch with his profound self. That is to say, he can fully experience the impressions he registers, but is incapable of seizing and enjoying when he is in direct contact with them.

These impressions are unique for each person; they make up a peculiar vision, the creation of a personal world. The artist can communicate his real self—in the form of a unique way of seeing—in his writings (III, 895–896). Marcel recognizes in all of Bergotte's books a common vision, which is what he appreciates rather than the specific matter of each book (94). The reader receives this communication in solitude, as the artist has created it in solitude. He responds to the author with his profound self, while he can relate to friends in everyday contact only through his social, superficial self. In the scale of Proustian relationships, friendship is the least valuable. Love at least puts us in touch with our deeper self, our emotions, although not with the loved one. Only art puts us in touch with others.[21]

Marcel reads novels in Combray, and he is able to understand the novels' characters as he could not understand the real people around him. Real persons are opaque in part because they and the person who observes them are both in perpetual flux. Erich Koehler has pointed out that in *A la recherche* the experience of the *autrui inconnaissable* is based (only in part, one would have to add) on the discontinuity of each person's selves—the *moi successifs* that make each moment of encounter between two people the meeting at one point of two lines of development that cannot be known as a whole.[22] For Marcel, the Swann he knew in his Combray childhood, the Swann he knows as the father of Gilberte who comes to fetch her in the Champs-Elysées, and the older Swann he knows later in society are entirely separate persons whom he can at no point integrate in his mind (19–20, 407). Both he and Swann are different persons at each of these stages.

Characters in a novel, on the other hand, can be grasped as a whole: the series of individual states make a curve which, because it takes its course in the short space of a book, can be experienced by the reader as a totality (85–86). The artist, on the other end of the connection, can recreate past states of himself and his perception of persons who were part of his life in the past, through "involuntary memory" (III, 872–873). These states would otherwise have remained forever closed to himself and to others, "vases clos et sans communication."

The artist does not always express his inner states with words, however. When Swann hears the Vinteuil sonata for the second time, "he was like a man into whose life a woman, whom he has seen for a moment passing by, has brought a new form of beauty, which strengthens and enlarges his own power of perception, without his knowing even whether he is ever to see her again whom he loves already, although he knows nothing of her, not even her name" (M 300). Swann's relation to the sonata is just the opposite of Marcel's relation to Mme. de Guermantes and Gilberte. Swann first receives a veritable communication through the music, then attempts to discover its name and the identity of its author. Marcel, before he knows Mme. de Guermantes and Gilberte, knows their names, around which he creates a mythical image. As he comes to know them personally, the mystery of the name gives way only to the mystery of the person herself.

Vinteuil's sonata, on the other hand, reveals itself even more fully to Swann as he comes to know it better. Although at first he appreciates the musical phrase principally to the extent that it corresponds to his feeling for Odette, and is irritated by the intrusion of an element that is proper to the artist himself (218–219), he later comes to realize that the piece expresses the ensemble of the experience of love—its joy, its suffering, and its final resignation—as Vinteuil has felt it (348–350). The fact that Swann has experienced similar emotions to those experienced by Vinteuil creates a fraternity between them.

The Proustian solution to the failure of communication in society, then, lies in solitude and art; yet the terms of the solution are widened beyond the elitist bounds of the late nineteenth century. Not only the artist, but all his readers, and beyond them all men, must find themselves and others in solitary withdrawal. And while the great artist is at first known only to an elite avant-garde of cultivated people who know how to understand him (although sometimes, as we noticed in the Verdurin salon, the so-called elite is no different from ordinary people and only pretends to understand a new work), his vision soon becomes accessible to wider and wider groups of readers or listeners. In Combray, Marcel is among the first admirers of Bergotte, along with the doctor du Boulbon: "And it was from his consulting room, and from a house in a park near Combray, that some of the first seeds were scattered of that taste for Bergotte, a rare growth in those days, but now so universally acclimatised that one finds it flowering everywhere throughout Europe and America, and even in the tiniest villages, rare still in its refinement, but in that alone" (M 133). The work of Vinteuil follows the same pattern (214).[23] We recognize here the conception of Romain Rolland's Jean Christophe and of others who at the turn of the century reacted against Decadent and Symbolist elitism.

At the end of his chapter on Proust in *Axel's Castle*, Edmund Wilson concludes: "Proust is perhaps the last great historian of the loves, the society, the intelligence, the diplomacy, the literature and the art of the Heartbreak House of capitalist culture; [he] dominates the scene and plays host in the mansion where he is not long to be master." [24] In this chapter we have looked at Proust's vision of human solitude—the universal isolation of the individual in society, which is one of the primary contradictions of modern capitalist culture. Although capitalism seems on the surface to be very distant from Proust's work, it is indeed the Heartbreak House in which he lives.

Yet Wilson's prediction, formulated at the beginning of the 1930s after the most shattering crisis that capitalism had ever undergone, proved of course to be inaccurate. What Wilson could not see is that Proust, although he draws his final solution to social fragmentation from a nineteenth-century perspective, is the first great historian of a whole new period of capitalist society. His novel stands first in a line of great twentieth-century novels of alienation, solitude, and man's effort to escape the modern condition.

5

La Condition humaine:
Solitude or Solidarity?

I

Proust's novel, a product of the period of transition between two capitalisms, elaborates a vision of universal solitude but offers a solution still based on the individual. With the domination of monopoly capitalism, however, the artist no longer conceives of self-realization in the isolated individual's *moi profond*. In a universally fragmented society in which the individual no longer has the importance he had as entrepreneur, isolation becomes a collective dilemma that requires a collective solution. The loneliness experienced by all individuals in the false collectivity calls for the recreation of bonds of solidarity in a true community. Consequently, during the period between the two wars, many writers turn from the individual as primary value to the collectivity.[1]

Some attempt simply to decree the reintegration of the individual in bourgeois society. Thus Jules Romains, one of the primary exponents of Unanimism, attempts to elaborate "a mode of composition that permits us to escape our habits of vision 'centered on the individual.' "[2] In his immense fresco of modern French society—*Les Hommes de bonne volonté* (27 volumes, 1932–1946)—Romains departs from the tradition that structures the novel on the life of an individual hero, creating a network of characters of equal importance and painting scenes that convey the movement of a crowd or a city as an ensemble that is more than the sum of the individuals who compose it. Here the individual's isolation in modern society is simply denied; although classes, groups, and different interests are part of the structure of group life as Romains depicts it, the ensemble is that of a "many-colored coat" rather than a dynamic totality in conflict and contradiction. A liberal ideology accompanies this novelistic conception: in spite of the variety of interests and passions in modern society, social progress will come from "men of good will" who give direction to and assure the unity of society.[3]

Some writers, on the other hand, reject the false collectivity of bourgeois society and attempt to integrate the individual in an alternate community. These are often elite collectivities made up of elite individuals. In the second half of the 1920s especially, a number of important novelists seek out the only communities that seem to have coherence and true fraternity: communities of *action*. In violent and dangerous action men are united in a necessary discipline and a common risk. In *Les Olympiques* (1924), Henry de Montherlant pictures sports as the only valid replacement in peacetime for the camaraderie, honesty, and naturalness of relations he experienced in World War One.[4] Sports and war also allow for the development of the elite individual, egotistical and proud of his value as part of the team or troop.[5]

Saint-Exupéry, whose first novels—*Courrier sud* and *Vol de nuit*—were published in 1928 and 1931, seeks both community and the full expression of the individual's powers in aviation, which was in its pioneering stage at that historical moment. The aviator escapes the alienated world of the *petit fonctionnaire* to a world of adventure which still exists only on the pioneering fringes of society. Here the individual has the status of a medieval warrior; he is joined in a strong bond of camaraderie to the elite brotherhood of flyers, which is compared to a medieval guild. Or, in another image, the flyer is a monk (solitary in his one-man cockpit) whose vocation is aviation and whose monastery is the airline. The human link grows directly out of the *danger* of the action: "We had met at last. Men travel side by side for years, each locked up in his own silence or exchanging those words which carry no freight—till danger comes. Then they stand shoulder to shoulder. They discover that they belong to the same family."[6]

This fraternity of danger is nonetheless doomed to be short-lived by the very purpose of pioneering aviation: the extension of a safe network of airlines around the world and the technological improvement of the airplane. Saint-Exupéry is aware of this when he writes *Terre des hommes* at the end of the entre-deux-guerres, as the heroic era of aviation comes to a close: "Pilot, mechanic, and radio operator no longer engage in an adventure; instead they are shut up in a laboratory."[7] The desert, once dangerous and mysterious territory controlled by tribes of *insoumis*, is now government-controlled and open

to exploitation by oil companies: "But they will have come too late
. . . [The sands] offered only a moment of fervor, and we were the
ones who experienced it." [8]

Although the literary "strategy" of André Malraux parallels those
of Saint-Exupéry and the early Montherlant—being in essence a
strategy that draws its force from violent and dangerous action—
there is an important difference. Malraux participated throughout his
novelistic career in the struggles of the political Left: revolutionary
anti-colonialism in the Orient and the Spanish Civil War. He engaged
himself in the combats of the Communist movement, which, unlike
sports, war, or aviation practiced for their own sakes, has not only
as its means but also as its end the transcendence of human isolation
and the creation of a new collectivity. In spite of this potentiality of
Communism as a project, Malraux comprehended and experienced the
Communist struggle almost exclusively in terms of its means—and
of these only the most violent. The alternate community it offered
him was the fraternity of armed combat alone. Thus Malraux's align-
ment with Communism does not contradict the deeper congruency
of his experience with the reactionary Montherlant and the apolitical
Saint-Exupéry.[9]

Malraux poses the problem of the isolated individual in his first
important work, *La Tentation de l'Occident* (1925), and in a lesser-
known short essay, "D'une jeunesse européenne" (1927). Here Malraux clearly defines solitude in historical terms. The isolation of man
has its roots in the concept of the individual soul at the beginning of
Western culture—in ancient Greece and early Christianity. The nineteenth century replaces the Christian world view with an individualism
that has the strength of a religion. Yet in the twentieth century, following the death of God and the triumph of individualism, man as an
absolute value is doomed to death as well. With no framework in
terms of which to understand and evaluate himself, the individual
falls prey to meaninglessness and total isolation. Malraux can only
pose the question: "What notion of Man is capable of rescuing the
civilization of solitude from its anguish . . . ?" [10]

In *La Tentation* the young Chinese, Ling, opposes this progressive
isolation and meaninglessness of man in Western civilization to the
individual's perfect integration in the universe in Eastern thought. But
he recognizes the inevitable corruption of the Oriental world view
by the present-day penetration of Western ideas. The old China is
dead, he says, and in the young, "the individual is being born." [11]
The present generation of young Europeans are left with only a lucid
despair in their solitude. They are unable to believe in any doctrine
that would replace the moribund religions of Christianity and nine-

teenth-century individualism: "Doctrines and religions, how difficult it is for man not to pay you homage with his solitude, and only to apply his disenchanted soul to those vain gestures that shine, at times, like the glitter of armor on the march." [12] Unable to believe, the young can only engage meaninglessly in action.

Several implications of Malraux's line of thought in these essays should be noted. First of all, although he interprets solitude as a modern phenomenon, and as the result of an historical evolution, his analysis is confined to the level of ideology: the idea of Christianity is replaced by the idea of the individual, and although Malraux does not say it explicitly, the "doctrine" available to twentieth-century man clearly is Communism. Individualism is another "religion" that supersedes Christianity, and Communism will put its own myth in the place of the old. Thus, although Malraux is already drawn to the Communist struggle, his analysis has little in common with the Marxist method. He makes no attempt to put forward a materialist interpretation of the historical developments he evokes; he does not ask what economic forces cause the decline of religion and the triumph of individualism. Nor is his interpretation in any sense dialectical, for religion, individualism, and socialism are related in a static juxtaposition of equal, interchangeable elements rather than in terms of progressive *dépassements* growing from the concrete, contradictory fabric of historical development. Since socialism has the status of a myth for Malraux, it does not carry the significance of its *telos*, the transcending of human alienation (and specifically solitude) under capitalism. Consequently, as Roger Stéphane points out, "Nothing fundamental, nothing that might give birth to loyalty, binds him to the idea of revolution." [13]

Of Malraux's first two novels—*Les Conquérants* (1928) and *La Voie royale* (1930)—only one has as its subject a revolutionary struggle, although the two are very similar in theme and structure. In both novels elite individuals of the adventurer type, alienated from and in revolt against bourgeois European society, engage in violent action—revolutionary and nonrevolutionary—that allows them temporarily to forget their solitude by complete absorption in the action, and to experience a fragile solidarity with the elite community of adventurers or insurrectional leaders: the *conquérants*. The adventurer-hero feels no solidarity, on the other hand, with the masses he manipulates from above—the Cantonese proletariat under Garine and the tribes of *insoumis* under Perken. The adventurer's sense of solitude, moreover, returns periodically whenever sickness or death brings him back to the concern that is always lurking in the back of his consciousness: his individual self and destiny, and his final annihilation as an individual in death. In both novels death and solitude triumph in the end over the power of action.

Garine and Perken can only engage in their action meaninglessly, for they believe in no doctrine that would give it significance. Perken wishes principally to create a powerful military force, to be used in whatever conflict develops; Garine is first attracted to the Communist Party not by its goal of creating a socialist society—for he believes that all societies are absurd—but by the efficacy of its insurrectional technique. Lack of commitment to the basic purposes of combat weakens its meaning for the hero, and its artificial solidarity is easily broken whenever the elemental force of death reasserts itself. Thus Trotsky's often-cited observation[14]—that with a more solid understanding of Marxism Malraux could have avoided the ideological mystifications of his hero Garine—has validity in a broad sense. Malraux did not tap the real significance of the socialist struggle in his obsession with the solitary individual. Had he been more concerned with the intellectual developments and implications of Marxist theory, he might have attributed a larger meaning to the struggle he was already engaged in: the telos of revolutionary activity is already contained, although only *partially and imperfectly* contained, in its means, the solidarity of struggle.

In spite of Malraux's limited definition of solidarity, however, its force in relation to solitude does not remain constant in the later novels. From the first novels to *Les Noyers de l'Altenburg*, the relation of solitude to solidarity describes a kind of parabola, with the importance and force of solidarity rising, then falling off.

In the first two novels solidarity plays no major role. The conqueror experiences occasional solidarity with fellow adventurers, but these ties are momentary, continually broken by the return of death, meaninglessness, and solitude. In *La Condition humaine* (1933), the obsession with solitude is still a central theme, but it is partially transcended in the group of the Shanghai revolutionaries. With *Le Temps du mépris* (1935), solitude is entirely transcended in a *fraternité virile*.

The growing dominance of bonds of solidarity is accompanied by a closer relation between the hero, or heroes, and the Party. In *Les Conquérants*, the central character is an adventurer who remains totally estranged from the ideology and goals of the Communist Party (although in agreement with its strategy). The group of Shanghai revolutionaries in *La Condition humaine*, on the other hand, is an integral part of the Party hierarchy and finds itself in conflict only with strategy decisions handed down from the Comintern. *Le Temps du mépris* celebrates the total accord of the hero Kassner with the Party.

In that work Malraux portrays the perfect solidarity of a Communist militant with his comrades—those who help him directly and those unseen all over the world. Here the solidary group is fully identified with the Party; there is no conflict between the ordinary militants and Communist workers and the Party's direction. Within this Communist bond, solitude is destroyed. Alone in prison, Kassner makes contact with another prisoner by means of a code they tap on the wall; then a comrade turns himself in for Kassner's release, and Kassner escapes Germany with the aid of a pilot who brings him through a dangerous storm. At the end, Kassner joins a meeting in Prague where the group expresses its community with its fellows who are prisoners in the German concentration camps. As in the earlier novels, the danger of torture and death plays a predominant role, and it is shared risk that cements Kassner's bond with all the others.

In *L'Espoir* (1937), the theme of *fraternité virile* is again dominant (and again cemented with the blood of violent combat), but now it is treated as an *illusion lyrique*. Solidarity is an *étrange fraternité* of anarchists, Communists, Catholics, and republicans fighting together against fascism in the Spanish Civil War. Garcia, one of the Communist Party leaders, calls the solidarity he senses out in the street "l'Apocalypse de la fraternité," and insists that apocalypse must be organized and disciplined by the Party. The fraternity of struggle is now separate from, and even opposed to, the need for obedience to Party discipline. The militant's strong bond with the Party in obedience or leadership must replace the romantic fraternity of the masses. But Manuel, who in the course of the novel transforms himself from a romantic revolutionary to a disciplined Party leader, feels increasingly isolated from his men: "There is not one of the steps that I have climbed in the direction of greater efficacy, of better command, that does not separate me further from men. Every day I am a little less human." [15]

Thus in *L'Espoir* the lyricism of solidarity is undermined, but its necessary alternative offers only solitude and blind devotion. Between romantic anarchism and Stalinism, Malraux sees no third option. Consequently the way is paved for his sudden change of political affiliation. If Stalinism does not provide solutions for his deepest obsessions, including solitude, if it raises moral problems (as it does especially after the Hitler-Stalin pact of 1939) and yet appears to him the only efficacious form of Communist struggle, then there can be only one outcome. He will reject not only Stalinism but the Communist struggle altogether.

Les Noyers de l'Altenburg, written during World War II, completes the parabola of Malraux's novelistic evolution: Communism is abandoned and solitude again prevails as it had in the first novels. The spectre of solitude lurked in the background already in *L'Espoir*, but was repulsed by the emotional force of the *illusion lyrique*. One character, Moreno, wishes to leave Spain after experiencing utter solitude while waiting to die in a convent-prison, where demoralized prisoners threw coins to guess if they would be shot next day. He tells Hernandez: "The two worlds don't communicate. There is the world where men die together singing . . . and then, pal, behind it there is that convent with . . ." [16] But Hernandez argues that camaraderie and hope are stronger than this memory of prison, and Moreno appears later in the novel, still engaged in the conflict and himself exhorting another demoralized soldier with Hernandez's words.

In *Les Noyers de l'Altenburg* the world of solitude has destroyed the illusion of the other world. In the symbolic introductory section, the prisoners in the Chartres camp compose letters to their wives and relatives that can only contain fixed formulas allowed by the Nazis. Even these are never delivered, for they are discarded by the Germans to be blown back into the camp by the wind. The narrator, moreover, feels a complete separation from the common soldiers imprisoned with him, as his father, Vincent Berger, had as an officer in World War One. Vincent is a conquérant figure, but he is even more alienated from the causes he espouses than Garine. He abandons his propaganda mission in the service of *touranisme* when he discovers that it does not exist in the people of central Asia, but is simply an ideological tool in the hands of the new Turkish government. As Lucien Goldmann suggests, the entire episode of Vincent's adventure with the Jeunes-Turcs probably is a transposition of Malraux's engagement and subsequent disillusionment with Communism.[17]

Although Vincent and other soldiers exerience momentary fraternity in action, there no longer exists the all-pervasive solidarity of men united against fascism that permeates *L'Espoir*. And the final nullity of fraternity in modern warfare is demonstrated in the episode of the gas attack. German soldiers, horrified by the effect of the gas on the enemy Russian soldiers, begin carrying them out of the area in an "assaut de la pitié." But the soldiers drop their fraternal enemies and run when they feel the effects of the lethal gas in themselves. When Vincent himself realizes that he is gassed, he thinks, as he runs desperately toward the ambulances: "Scruples, dignity, pity and thought were nothing but a monstrous fake . . . In this savage flight from the clutches of death, there remained only a wild hatred of everything that had kept him from being happy." [18] Man is again a solitary individual in his confrontation with death. Moreover, in this passage Vincent longs for a personal happiness that the destruction of his self in death will render forever impossible. Thus in *Les Noyers* not only is Communism renounced but the validity of dangerous adventure is placed in doubt as well. World War Two in fact marks the end of Malraux's own career in combat.

In the parabola that describes the successive relations between solitude and solidarity in Malraux's novels, *La Condition humaine* stands at the midpoint of the rising side of the curve. It comes at a moment of contradiction and ambiguity in Malraux's development. The work comprehends, in a delicate balance, both the anguish of solitude and the possibilities of solidarity; a close examination reveals to us Malraux's world in the process of transformation.

II

La Condition humaine is comprised of a multiplicity of isolated consciousnesses, each its own world (with the exception of the revolutionaries). The novel begins with a single character—Tchen preparing to murder a sleeping man—and he is the center of consciousness. Then, unlike *Les Conquérants*, which retains a single point of view, the novel goes on to explore the consciousness of other characters. The point of view shifts continually, sometimes remaining fixed in one person during an entire scene, but more often jumping from one interlocutor to another within a single scene. Malraux employs occasionally, and briefly, his authorial omniscience to inform the reader of something in one character's consciousness that another could not know. Ferral, we learn, is unaware that Valérie is waiting for him to fall in love with her. And, conversely, "she was not aware that Ferral's nature, and his present struggle, shut him into eroticism, and not love." [19]

In *La Condition humaine* each person is a universe, enclosed in his own desires and fears. Conversations between characters are largely noncommunicative. Each person speaks of himself and his obsessions, incapable of responding to those of others. These noncommunicative conversations contribute to produce Malraux's characteristic style, abrupt and transitionless; the declarations of one character are only juxtaposed, without the close relation of true dialogue, to those of another.[20]

Symbols of human solitude recur throughout the novel to reinforce the sense of isolation in the characters' encounters. Kyo does not recognize his own voice on the coded phonograph record he has made. Gisors spells out its significance when he reflects: "Just as Kyo had not recognized his own voice because he had heard it with his throat, so the consciousness that he, Gisors, had of himself was doubtless irreducible to that which he could have of another being, because it was not acquired by the same means." [21] If our awareness of our inner selves is of a fundamentally different nature from our awareness of others, then no one can know us as we know ourselves, nor we them. Each individual is doomed to isolation within his own consciousness.

Still more important as a concrete object symbolizing isolation is the armored train. Like many of the characters in *La Condition humaine*, the government train has come to combat and conquer. And like the human combatant it is helpless and solitary in the face of its death. It fires desperately in its last moments, cut off and surrounded by the enemy on all sides, paralyzed and shaking in its final agony. Although all are not combatants, each of the characters who is not part of the revolutionary collectivity—Tchen, Gisors, Clappique, and Ferral—experiences the absolute solitude that this train embodies.

Tchen's solitude in the act of murder is the subject of the opening scene of the novel. Although he is still part of the revolutionary group, Tchen feels utterly alone as he prepares to stab the sleeping man. After accomplishing the murder he avidly wishes to reenter the world of men. Once back in that world, however, he still feels apart. He tells Gisors that his murder reminds him of the first time he made love with a woman; he has contempt for and is isolated from the "virgins" who have never experienced it. Henceforth he remains alone in his universe of murder, alternating between the urgent desire to break out and the passionate affirmation of his solitude.

The solitude of Tchen is more absolute even than that of the conquérant type. Tchen cannot for a moment forget his isolation in action. Gisors reflects that political action gives Tchen "a meaning to his solitude." [22] At first he finds this meaning in the framework of organized revolutionary activity, but later can find it only in individual terrorism, which places him in confrontation with himself and his own death.

Like the heroes of Malraux's first two novels, Tchen is obsessed with his own death. Kyo realizes that because Tchen fears his death, he will be brought to kill himself. Isolated in his self, and not believing in an afterlife for this self, Tchen fears its dissolution. The only form of immortality possible lies in the perfect possession of himself that comes at the moment of a death that he *wills* rather than suffers. Since this project is individual by its very nature, it must be carried out in total solitude. Thus Tchen progressively separates himself in action as well as in spirit from the revolutionaries, perfecting his solitude and giving final meaning to his isolated self in his death under Chiang Kai-shek's car.

Although his special virtue is his concern with defining what is unique in others, Tchen's former professor Gisors is as isolated as Tchen himself. He can sometimes define intellectually the deepest principles at work in others, but he knows that intellectual knowledge is a poor substitute for real communication, which he does not achieve even with those closest to him—his son Kyo as well as his student Tchen. Gisors' knowledge of others really only amounts to self-knowledge: "Gisors' penetration had its source in the fact that he recognized elements of his own personality in those he spoke to." [23] Knowledge of what he has contributed to another's personality, or more generally what fragments of his personality coincide with another's, is not enough to allow him to enter their universe, as Gisors' conversation with Tchen after the murder indicates. Only the long familiarity that comes with passing time can make him forget that he does not know either Kyo or Tchen. As Gisors tells Ferral: "One never knows a human being, but one occasionally ceases to feel that one does not know him." [24]

Gisors has not simply awaited the passage of time, however. His escape from the condition of solitude—his *domaine*, as he calls the personal escape each person finds from the human condition—is opium. Opium is his own world; within it both solitude and death are tranquilized, bereft of their power to disturb. Opium transforms the pain of the real world into images of serenity and acceptance.

The domaine of Clappique—his perpetual fantasies and role playing (*mythomanie*)—is similar to Gisors' opium world, for it too involves a refusal of the real world. Like Gisors, Clappique talks to himself when he converses with others. His monologue in the night club with his two female companions is entirely beyond their comprehension, but the performance is addressed to himself and does not require a responsive audience. He has made his make-believe so much a part of him, however, that he no longer responds to a deeper dimension of his self in which his isolation would be experienced as suffering. Only when he is forced to act in the real world, as he learns that his life is in danger if he does not leave Shanghai, does he become aware of the pain that is always with Gisors when he is not smoking opium. And once safe on the departing ship, the realities of death and solitude, glimpsed for just a moment, again cease to exist for Clappique.

Tchen was temporarily a part of the revolutionary enterprise, but soon left it to pursue his personal destiny. Gisors and Clappique, although the former is sympathetic and the latter unwittingly aids it, are essentially neutral, indifferent to the revolution. Ferral, the director of the principal consortium of colonial business enterprises in China, stands in opposition to it. In *La Condition humaine* the conqueror, who acts to forget his solitude and death in domination, passes to the counterrevolutionary camp. This shift was already latent in *Les Conquérants*, at the end of which Garine prepares to leave China for England, hoping to engage himself there in the imperial venture.

As Gisors once explained to his students in sociology, "modern capitalism . . . is much more a will to organization than to power." [25] Ferral, however, refuses the situation of the monopoly capitalist, powerless as an individual within his organization, and seeks the individualist, entrepreneurial role in the only area where it can still (temporarily) be exercised: on the frontiers of capitalism, in imperialist penetration and control.

As a capitalist conqueror Ferral has only *rapports de force* with others; in all his dealings he does not attempt to discuss and convince, but to *force* with the power of his intellect in the service of his interests. As the action of the novel commences, though, Ferral's power is endangered by the Shanghai insurrection; with a Communist victory his consortium would fall out of his hands. As his whole enterprise of action and domination is menaced, his sense of isolation returns.

Ferral's enterprise is not only menaced by Communism; it is on the verge of bankruptcy as well. He returns to Paris in an attempt to get the necessary financial backing to save the consortium. After the unsuccessful meeting with bankers at the Finance Minister's office, Ferral is obliged to recognize that he is fatally dependent upon, and has finally been defeated by, the organizational capitalism he has shunned. He is in fact defeated by the very nature of the modern economic system. Here the conquérant ideal is undermined not by the unavoidable return of death and solitude breaking in upon the action, but by the failure of the action itself. In a modern capitalist economy, the adventurer-as-entrepreneur is a prehistoric creature doomed to extinction.

The secondary and parallel domination that eroticism affords in the early novels is also undermined for Ferral in the failure of the action itself, rather than in the return of the obsession with death. Ferral's fate in *La Condition humaine* is the simultaneous failure to dominate through his consortium and through erotic power over his mistress Valérie. Eroticism is a combat for him, parallel to combat in the world of business. Women are the enemy; he can only forget his lack of human contact with them by succeeding in his conquest of them. From enemies he must reduce them to dependent, sensual beings that exist only to respond to his stimulation.

But Valérie is a stronger-willed adversary, and a human being more insistent on being treated as one, than Ferral has anticipated. Angered by his having kept the light on while they made love, to watch her enslavement to him, Valérie humiliates him by means of a practical joke. She turns the tables, making him into an interchangeable object (the joke demonstrates that he is one lover among many for her), and he feels painfully alone. He must sleep with a woman to escape his solitude, and he goes to a courtesan. But as she undresses, Ferral realizes the truth: "In reality he never went to bed with anyone but himself . . . He looked at the Tibetan painting . . . on a discolored world over which travelers were wandering, two exactly similar skeletons were embracing each other in a trance." [26] With the failure of his erotic enterprise, Ferral is faced with the image of his narcissistic solitude and inevitable death: identical skeletons embracing.

In contrast to the multiple isolated consciousnesses, the personal domaines, or universes, in *La Condition humaine*, stands the revolutionary community.[27] The existence of such a collective entity in the novel constitutes at least one reason for the necessity of the technique of multiple points of view. In Malraux's earlier novels, no veritable collective solution to the problem of the individual's isolation is posed. Thus the problem of solitude can be expressed from within a single individual's consciousness, although this individual becomes aware of the isolation of others as well. With *La Condition humaine* Malraux has moved beyond the purely individualistic perspective of the early novels, toward the celebration of group solidarity that reaches its peak in *Le Temps du mépris*. At the same time, he is still preoccupied with the isolated individual. A novelistic world of multiple consciousnesses allows him to explore the problem of solitude by juxtaposing several human types whose consciousnesses are isolated in relation to one another, and also to create a community of individuals who by contrast are shown to be in some measure permeable to one another. A series of isolated individuals coexists with a solidary group that is pictured *as a group* rather than through one individual's relation to it.

This group—comprised of Kyo and Katow, May and Hemmelrich, as well as the anonymous militants and workers who surround them— supplants an older (and more perfectly unitary) one: the ancient Oriental culture and community. In *La Tentation de l'Occident* Malraux already showed the latter community to be in the process of dissolution. Its demise is completed in *La Condition humaine*. Although it continues to survive in a few individuals, especially the Japanese painter Kama, its values are seen by Gisors, who of the major characters stands in the closest relation to it, as a thing of the past based on considerable injustice. Although immersed in this culture, Gisors is, as we have seen, plagued by the Occidental concern with solitude and death. And the Oriental conception of the universe is dead for the Chinese masses as well. The replacement of the old community by the new, revolutionary one is clearly pointed to in the scene of the imprisoned revolutionaries awaiting death. As the men achieve a final communion in the mystical body of the Revolution, one Chinese vainly calls up the old collectivity: "Lu was reciting in a loud voice, without resonance, the death of the hero in a famous play; but the old Chinese solidarity was indeed destroyed: no one was listening." [28]

The revolutionary community, then, represents a reintegration of the individual after his "Fall" into isolation from an earlier culture of integration. Yet *La Condition humaine* as a whole reveals a developing contradiction in Malraux's conception of the nature of solitude. On the one hand, as in *La Tentation* (and the essay, "D'une jeunesse européenne"), isolation is the product of a given historical culture, and the fraternity of the revolutionary group allows the reintegration of the individual. On the other hand, isolation is also seen as an immutable element of "la condition humaine." Kyo laments: "First of all there was solitude, the inescapable aloneness behind the living multitude like the great primitive night behind the dense, low night under which this city of deserted streets was expectantly waiting, full of hope and hatred." [29] Behind the night of fraternity lurks the more primitive, essential night of solitude. According to this conception, the revolutionary group would not be a true reintegration of the individual, but an attempt to *escape* an unchangeable human condition. It is an escape analogous to the domaines of the other characters, which allow them to forget or give meaning to their solitude. The contradiction between solitude as an historical and as a metaphysical problem is not resolved in the novel. It constitutes one of the reasons for the ambiguity—the combined weakness and strength—of the collective solution.

The main characters that constitute the Communist collectivity are of a type without precedent in Malraux's earlier novels. Katow, the Russian militant, has engaged his life totally in the revolutionary community and has repeatedly demonstrated selflessness and fraternity toward his comrades in struggle. Concern for his individual life is entirely subordinated to the requirements of the revolutionary action. Since he has merged his individual self with the revolution, Katow is not obsessed with isolation; yet he is aware of the danger of solitude for others.

Thus he is even able momentarily to alleviate the isolation of Hemmelrich,[30] who is at first cut off from participation in the full solidarity of the revolutionary action by the necessity of protecting and providing for his wife and sick child. Later, after his wife and child are massacred in the repression of the Communists, Hemmelrich breaks out of his isolation permanently. Private and public life become one: in the final battle to defend the Communist headquarters, he both seeks vengeance for his dead loved ones (united with them through an action that places his life in danger) and finally participates in the revolutionary fraternity through mortal combat.

As for Katow, he experiences his most intense moment of solidarity as he faces not just the risk of death but the assurance of torture and death. As he and Kyo lie awaiting death, Katow is linked to him "by that absolute friendship, without reticence, which death alone gives." [31] Later that night, surrounded by his comrades, he dies united with them. His perfect union with the collectivity is appropriately expressed in a shift in the point of view. From Katow's consciousness, we turn to the collective consciousness of the other prisoners. When the soldiers come to take Katow away, the group rhythmically joins in his final walk to death: "All the heads, moving up and down, followed the rhythm of his walk, with love, with dread, with resignation; it was as if, in spite of the similarity of the movements, each one revealed himself by following that jerky departure." [32] In this *moment privilégié*, the group as a whole, and each member individually, is "revealed"; the obscurity of the "other" no longer exists.

For Katow, death brings the perfection of his oneness with the collectivity. But we have already noted that in Malraux's early novels (and in the case of Tchen in *La Condition humaine*), death and solitude are indissolubly related: solitude is felt most intensely at the approach of death. Why this strong connection? I have indicated that, with the decline of the individual's importance in the modern form of capitalism, there occurs a crisis of individualist values that Malraux was among the first to articulate, in *La Tentation de l'Occident*. If the individual's life no longer is an absolute value—as it was in eighteenth- and nineteenth-century ideologies that tended to reduce the significance of the individual's death as a problem—then the moment of his cessation in death again takes on importance, without regaining the security of the earlier religious conception of a communal afterlife.[33] If he faces death alone, still as an individual unrelated to any community either human or divine, his death must carry to its greatest intensity the individual's sense of isolation.

It is within this context that Malraux portrays the double anguish of death and solitude in the early novels. The individual reintegrated within the revolutionary collectivity, on the other hand, is part of a struggle that will continue beyond the limits of his individual life. Within the revolutionary's scheme of values, then, an obsession with his own death has no place; the values his life has incarnated will be perpetuated in others. Nor is his death solitary, since he dies with and for all the others. This trancendence of individualism gives a collective meaning to the death of Katow.

Kyo, like Katow, has fully integrated his individual life in the revolutionary action. He too dies united with the revolutionary community. Yet in his life more than in Katow's—probably because he is a more important character and his consciousness is more thoroughly explored—we are aware of the limitations of the revolutionary community. In spite of his solidarity with the group, Kyo is troubled by solitude as Katow is not. Repeatedly throughout the action, the identification of individual self and revolutionary group is broken. One of Kyo's ideas, reported by Gisors, is that men fight and die in the revolution to *justify* the human condition "by giving it a foundation in dignity." [34] According to such a conception, solitude is inevitable and can only be justified, not transcended, in the revolution. The metaphysical rather than the historical notion of solitude unquestionably is dominant in Kyo's psychology; for him the revolution is in the final analysis only an escape, like Gisors' other domaines, from the human condition. The existence of this conception at the very heart of the collectivity, in its most fully developed representative, undermines its meaning and binding power.

Another weakness in Kyo's revolutionary solidarity results from Malraux's representation of Communism and revolutionary struggle. Solidarity develops only out of violent combat and common risk of life. As W. M. Frohock emphatically states, "Malraux's fictional world needs to be violent to be complete." [35] Consequently, the purely *military* aspect is foremost in Malraux's representation of Communist activity. The author of *La Condition humaine* passes over the organization of the combatants (and beyond that the more basic organization of workers into the Party framework), and concentrates the dramatic moment on the acquisition of arms and the insurrectional combat. Moreover, the combat itself is viewed exclusively through the eyes of the leaders: Kyo, Katow, and Tchen. The ordinary fighters, the "masses," remain anonymous.

Kyo's only *concrete* relationships are with other leaders. At his death, like Katow, he is united with the revolutionary collectivity. Yet Kyo's communion, not only with the prisoners but with the invisible masses everywhere, is experienced by his own consciousness—the consciousness of the leader-hero dying for the Revolution. The relation of Kyo to the masses is not only elitist but religious in nature. The Revolution is a new religion of the people, and Kyo one of its revered martyrs. [36]

Kyo also feels united with his wife May at his death. But their relation in life is a highly ambiguous one, a constant tension between separation and complicity. Although May is both a lover and a comrade, joining public and private solidarities, Kyo realizes that ultimately he is isolated from her as well as all the others.[37] Whereas his relation to May is one of love between equals as opposed to the domination-submission of eroticism in the relation between Ferral and Valérie, both couples finally share the same essential isolation.

The possibility of overcoming the isolation of the individual in the revolutionary group is thus fatally weakened by the predominance of the metaphysical definition of solitude and by Malraux's elitist and religious conception of revolution. His cult of the hero-leader and of effective power in military action brings him close to the Stalinist perspectives of the period, and although the revolutionaries oppose the strategy of the Comintern, the novel ends with the surviving remnant—Pei, Hemmelrich, May—leaving China to work in the Soviet Union. Hemmelrich, who goes to work in a Soviet electrical plant, remembers Gisors' professing in his sociology course: "The factory, which is still only a kind of church of the catacombs, must become what the cathedral was." [38] Here the religious conception (Communism replaces Christianity) is joined to the Stalinist definition of Communist goals: rapid industrialization under the five-year plan. For Malraux, beyond the violent struggle for Communism there stands only the glorification of socialist work and the factory of the future. And behind the struggle stands the solitude that is man's fate.

Since Malraux never conceived of the Communist project outside the limits of Stalinist methods and goals—Stalinism was of course the dominant Communist ideology of the period—he could establish no meaningful connection between the telos of the struggle and the solitude he felt lurking behind it. And even if the struggle itself could not fully innoculate the individual against isolation, there remained no reason for fidelity to the struggle. The contradiction between a metaphysical obsession with solitude and death and a Stalinist conception of revolution, present already in La Condition humaine, led to Malraux's abandonment of the revolution, signaling the failure of his attempt to reintegrate the individual in the collectivity of revolutionary action.

6

༄

Journal d'un curé de campagne:
The Saint's Gethsemane

I

Concurrent with the novel of adventure in the entre-deux-guerres, another literature in a different perspective rejects the fragmentation and inauthenticity of bourgeois society. In the novels of François Mauriac, Julien Green, and Georges Bernanos, the portrait of modern society is similar: relations between people are ruled by money. Each person lives alone, hating himself and others, within the bourgeois family—the "noeud de vipères." Love and communication is impossible between both individuals and classes in a world that has become a "désert de l'amour." The heroes and heroines of these novels are stifled by the world in which they live and revolt violently against it. They attempt to escape through flight and suicide, and through acts of violence.

Although these novelists share a Catholic perspective, the novels of Mauriac and Green portray only the negative revolt of characters for whom God is just as absent as he is in the world they reject. Green experienced a long crisis of religious agnosticism and inquietude during his period of novelistic production between the two wars. Thus in his *Léviathan* (1929), the protagonist Guéret's blind revolt leads him not to God but to rape and murder. Mauriac, although he never underwent such a crisis, refused to consider himself a Catholic writer. In his novels the supernatural is either entirely absent, as in *Thérèse Desqueyroux* (1927), or only alluded to at the very end as a hidden reality to which the characters of the novel were never able to find access. At the end of *Le Désert de l'amour* (1925), the author suggests that the protagonist Raymond's passions, like his father's, will cause him to repeat sterile and painful relations with women, unless, "before the death of the father and son, He finally reveals Himself to them, He who without their knowing it calls, draws towards Him that burning tide from the deepest recess of their being." [1] In *Le Noeud de vipères* (1932), the narrator discovers this hidden reality, but only in the last sentence of his diary, which is broken off by his death.

In the works of Bernanos, on the other hand, the supernatural is present in the novelistic world. For Bernanos, although the mass of man are unaware of its presence, the supernatural manifests itself in a positive struggle which counterbalances the negative revolt: the heroic efforts of the "saint" to win the souls of the *révoltés*. Several of Bernanos' novels are set in country towns similar to the one in Green's *Léviathan*. But unlike the village in *Léviathan*, Bernanos' towns have their center, or one of their centers, in the country priest. This country priest, like Bernanos' other "saints," is principal actor in a supernatural conflict, within himself and within the *révoltés*, between the forces of good and evil.

This heroic action of the saint relates Bernanos' novelistic world to the literature of adventure. Like Malraux's revolutionaries, Bernanos' saints are elite individuals who risk themselves totally and who attempt to create an authentic community in opposition to bourgeois society. [2] Yet though Malraux's characters engage in physical combat beyond the bounds of bourgeois European society, Bernanos' saints undertake an inner, spiritual adventure within that society. French society as Bernanos portrays it—in Paris and in the country town—renders the individual both solitary and mediocre; personal honor and risk of self have no more place within it than true community. Yet the individual may have access to another world in which he risks his soul in a spiritual adventure and may win the communion of sainthood. He enters this supernatural reality *without leaving* the bourgeois world.

Bernanos' ideological convictions are directly related to this opposition between modern society and the domain of the supernatural. The saint has access to the realm of the supernatural by retaining the spirit of childhood, with its dreams of adventure and joy, and its ultimate security under a guiding authority. Bernanos' political faith involves a parallel ideal that is reactionary in the strictest sense: a return to the *ancienne France* of monarchy and Christendom (the "childhood" of the French people.) [3] Only under such a regime did the domains of the supernatural and society meet; the individual found self-fulfillment as an inseparable part of the joined human and divine community. The modern saint of Bernanos' novels, as an incarnation of the spirit of childhood, struggles to win souls in the hopeless battle to begin to recreate the lost *chrétienté*.

Thus, unlike Malraux's Communism, Bernanos' political ideology is indissolubly linked to the totality of his vision. The ambiguity we observed in Malraux's conception of solitude does not exist in Bernanos. For the latter, the solitude of modern man is never conceived to be part of an immutable human condition; solitude is rather a function of capitalist society, as Bernanos states explicitly in *Les Grands Cimetières sous la lune* (1938): "Man is naturally resigned. And modern man more than others, on account of the extreme solitude in which he is left by a society that scarcely knows any other than money relations (*rapports d'argent*)." [4] Modern society is presented in an image that gives the book its title: it is a land of the dead, an expanse of cemeteries under the silver moon of Money. In later polemical writings during and after the war, Bernanos sometimes located the root of evil in technology (the machine) rather than the rule of money. And in earlier writings the rule of money tends to be identified with the rule of Jews. Yet antisemitism and antitechnology are essentially deviations (growing out of a reactionary Catholic perspective) from Bernanos' basic perception of the corruption of society by money.

Whereas Malraux abandoned Communism under the pressure of the contradiction between his interpretation of it and his vision of the human condition, Bernanos maintained an absolute fidelity to the idea of a Christian monarchy, which he saw as the only remedy for the alienations of modern society. But as a pure—and by definition unattainable—ideal, it was incompatible with any concrete attempt at political reaction. Consequently, Bernanos' only political evolution was from engagement—in the monarchist *Camelots du Roi* (1908–1914) and *L'Action française* (until 1932)—to progressive disengagement and political wavering as it became clearer that the Right was tending toward fascism rather than pure reactionary monarchism.[5] In *Les Grands Cimetières sous la lune* Bernanos points out that it is not he, but the Right, which has changed.[6]

There is likewise no evolution in Bernanos' novels of the kind we saw in Malraux. His novelistic vision remains fixed because no elements in it are subject to internal contradiction and mutation. On the one hand, the alienated, godless modern world and, on the other, the lost world of order and integration: the modern saint struggles hopelessly between the two. No resolution can ever be reached, and each novel repeats the drama of the saint crucified by modern society. In sainthood he wins an ambiguous communion with others and God which is only a shadow of the lost Christendom.

Bernanos' major preoccupations are already present in the letters he wrote to L'Abbé Lagrange in 1904–1906, as an adolescent just emerging from the childhood to which he would always look back nostalgically. He tells the abbé that as a child he was often sick, and continually feared death. His remedy for this fear was to dream of worldly adventure. With his first communion in the Church, however, the boy realized that the only way to conquer the fear of death is to live not for oneself, but for God, making one's life part of God's cause.[7] The real remedy for fear of death, in other words, is the participation of the isolated self in a struggle that transcends the individual, and only spiritual adventure in God's service can assure this transcendence.

In Bernanos' early short stories, some written before, some after World War One, specific themes and characters of the later novels appear repeatedly. One character in particular appears again and again: the successful and wealthy author, superficial, insincere, ambitious, and therefore incapable of love, joy, adventure ("Mme. Dargent," "Dialogue d'ombres," "La Tombe refermée"). This figure of the *auteur mondain* is the image of what Bernanos feared becoming; it represents the corruption of a literary vocation by the values of society. In "Une Nuit" Bernanos again signifies refusal of his other temptation: the worldly adventure pursued by Malraux. A young Frenchman come to seek adventure and fortune in a distant colony is shown to have risked nothing essential since he has not risked his soul. In this story, exceptional among Bernanos' works for its exotic setting, Bernanos suggests that the only true adventure is supernatural.

Thus Bernanos' vision of modern society, his rejection of it and engagement in a spiritual adventure (as well as his political engagement in *L'Action française*, indicated in a letter to Lagrange in 1906), is elaborated already in adolescence. But only in his novelistic cycle (1926–1936), which covers roughly the same period as Malraux's, does Bernanos discover the specific form of spiritual heroism which the adventure will take—the heroic struggle that, as the principal subject of his novels, gives his vocation as a writer the quality of a supernatural enterprise rather than a bourgeois career. The novels introduce the saint, who struggles for the souls of the other adventurers—the *révoltés* or *héros du mal*[8]—against a background of *médiocres*, the mass of men thoroughly corrupted by modern society. The social corruption is also brought to the foreground in major characters, often successful authors or academicians. In the novelistic cycle as a whole there exists an equilibrium between these three principles—the saint, the rebel, and society.

Although the force of each element in the trio varies substantially from novel to novel (in only one case, the novelette *Nouvelle Histoire de Mouchette*, the saint disappears altogether), there is no evolution in favor of any one element. One of Bernanos' most positive treatments of the saint—*Journal d'un curé de campagne*—was written concurrently with novels in which the rebel or the corruption of society dominate: *Un Crime, Un Mauvais Rêve, Monsieur Ouine* (1934–1936).

Because of the stability of Bernanos' novelistic world, the choice of a single novel for study is somewhat arbitrary. Almost any novel would reveal most or all of the elements of his universe and their typical interrelationships. Yet the *Journal,* Bernanos' best-known novel, has the advantage of exploring the positive, spiritual adventure of the saint more intimately than any other: unlike the other novels, the world of the *Journal* is experienced solely through the consciousness of the saint.

II

The very first sentence of the *Journal d'un curé de campagne* defines the context in which the priest's adventure will take place: "Mine is a parish like all the rest. They're all alike. Those of today I mean" (PM 1).[9] The priest's village parish is representative of all others— both rural and urban—and is thus a microcosm of society. Moreover, the parish society is specifically *modern;* the vices it exhibits are peculiar to the contemporary period of history. The priest's diary develops a meditation on this modern society, stimulated by conversations with his friend Curé de Torcy (and at the end of the novel, with his new friend Olivier). Society's primary characteristic is the rule of money. As Olivier comments, "The titulary gods of the modern world—we *know* 'em; they dine out, they're called bankers" (PM 248). Society is a "huge machine-for-the-making-of-rich-men" (PM 244), but more important, it creates on all social levels a reified mentality. The true definition of the rich is the "riche en esprit": "the real rich, rich in cunning, were they to have but a farthing in their pockets, moneyed men as they are called" (PM 66). In school the child is taught to think in terms of *things;* he is "man schooled by things" (1050).

Modern man is not only degraded by the reification of a society ruled by money. He also no longer has any stature as an individual; he exists only as part of a mediocre mass. Thus the priest notes that, in modern parishes, "the center of gravity is set low, very low" (1031).

Even in warfare modern men do not affirm their powers. World War I inaugurated the era of generalized, mass wars, which lead the apathetic herd to slaughter (1143–1144). Men live inauthentically, out of touch with their inner needs. Alienated from themselves and others, they are tortured by ennui and solitude. The life of modern men is a living death, and the curé's parish is a *paroisse morte*.[10] The recurrent funerals throughout the novel (there are no baptisms or marriages) symbolize this collective death.

Men who are dead to the inner life and adventure experience the solitude of God's absence. They do not revolt against God, but are simply closed to his presence. The peasants' faces cloud over whenever the priest begins to speak of God, or when God's presence seems to emanate from him. Thus although the priest knows that a parish should be a unified part of the larger community of the Church—"a living cell of the everlasting Church" (PM 28)—he does not see either spiritual life or unity in his parish. Modern society no longer preserves the ancient Christendom of the Middle Ages; its ennui is "like the fermentation of a Christianity in decay" (PM 3).

In childhood, says the Curé de Torcy, we suffer (especially from fear of death) but are protected by the love and guiding authority of our mother. If a unified Christendom had survived into the modern era, it would have given this authority and community to men: "But man would have known he was the son of God; and therein lies your miracle . . . What we would have got rid of, what we would have torn from the very heart of Adam, is that sense of his own loneliness" (PM 19). Thus in the opening scene of the *Journal* the priest has the impression that his village "seemed to be waiting . . . without much hope after so many nights in the mud—for a master to follow towards some undreamed-of, improbable shelter" (PM 2). The priest feels that a saint might have called the village as a cowboy calls the cows; although he himself will be the saint who calls this village, most of the villagers will not hear.

The image of modern society which the priest and Torcy develop discursively in their discussions and reflections is illustrated in characters and events of the priest's daily life in his new parish, recounted in his diary. From the very start he encounters in the villagers a mentality that deforms human relationships into reified forms. The priest's grocer, for instance, offers him aperitifs in the back of his store, then puts three extra bottles of the drink in the curé's grocery order—not as a gift but to make a bigger sale (1035). Later the priest learns that the grocer's family has recently risen from the working class. They are avid petty bourgeois who are making money by hard dealing, and gaining respectability by sending their children to private Catholic school. Moreover, the family has gained the steady trade of the clergy in the region. In the light of this background, the merchant's offer of aperitifs in the back of the store seems to be further motivated by the need, for the sake of both interest and bourgeois respectability, to cultivate good relations with clergymen.

The Church—whose role should be to struggle to recreate the lost Christendom—has itself been corrupted by the evil of modern society. Its hierarchy often identifies itself with the bourgeoisie and reflects their mental structures. Thus the curé is reprimanded by a superior— the Doyen de Blangermont—for not paying his debts promptly and for not cultivating good relations with the merchants. For if the merchants need the clergy's business, the reverse is true as well. The petty bourgeoisie, according to the doyen, is the best clientele of the modern Church: "Besides, the Church has needs—let's use the word—it has financial needs . . . From whom does the State receive most of its revenue? Isn't it precisely from that petite bourgeoisie, greedy for gain, hard on the poor as on itself, mad on saving?" (1083). For a "realistic" priest like the doyen, then, the Church has a stake in preserving the present social order against socialist agitation, and the petty bourgeoisie knows that its best ally is the Church. With this status quo to preserve, the doyen also fears the subversive power of saints whose spiritual life breaks in upon the commercial mentality of the established Church—"the supernatural adventurers who sometimes shake the framework of the hierarchy" (1083).

While the doyen is an example of the *prêtre médiocre*, unproblematically integrated in modern society,[11] the Abbé Dufréty, one of the curé's seminary friends, is a priest who, in spite of an intense disquietude, refuses the call to sainthood and attempts to integrate himself into society. In a series of letters addressed to the curé, Dufréty makes it clear that he has left the ministry after a prolonged sickness. He rejects the seminary education as having made of them "individualists, solitaries" (1062). He adopts a new motto—*Aurea mediocritas*— and accepts a job in a company: "I am earning my living—a big saying and a big thing. To earn one's living! The habit which begins in the seminary of receiving our daily bread or dish of daily beans from the hands of our superiors, like a dole, makes schoolboys of us, children to the very end of our lives" (PM 73).

Dufréty's definition of the seminary education—and by extension, of the vocation of priesthood—is significant. It involves a solitary development of the individual, a childlike acceptance of authority and an ignorance of the commercial mentality. Life in modern society involves just the opposite: the diminution of the individual and at the same time the absence of traditional authority in the egalitarian market. Dufréty seems bent on pressing himself into the mold of the modern organization man. Yet the curé doubts that with his extreme sensitivity he will succeed in fully integrating himself (1089), and in fact Dufréty seems to vacillate in his conception of his future role. At one point he attempts to set up his own independent business and conceives of his new life in the mode of the adventurer-capitalist (1247). Although he dreams of capitalist conquest—the individual self-assertion that even Ferral failed to achieve in *La Condition humaine*—Dufréty is still the modest representative of a pharmaceutical concern at the end of the novel and shows all the signs of corruption by the modern ethos of mediocrity.

Thus the clergy often renounces its difficult role of spiritual leadership to become bourgeois. Likewise the class that once exercised supreme leadership in society—the nobility—has fallen irremediably into the bourgeoisie. Because of his ignorance of modern society the curé only learns this slowly and painfully through the course of the novel. The owner of the nearby château is a count, but the priest discovers that he is no less bourgeois than the other villagers. A worldly clergyman, the uncle of the count, tells the priest not to be misled by his nephew's titles of nobility: "There's no longer any aristocracy, my friend, get that into your head . . . No family can hold out against the slow sapping process of greed, when the law is the same for everyone, and public opinion the standard. The aristocrats of to-day are only shamefaced *bourgeois*" (PM 187).[12] When the count insists on renting rather than loaning land to the priest for his projected village soccer field—and stipulates advantageous legal conditions for himself—the priest still does not see the count's true nature. Later, however, the priest finds his cordiality affected, even vulgar (1124). And when at the death of his wife the count comes to speak with the priest solely about the price of the funeral and its concrete details, the priest finds that he resembles "an ordinary rich peasant" (1175). The count now even looks bourgeois to the priest, since he has finally understood what is behind the count's appearance.

Instead of fulfilling the role of a nobleman as the guiding authority of an aristocratic household, the count is a bourgeois father and husband in a "noeud de vipères." His daughter Chantal once adored her father as the ancient seigneurial figure of loving authority—"a master, a king, a god—a friend" (1136)—but now she despises the common bourgeois who has adulterous affairs with other women as the wife pretends not to notice. The count, his wife, and daughter incarnate the frightening reality of the bourgeois family as opposed to the idealized stereotype of the "Family" invoked in speeches (1149, 1175). They have lived for years in total isolation and hidden antagonism. Chantal tells the curé that she and her mother often sat seemingly calm at their needlework, while they held back their anger at each other: "We could remain for hours, stitching side by side, each immersed in her own dream, her own anger, and papa, of course, didn't notice a thing" (1178).

With the transformation of the nobility into bourgeois, the traditional ideal of the country estate as a tranquil retreat from society is cruelly contradicted; the chateau of the count and countess now harbors the worst evils of bourgeois society,[13] as does the village it once protected. The curé looks out from the chateau at its grounds: "Through dripping panes I could see the park, noble and calm, its lawns majestically curved, its grave old trees . . . When Providence miraculously spares some haven in which peace might flourish, human lusts must needs creep into it, and once ensconced, howl bestially, night and day!" (PM 158).

The alienations of modern society, then, are everywhere—in city, village, and country estate, in nobility and clergy as well as in the bourgeois, petty bourgeois, and rich peasantry. Only the lowest stratum of society is free of the all-pervasive bourgeois mentality: the worker and the poor peasant. Thus the mistress of Dufréty—an attendant in a sanatorium and then a cleaning woman—is totally untouched by the dominant ethos. She is perfectly selfless in her love for Dufréty, and she is never tempted by revolt against her condition:

When I can't go on no more, and me legs are givin' way with that pain in me side, I creep into a corner by meself . . . I think of all the people that I don't know of like me . . . I slip into the crowd of 'em, makin' meself small, and it's not only the livin' but the dead as well who was sufferin' once, and those that are comin', an'll be sufferin' too . . . 'What's it for? Why suffer?' they all keep sayin' . . . I feel I'm sayin' it too, with 'em, I can hear it like a great murmurin', sendin' me to sleep. I wouldn't be changin' places then with a millionaire, it's so happy I'm feelin'. (PM 289)

In these moments of resignation shared with all the *misérables* of the earth, she achieves a kind of mystical communion in poverty and suffering—a communion unknown to the bourgeois. But because of the sheer brutality of her daily life she does not escape solitude; she does not know the consolations of religion (1251), and the priest is aware that she has never told her life and feelings to anyone as she does to him (1253).[14] She is entirely misunderstood by the bourgeois-minded Dufréty, who is ashamed of her and wishes only to make her "respectable."

The character of Dufréty's mistress is an illustration of the purity of poverty, a Bernanosian idea also developed discursively by the curé and Torcy. Although Torcy is painfully sensitive to the oppression of the poor and has been tempted to preach insurrection to them (1075), he knows that Christ and the Church teach that poverty is glorious in the eyes of God and, that far from being eliminated, it should be honored. The secret of its purity, the curé reflects, is that while others in bourgeois society live by taking advantage of everyone else, the poor live by *charity* (1104). To eliminate poverty would be to eliminate this purity; according to Torcy, the Soviets are transforming the poor into rentiers and fonctionnaires, and therefore corrupting them (1068–1069). Dufréty's mistress is the perfect *pauvre* from this point of view, since she not only is unsullied by bourgeois society but also does not wish to be freed from her oppression by that society.

Thus Bernanos' reactionary Catholic form of anticapitalism—as expressed here through the curé and Torcy—ends in a contradiction. By glorifying poverty, one justifies exploitation. Although they sharply distinguish themselves from the political priests whose role is to profit from and protect bourgeois society, the saints finally aid in the preservation of that society in spite of their abhorrence of it. Both Torcy and the curé are aware of the problem. The former sees that even he and other authentic clergy who refuse modern society "are used as hostages by the Powerful, each time the army of the poor returns to assault the walls of the City!" (1078). And the curé notes in his diary: "*Insoluble problem:* to give back his rights to the Poor Man without investing him with power" (PM 93, italics mine).

III

Those who revolt in Bernanos' world do not do so against material oppression but against the spiritual misery of bourgeois society. Since they revolt individually rather than collectively, the solitude they experienced in society only deepens in their revolt, and the revolt itself is hopeless and self-destructive. Many of these desperate rebels from society are adolescents who refuse to give up their childhood dream and accept the degraded adult world. But since their dreams of adventure and love can find no opportunity for positive expression in reality, they turn into an adventure in evil, and from love into debauchery. The rebels revolt under Satan's power.

Thus Séraphita Dumouchel, the granddaughter of the *avare* who at the beginning of the *Journal* bickers with the priest over prices for his wife's funeral (1037), rebels through cruelty, debauchery, and self-humiliation. She is differentiated from her ordinary classmates in catechism precisely because she is not satisfied with the mediocre evil of the group that looks on. She *excels* in evil, inhabited by Satan. Her cruelty to the priest is a distorted expression of her frustrated need to love and to communicate with another person. Séraphita's frustration also leads her to precocious sex with boys whom she despises, causing her to hate herself and wish her own destruction. Unlike the médiocres, Séraphita bears her suffering proudly and independently. She never weeps, never shares her pain with others (1206–1207).

Another adolescent, whose background and revolt are more fully developed than those of Séraphita, is Chantal, the daughter of the bourgeois count. Her revolt against her solitude in the family and the degradation of her elevated image of the father takes violent forms. As the priest realizes, it is precisely because Chantal fears death so greatly that suicide is her strongest temptation (1152; she resembles Tchen of *La Condition humaine* in this respect). Fiercely proud like Séraphita, Chantal voluntarily deepens her own solitude. She closes herself to love, angrily defying the priest, by whom she is fascinated and attracted, and who offers the only opportunity to break out of her isolation and establish a human bond. Chantal renders herself inaccessible to him, her face impenetrable (1138).

Also like Séraphita, she resists the presence and love of God to which the curé might give her access. The priest often recognizes signs of her possession by demons—whose presence brings cold solitude rather than communion (1133, 1136, 1139, 1177).[15] And yet her negative revolt itself creates the preconditions for her salvation. Without a total refusal of the degraded world, one does not possess even the potentiality of communion with God and others. When, during their last conversation together, Chantal tells the priest that she will taste all experiences and if life disappoints her will take vengeance in evil, the curé answers:

And when you do . . . you'll discover God . . . You are setting off with your back turned on the world, for the world does not stand for revolt, but for submission, submission to lies, first and foremost. Go ahead for all you're worth, the walls are bound to fall in the end, and every breach shows a patch of sky. (PM 255)

A third adolescent throws himself, turning his back on the world, into a different sort of adventure. When he meets the curé, Olivier is on leave from service in the Foreign Legion. Speaking of their common alienation from the bourgeois order, Olivier insists to the priest: "Admit it: our order is not theirs" (1216). The order of the Legion is one of risk and poverty. With the modern transformation of the soldier from a chevalier fighting for Christendom to a passive *militaire* in a mass army, heroism of the kind Olivier desires can be sought only on the outlaw fringe of the army—the Legion, which engages in the most dangerous and ruthless forms of colonial combat.

While on leave Olivier rides a powerful motorcycle the sound of which expresses his own soul: "It was like a cry—savagely imperious, menacing, desperate" (PM 234). Descending from a family of rebels whose motto is "all or nothing," Olivier like his fellow légionnaires carries risk into the metaphysical realm: believing in God, they blaspheme in the teeth of death, taking the ultimate risk of eternal perdition (1214–1216).

Olivier is an exceptional case in Bernanos' works of revolt taking a form of adventure similar to that in Malraux or Saint-Exupéry. The existence of Olivier in the novelistic world of the *Journal*, in a parallel relation to Chantal and the other rebels, indicates that his adventure, arising from the same impulse to escape modern society, remained a fascinating image for Bernanos. Conversely, Malraux remained fascinated by religious disquietude. The pastor Smithson, appearing briefly to juxtapose his spiritual adventure against Tchen's concrete one, stands in the same relation to *La Condition humaine* as Olivier to the *Journal*. Yet for Olivier's worldly adventure to be validated in the Bernanosian perspective, it must project itself into spiritual risk as well, and thus Olivier's supreme *pari* is not merely on life and death, but on his salvation.[16] Moreover, since in Bernanos' view no human fraternity is conceivable outside divine communion, solidarity with his fellow légionnaires is not one of the sources of Olivier's enthusiasm for his service. Such solidarity can only exist in Christian soldiers united in an "immense fraternité" (1219), fighting to preserve the divine-human community of Christendom. But the Christian soldier and Christendom are both extinct.

All of the adolescent rebels—Séraphita, Chantal, and Olivier—are elite souls in the sense that they have the moral strength necessary to reject an easy mediocrity and conformity, and to express their individual self to the extreme limit. Not all the alienated and disturbed of Bernanos' world have this stature. Dufréty, Mlle. Louise, and Sulpice Mitonnet are each a case of a *révolte manquée*. They are solitary, maladjusted persons whose disquiet never explodes into rebellion and escape but putrifies in a partial, unhappy complicity with the world. The elite souls who do rebel, however, remain as solitary as the médiocres and can achieve only destruction as long as they refuse God.

They can have access to community only through the agency of the saint.

Revolt does not always take the active, violent form that it does in the adolescent's furious refusal of the adult world. There also exist in the *Journal* adults who have the pride and spiritual nobility to refuse the world. But their revolt is most often passive and interior, a silent and tortured isolation that makes no concessions to the world while continuing to live within it. The emotions that in the adolescents break out in evil and violence remain hidden (until brought out by the curé) in the adult rebels. Whereas the adolescents manifest their superiority to the mass in extremes of action or behavior, the adults excel in proud endurance. Thus the doctor Delbende is of the race "that isn't got down," and his motto is "face up to it" (PM 78–79).

Delbende is the closest to a saint of the rebels, since his revolt partly takes a positive form in his aid to society's oppressed (1120). He is in fact a saint manqué, since his adolescent wish was to become a missionary; he lost the faith during his medical studies and thereafter remained in spiritual torment. The countess, mother of Chantal, is similarly separated from God, whom she began to hate when her son died. The memory of her dead child holds her in the most complete solitude, from which only a saint can release her (1165).

Although the countess and the other rebels live in total solitude, they are united, *without their being conscious of it*, to others in evil. In spite of their superiority they are bound to the médiocres in a "solidarity in evil" (PM 144). The curé explains the nature of this union to Chantal:

The world of sin confronts the world of grace like the reflected picture of a landscape in the blackness of very still, deep waters. There is not only a communion of saints; there is also a communion of sinners. In their hatred of one another, their contempt, sinners unite, embrace, intermingle, become as one; one day in the eyes of Eternal God they will be no more than a mass of perpetual slime over which the vast tide of divine love . . . passes vainly. (PM 138–139)

Thus the entire family—the count and countess, Mlle. Louise and Chantal, both the médiocres and the révoltés—are bound together in a community of evil. This indivisible evil grew like a plant with its seed in the countess' hidden hatred (1158–1159).

In a degraded and unconscious solidarity, the rebel's aspiration to be apart from and superior to the médiocres is annihilated,[17] without being compensated by a sense of fraternity. Men are not conscious of their union in either good or evil; if they were, the understanding of their mutual responsibility to each other would be unbearable. As the curé tells the countess: "I don't suppose if God had given us the clear knowledge of how closely we are bound to one another both in good and evil, that we could go on living, as you say" (PM 166).

IV

In all the other works of Bernanos, the novelistic point of view lies with the author, who is present rather than invisible in the narration, commenting, expressing emotions concerning the characters' fates, even blessing his characters. The author enters and reveals the consciousness of his major characters, not by a minute analysis of the complexities and interrelationships of psychological patterns (as in Proust, for instance), but by a description of the major passions and sins that drive the characters, a dramatization of the spiritual conflicts and adventure they are experiencing. As Albert Béguin has noticed, this form of presentation, this relation of the author to his characters, corresponds to the priest-saint's form of knowledge of the souls he encounters:

Vis-à-vis his characters, Bernanos the novelist attempts not to perform the analysis of the psychologist but rather to obtain a kind of knowledge that much more resembles the knowledge that he bestowed upon his priests . . . We must go so far as to define him as a *sacerdotal novelist*—by which I mean a novelist who performs for the creatures of his fictional universe the very functions of the priest.[18]

In the *Journal* the priestly function of the novelist is given its most perfect formal expression. The author becomes one with the priest-saint; the novelistic world is experienced exclusively through the consciousness of the curé, as it is presented in his diary. The measure of knowledge we come to have of other characters derives from the special nature of the priest's consciousness. He alone may partially transcend the isolation in which modern men live—both rebels and médiocres—to achieve some knowledge of and communication with others. Unlike Proust's world, which is also experienced through a single narrative point of view, the "other" that remained irremediably mysterious for the Marcel of *Du côté de chez Swann* is revealed in sudden supernatural illuminations.

The specific form in which the priest's consciousness is presented—the diary—itself raises several questions. What is the function of the diary in relation to the priest's vocation, and to whom is it addressed? Is it a communication? The answers to these questions are ambiguous. The curé sometimes, particularly when first taking up the diary, fears that it could be simply an expression of his own egoism (1034), and that by indulging himself in this activity he is sinning. Although he knows that his diary should be "a conversation between God and myself, an extension of prayer" (1048), he is sometimes aware while writing of another presence than God's: "rather a friend made in my image, although distinct from me, a separate entity" (PM 24). This mirror image of himself is Satan taking the form of the priest's self-concern.[19] If this presence did dominate the diary, it would be a communication only with himself, a union with Satan which amounts to narcissistic solitude.

Later, communication with a future reader is added to the idea of communication with self, although the priest mistrusts its value (1117–1118). If the priest's diary is an egotistical exaltation of himself through a self-pitying portrayal of his spiritual anguish, and "literary" in the sense of being elegantly composed to bring acclamation from the public (like Dufréty's diary, written to be published, entitled *My Stages*), it will not be a true communication with the reader, but only another expression of narcissism.

During his crisis the priest lives in "a landscape of mists, without guideposts, without routes. If I keep it scrupulously, morning and evening, my diary marks out this solitary wilderness (*jalonne ces solitudes*)" (1171). The statement is ambiguous: does it mean that God aids the curé through the medium of the diary? Does the diary finally express a communion with God and, through him, with others? The answer is suggested in the last allusion the priest makes to his diary, when he speaks of "the power of presentiment that allowed me to bring together by association events unimportant in themselves" (1183). God expresses his presence in the diary precisely by giving the priest the supernatural ability to "see" the souls of other human beings in the banal pattern of daily occurrences that would otherwise have remained meaningless or obscure. For the reader of the *Journal*, this assertion must be tested in reference to the content of the diary itself, as it exposes the priest's daily relation to the world of the village, to the rebels he encounters, and to God. The diary reveals the essential ambiguity of the priest's destiny, both what he does and does not see, both his solitude and his communion.

The priest's isolation from the world of the bourgeois village is symbolized in the opening entry of his diary. From a road on a hill, the priest looks down on the village below as it disappears into the advancing night: "Never had I so cruelly felt its solitude and my own" (1031). He is aware not only of the isolation of those who live in the village, but in the darkness and distance he feels his own separation from the totality of the village. He stands above it as one whose calling is to lead it (and as one who is spiritually superior); yet he will never be able to make contact with it. Later the priest notes that almost every day he stops on another hill to sit on a tree trunk and gaze down on the village:

It is here that the idea of this diary first occurred to me, and I don't feel I could have thought of it anywhere else . . . It would be hard to find such another place from which to overlook the whole village, gathered together, as it were, in the palm of a hand. I look down, but it never seems to look back at me. Rather does it turn away, cat-like, watching me askance with half-shut eyes. (PM, 40)

The idea of the diary grows directly out of the priest's experience of solitude in relation to the village, of the mystery and apparent hostility in the way the village seems to "look" surreptitiously at him. Through the diary he will attempt to come to terms with the "other" from which he is separated.

Although he is spiritually isolated from them, the priest's vocation is to live *among men*. The Bernanosian saints all live in society; they are tempted to retreat from it to a monastic solitude, but invariably refuse this solution.[20] The role of the saint must be to attempt to recreate community among men. Thus at the start the curé accepts the task of priesthood knowing it to be more difficult than monastic virtue (1033). And later in the novel, although he recognizes the curé's profound lack of "l'expérience des hommes," Torcy insists that the curé must continue his vocation and not retire to a monastery (1102).

A parallel to the priest's supernatural vocation to live among men and to reestablish community, exists in the psychological domain. The curé has a deep need for companionship, a "vocation for friendship," as another priest tells him. This need is repeatedly frustrated as the priest attempts to establish friendships in the bourgeois world. He seeks companionship in the count, but is disappointed when he discovers the count's true mentality. The priest also seeks friendship and understanding in the adolescents in his catechism class. He expects in them the innocence of childhood, but most of them are already becoming corrupted adults. He soon rejects as egotistical his purely human desire to share his joys and sorrows with the catechism class, for catechism is a preparation for Holy Communion, not a meeting of friends. Henceforth his efforts at communication will be selflessly aimed at breaking down the isolation of others (through God).

But the priest never succeeds in establishing any contact with the mass of médiocres in the village. Again and again the priest creates misunderstanding and hostility because he does not know the "value of money" and has no sense of property as the villagers and worldly priests do. This lack of corruption by bourgeois society, and therefore complete unfitness for life in it, derives both from the curé's spiritual vocation and from his background of extreme poverty (1033, 1055–1056). The purity of the child, the poor, and the saint meet in the curé.

The priest's persecution is such that he sometimes feels "crucified" by the village (1061). The bread and wine, which is the only nourishment he takes, suggest the Last Supper. Moreover, he is betrayed to the villagers by Séraphita and Chantal, who have started the rumors about him, as Judas betrayed Christ. Bernanos establishes a symbolic parallel, then, between the vocation and agony of the curé and that of Christ. Christ also came to reunite men in love, but was not understood.

But the heart of the symbolic analogy between Christ and the priest lies in Jesus' trial in the garden of Gethsemane. When Torcy tells the curé that he imagines a person's vocation to be determined by the moment in Jesus' life when he "meets" that person, the curé weeps and thinks to himself: "The truth is that *my* place for all time has been Mount Olivet, yes, in that instant—strangely in that very instant, when He set His hand on Peter's shoulder asking him the useless question, almost naive yet so tender, so deeply courteous: *Why sleep ye?*" (PM 203). Like Pascal and Vigny, Bernanos gives a modernist interpretation to Jesus' experience in Gethsemane. The specific moment of the biblical account which remains fixed in the priest's mind as the symbol of his condition, reveals the essential meaning of Gethsemane for him. Peter, who as a faithful disciple should be sharing his agony, is asleep; in the same way the priest is alone among the villagers, the médiocres who are spiritually asleep. Their active cruelty to him, their "crucifixion" of him, is finally less important than the terrible isolation to which their essential otherness abandons him.

Having learned that he is soon to die, as he is sitting in a café in Lille, the priest has an experience that sets off a meditation on a special function of the saint as supreme representative of the indivisible Church—"one of the most mysterious aspects of the Communion of Saints" (PM 260). Although he fears that it may be absurd to assume such a role for himself, the priest feels that he has fulfilled this function at least at some moments in the past as well as in the present moment:

Some people had just come in, workers who were going to have lunch. One of them saw me over the partition, and his friends burst out laughing. The noise they make doesn't bother me, on the contrary. My inner silence—the silence that God blesses—has never isolated me from other human beings.

It seems to me that they come into it; I receive them at the threshold of my dwelling, as it were. And they doubtless come to me, they come without knowing it . . . But I imagine the silence of certain souls to be vast places of refuge. Poor exhausted sinners come in gropingly, fall asleep, and leave consoled, without retaining any memory of the great, invisible temple . . . (1229–1230)

But this communion of the saint with sinners—like the communion of sinners in evil mentioned above—does not take place on the conscious level, either for the saint or for those who unknowingly find repose in his soul. It is in fact contradicted, on the conscious level, not only by the incident that occasions the meditation (the workers only laugh at the priest's strange appearance, unaware of his inner anguish in confrontation with death), but also by the daily experience of the priest throughout the novel. Since the communion has no basis in the priest's conscious experience, it has no reality in the novelistic world. More important, since it is based on an ideal conception of the Church—or Christendom—that the novel negates, its reality is positively undermined by the novel. The saint's isolation from the mass of mediocre sinners—like their own isolation from each other—is absolute in the *Journal*.

For the saint living in bourgeois society, the only communication possible is with those who have totally rejected that society, and who are therefore not of a nature irreconcilably foreign to his own. Indeed, the sensibilities of the saint and the rebels are profoundly similar. The doctors Delbende and Laville, Olivier, the countess and Chantal, are of the "same race" as the curé. Like them, the priest has a stature superior to the médiocres; he has the courage and strength to struggle, to risk, to endure. The rebels often speak of themselves and the priest as *nous* (1092, 1215–1216, 1237). The priest also experiences revolt against the world's injustice and degradation, and the temptation of despair and suicide (1116–1117, 1162, 1185). The curé is tempted by Satan; his soul, like theirs, is a battlefield of the forces of good and evil, although the *rapport de forces* is reversed.

The possibility of communication exists between the saint and the rebels from society, and only through this communcation can the rebels have access to community and love. The saint's role is to break down their resistance to God and bring them into God's presence. Were he to succeed in this task, the converts might constitute the beginnings of the recreation of a true Christian community, a Christendom. But the saint does not succeed in bringing even the rebels to God, or when he exceptionally does, it is at the very moment of their death. In his confrontations with the rebels, however, the saint is blessed with the only veritable communication that can exist in the modern world: a momentary vision of their souls.[21]

These visions provide a sudden illumination of the consciousness of the rebel, whereas the priest's ordinary task of listening to the confessions of the médiocres leaves their consciousnesses veiled. After listening to Mlle. Louise's confession one morning, the priest notes: "Those people who think the Sacrament gives us instant power to read the hidden places of a soul are indeed credulous! . . . I still cannot manage to understand what horrible metamorphosis has enabled so many people to show me their inner life as a mere convention, a formal scheme without one clue to its reality" (PM 86).

But the visions that the priest has of Chantal and the countess reveal a central, hidden passion in each of them. As Chantal tells the priest of her hatred of her father and her desire to revenge herself, he receives a vision of her which contradicts her words: "It seemed I could read other words on her lips as she was speaking—words to which she gave no voice, yet they burnt their way, one by one, into my brain" (PM 136). The priest suddenly sees that Chantal is not tempted to flee to Paris and dishonor herself, as she claims, but to commit suicide. This supernatural clairvoyance, which is unaided by anything Chantal has said, even guesses the concrete detail that she has written a suicide note and has it with her (1137). But the detail is simply an extension of the basic perception that Chantal's hatred has turned in upon itself, that her passion has become self-destructive.

The next day, when the priest visits Chantal's mother, his interview with her turns into a supernatural encounter in which he sees into the countess' soul as well (1147). Here the inner reality is suggested to the priest by the countess' comportment rather than by her words. Indeed, the relations between the priest and the rebels often involve a sensitivity to the gestures, looks, and tone of voice that may reveal feeling hidden on the verbal level. Many times the priest and the rebels "read" each other's eyes (for example, 1151, 1216, 1240), in marked contrast to the impenetrability of the "regard de la paroisse."

However, the priest's vision of another may be contradicted by, or unrelated to, the other person's nonverbal expressions. If his vision sometimes has its point of departure in the other's expressions, it always transcends them, since in Bernanos' world communication can *only* come through the agency of God. The gift of vision is given by God to those like the curé who exercise charity with others—that is, in the Bernanosian perspective, the human relation that is the opposite of the reified relations in bourgeois society.

The vision is given directly by God; it is not only a communication with the other person, but also an expression of the presence of God: "God is speaking" (p. 1135). With the countess, the priest not only experiences communication with her and with God, but also brings her face to face with God (1160), thus creating a triangular relationship between two human beings and God. The relationship is only momentary, however, for the countess dies on the night following their confrontation. The saint's only communication with others is rare and of short duration. Once the vision is past, the game of *regards* begins again—the play of closed, impenetrable looks, hard, defiant ones, misleading or only suggestive ones. This tortured relation with the rebel may give glimmers of the inner reality of the other, but never the full revelation. The priest even places in question the infallibility of the visions themselves, for he tells the countess: "God alone knows the secret of souls, He alone. The most discerning of us are brought into error" (1145; also 1160).

Though the rebels never accede to the presence of God—with the exception of the countess, who dies immediately thereafter—the saint does experience God's presence at exceptional moments—especially in the moments of his vision of souls. Yet these moments are won dearly out of his perpetual struggle to pray. Although at the beginning of his diary the curé speaks of the priest's vocation to accept "the terrifying presence of the divine in each moment of our poor life" (1034), God's presence is nowhere evident in the degraded world in which the curé lives. In a world that seems to deny the existence of God altogether, the curé undergoes a crisis. He becomes unable to pray and is thrown into the anguish of metaphysical solitude: "Behind me there was nothing. And in front of me a wall, a black wall" (1111).

In his moments of vision the priest is miraculously able to pray again, to hear God speak. Communication with others and with God is simultaneous. The prayer and the presence of God evaporate, however, when the *moment privilégié* is terminated (1145, 1186). The priest faces his cruellest solitude confronting death: "However hard I try now, I know I shall never understand by what terrible mischance I was able at such a time even to forget the very name of God. I was alone, utterly alone, facing my death—and that death was a wiping out, and nothing more" (PM 275). Without God's presence, death means for the priest himself that destruction of the self which obsesses many of Malraux's characters as well as Bernanos' rebels.

The priest is periodically awakened by mysterious sounds at night: the gate banging open and shut, steps in the garden, a voice calling him. Yet each time he gets up to find nobody there (1104, 1105, 1123, 1140). Were these strange presences some person who strayed into his yard, was he dreaming, or were they signs from God? The priest never knows, and once reported the incidents are not mentioned again; nor are they linked in the priest's mind. For God does not manifest himself visibly and unambiguously in the world. In the Bernanosian universe he is an *absent* God, even for the saint. Since the priest questions even his visions, God's apparitions—both in the world and within the priest—are irremediably doubtful.

The curé is able to establish contact only with the rebels, and with limited results, but a secondary "saint" of the novel is principally concerned with the relationship between the priest and *all* of his parish: the Curé de Torcy. Although he in no way integrates himself in society by accepting its terms, he *knows* society in a way the curé, continually embroiled in blunders and misunderstandings, does not. Torcy sees the need to transform this society; to do so, priests are needed who comprehend the world and are unafraid of it and, at the same time, are superior to it, able to provide it with firm leadership. He tells the curé:

When I was your age we had *men* in the church . . . heads of a parish, masters, my boy, *rulers*. They could hold a whole country together, that sort could—with a mere lift of the chin . . . Nowadays the seminaries turn out little choirboys, little ragamuffins who think they're working harder than anybody because they never get anything done. They go snivelling around instead of giving orders. (PM 9)

The purpose of the leader-priests of Torcy's generation was not to attempt to vanquish evil heroically, an impossible and absurd task, but to make order, to make a Christendom (1038–1039). Torcy and his generation look back for their model to the thirteenth century (1044).

Yet, as Torcy recognizes, the medieval Christendom exists no longer, and the priests of his generation have not been able to recreate one. Thus, in spite of his scorn for "choirboys" like the curé, expressed during the first conversation between the two when the curé has just begun at his new post, Torcy does not subsequently offer an alternative to the curé's spiritual adventure, which touches only the rebels. Indeed, Torcy's admiration for the curé quite obviously grows throughout the course of the novel.

The tension between the minor and the major saint in the *Journal* dramatizes an insuperable contradiction in Bernanos' world.[22] The curé is finally unable to create a spiritual community even among his rebels. His intense suffering and struggle bring a mere evanescent hint of what a Christendom might be. The simultaneous communion with God and another human being which the vision of souls offers the curé is only a microcosm, destroyed as soon as it is born, of the global and continuous unity throughout society that was lost with Christendom.

And yet the curé's rather than Torcy's struggle is the subject of the novel. Torcy's conception of a pastoral vocation to the médiocres (1123), which aims at the ideal of a Christian society, can exist only on the discursive level. Torcy can be no more than a secondary figure who converses with the central actor in the spiritual drama, since the task that he knows to be necessary is also unrealizable. As Bernanos writes in conclusion to the preface of *Les Grands Cimetières sous la lune:* "My profound certainty is that the part of the world still capable of redemption belongs only to children, heros, and martyrs." [23] The reactionary project of a return to the past is impossible. The real drama for Bernanos, then, must be the saint-hero's solitary Gethsemane in the immutable modern world, and his dearly won visions of what might have been.

7

La Chute: The Egocentric Individual

I

During and after World War Two some important changes in the literary treatment of solitude occur—changes that correspond to modifications of the economic system as well as to political developments. The most important new feature of the postwar economy—in Western Europe and most markedly in France—was the increase of state intervention in the economic system. This intervention took the form of massive government expenditures, notably in armaments, partial or complete government control or ownership of enterprises, and long-range centralized economic planning. In France, state control of the economy operated principally through the interrelation between the "mixed enterprises" (companies partially owned by the government or partially controlled through agreements) and the Commissariat du Plan, which set up and coordinated long-range economic goals.[1]

The beginnings of significant state intervention in its modern form (the state has always played a larger role in French capitalist development than in other Western countries) dates back to the entre-deux-guerres period. The French mixed enterprise (along with the first attempts at planification) was already developing in the 1920s, and the slow recovery from depression through the 1930s in all Western countries was due in large part to government intervention and expenditure.[2] However, as Maurice Dobb states, "the Second World War and its aftermath witnessed a sufficiently large extension of the economic functions of the State as to make it a qualitative dividing line in this respect." [3] Although this new aspect of the postwar economy has significant consequences, it is important to note that state intervention does not entail a basic structural change in the capitalist system. Monopolies are by no means weakened or eliminated by state power; monopolistic concentration is, on the contrary, supported by state capitalism.[4]

Thus state monopoly capitalism, as it is also termed, has the effect of *intensifying* an essential characteristic of monopoly capitalist culture: the decline of the individual's power and importance and the decadence of individualist values. For the aim of economic planning is to reduce the dangerous conflicts of the market, to attenuate risks and submit the economy to a predictable functioning based on calculated, centralized guidance and cooperation between companies.[5] Already in *La Condition humaine*, Ferral stands in defiant contrast to the impotent bankers caught in the organizational network that binds them to their enterprise and their enterprise to the state. The state-private conglomerates that defeat Ferral become widespread and combine with full-scale planning in the postwar period.

Certain major developments in the political sphere coincide with the advent of state capitalism. World War Two revealed the terrifying destructiveness and inhumanity of fascism, under the Occupation in France and especially in the Nazi concentration camps. The fascist powers were defeated and humiliated; collaborators were imprisoned and shot. The ideology of fascism was thus defamed and, with it, the glorification of sport and the warrior ethic. On the other hand, a massive disenchantment of Western intellectuals with Communism occurred after the Stalin-Hitler pact of 1939, and intensified with the revelations of Stalinist repression during the Cold War years. After the intense social agitation and Popular Front government of the 1930s, and the hopes of the post-Liberation period, revolution did not occur in France and other Western countries. The Communist parties of these countries sought to increase their power solely through parliamentary politics, and secreted their own Stalinist bureaucracies.

Thus the political movements to the Right and Left which offered to the individual stature and reintegration in a collectivity seem to have failed or foundered. We have seen the heroic attempts to achieve community, and their final failure, in the novelistic worlds of Malraux and Bernanos. Malraux's conception of the Communist enterprise did not transcend the dominant Stalinist mode, and consequently solidarity finally fails to become true community. Bernanos, by refusing the dominant trend of the Right toward fascism, condemned his community to an ideal, unattainable past; Montherlant, by accepting that trend and by following the logic of his ethic of sport and war, ended by adding his voice to those who praised Nazism as it occupied and oppressed their country. And Saint-Exupéry's fraternity of pilots, outside all political movements, was doomed to extinction by technological advances that greatly reduced the adventure of flying. With the coming of World War Two, then, both the political and literary adventures of the entre-deux-guerres seem bankrupt.

A new group of writers began publishing just before the outbreak of World War Two, but with the better part of their literary careers stretching from the war and Occupation through the postwar period. These writers include those often termed "existentialist"—Jean-Paul Sartre, Simone de Beauvoir, Albert Camus (although he refused that designation himself)—as well as others not directly related to existentialist currents of thought but sharing some similar perspectives in their literary works—for example, Michel Leiris and Samuel Beckett. They were confronted with the economic and political situation described above: on the one hand, after a period of crisis, the stabilization and reinforcement of monopoly capitalism under the aegis of the state and, on the other, the failure and devaluation of previous political and literary ideologies.

In this context, their works reflect a deepening and an extension of the anguish of solitude and death already central to Malraux and Bernanos. Existence in the face of death becomes totally absurd, and men hopelessly alienated from themselves, from nature, from other men and society, fall prey to a generalized *étrangeté*. Man's isolation now extends through all levels of being; from the metaphysical it descends to the physical in recurrent images of masturbation, impotence, and paralysis. Sartre's first fictional works, *La Nausée* (1938) and *Le Mur* (1939), Leiris' *L'Age d'homme* (1939), and Beckett's first novel in French, *Molloy* (written in 1947, published in 1951): each of these early works develops in its own way this radical pessimism.

Whereas Beckett has continued throughout his career to explore the nihilism that was a common *point de départ*, the two dominant figures of literary "existentialism"—Sartre and Camus—renewed the struggle, immensely difficult in the contemporary situation, to discover the path to a new collectivity.[6] From a similar point of departure and with a common impetus to find a "way out," however, the two writers followed diverging courses of development. Sartre, though most of his fictional works portray the basic solitude of the individual even when engaged in political action, has maintained a critical dialogue with the theory and practice of socialism. In the postwar period he attempted to define a revolutionary strategy outside Stalinism, and recently he has drawn progressively closer to a Marxist theoretical stance. Camus, on the other hand, turned from his early nihilism to the exploration of liberal forms of community and solidarity, becoming more anticommunist in orientation and ending in disillusionment and isolation.

Camus himself divided his work into three "series"; in the *Carnets* he lists his major works under the headings of the Absurd, Revolt, and Judgment.[7] He does not include his earliest works, which represent a fourth discrete period. Although they overlap to some extent chronologically and thematically, these series do mark the basic outlines of a literary evolution; for Camus' vision, like Malraux's, is not static.

The early works—*L'Envers et l'endroit*, *Noces*, and the first piece in *L'Eté*—are lyrical essays written from 1935 to 1939. In them Camus already discovers absurdity and estrangement. In "La Mort dans l'âme," he recounts a visit to Prague which, by tearing away the veil of familiar routine, reveals to him his true condition. He finds himself in the streets of the city among crowds of strange people whose language he does not even understand. To this solitude in the crowd his only alternative is the lonely hotel room where he fears being "reduced to myself and my miserable thoughts." [8] He vainly seeks to lose the sense of strangeness and isolation through religion: "I lost myself in the sumptuous baroque churches, looking for a homeland in them, emerging emptier and more depressed after a disappointing confrontation with myself." [9] Later, in the hotel a man is found dead. The author is deeply disturbed by the idea that the man died alone in his room and that life goes on indifferent to death. He is on the point of suicide when some friends arrive and unknowingly save him from this act.

In the northern city of Prague the anguish of absurdity and solitude is ineluctable, whereas in Algeria, and in the Mediterranean south in general, there exists a way of overcoming it. In the second half of "La Mort dans l'âme," the author travels from Prague to Italy where he "recovers" like a convalescent from his experience and finds happiness in love for the people in the streets of a town and for the countryside around it. The solution to the anguish he feels in an absurd universe lies in total acceptance of life as it is; by living as intensely as possible in the present, tasting deeply the pleasure of sun and sea, he can become united with the universe from which he felt estranged. In the hot Mediterranean countries he can overcome his isolation in the *noces* that provide the title of his second collection of essays.

Yet Camus' description of this marriage with the world seems to vacillate between two meanings. In some passages, the union with nature involves ecstatic, sensual pleasure and includes a complementary sensual communion with other human beings. The opening pages of the first essay—"Noces à Tipasa"—are narrated in an unspecified first person plural, *nous*, and the author insists that he would not wish to visit Tipasa (ancient ruins on the Algerian coast) alone. Similarly, in "L'Eté à Alger," Camus seems to link the experience of communion with natural surroundings and that with other men: "To feel one's ties to a land, one's love for certain men . . . At certain moments everything yearns for this homeland of the soul." [10] The true self expresses itself in these sensual relations; at Tipasa the author feels that "everything here leaves me intact, I surrender nothing of myself, and don no mask." [11] After a day with the "other" in the sun of Tipasa—"a day of nuptials with the world." [12]—solitude returns but now bereft of its anguish: "Then we are alone again, but satisfied." [13]

Although it can be achieved only in relatively short-lived, ecstatic moments, this form of *noces* encompasses the human world, allowing a sensual tie with another person, or with many, as in the dancehall in Algiers. At the outer limit, Camus suggests a community that he shares with the youth of Algeria (by which he means French Algerians).[14] But another conception of the *noces* alternates with this one. Appearing especially in "Le Vent à Djémila" and "Le Désert," the alternate conception annihilates the human personality and excludes other men. One must give up "the small change of his personality," [15] to enter into communion with the world. Union with a world bereft of other human presences paradoxically expresses itself as a solitude:

Like a pebble polished by the tides, I was polished by the wind, worn through to the very soul. I was a portion of the great force on which I drifted, then much of it, then entirely it, confusing the throbbing of my own heart with the great sonorous beating of this omnipresent natural heart. The wind was fashioning me in the image of the burning nakedness around me. And its fugitive embrace gave me, a stone among stones, the solitude of a column or an olive tree in the summer sky.[16]

Oneness comes from the physical contact between the self, reduced to an isolated object like a stone, and nature's larger forces, like the wind. Rather than the sense of a bond, the author has an experience of isolation, of an insentient mineral solitude.

Thus the solution to absurdity and solitude of Camus' early essays is contradictory and at one of its poles negates the human world altogether, approaching the death wish in its yearning for the unfeeling condition of the stone. In the second series of works (the first series in Camus' enumeration), the communion of *noces*—in either its human or inhuman, binding or isolating form—is no longer a realizable or an acceptable solution. Men must remain throughout their lives alone in confrontation with the Absurd. This series, in which the world of absurdity revealed to the young Camus in Prague can no longer be escaped, includes *L'Etranger*, *Caligula*, and *Le Mythe de Sisyphe*.

The composition of works in this series falls in the period from the immediate prelude to and beginning of World War Two, to the active engagement of Camus in the struggle against the German Occupation (the period also begins with the influence on Camus of Sartre's *La Nausée* and *Le Mur*).[17] At this time Camus suddenly found himself obliged to submit to human history, in the form of war and foreign conquest, rather than to participate in its making. He writes in a later essay of *L'Eté* that in 1939 he had planned to visit Greece, another Mediterranean land of sun and sea. But because of the outbreak of the war:

I did not get on that ship. I took my place in the queue shuffling toward the open mouth of hell. Little by little, we entered. At the first cry of murdered innocence, the door slammed shut behind us . . . Now we glimpse the warm ghosts of fortunate islands only at the end of long, cold, sunless years that lie ahead.[18]

Emerging from his dialogue with a timeless Algerian nature, Camus perceived history as an *enfer*, a chamber of human horror; history imprisons him, keeping him from the lost paradise of noces.

Camus's sensibility was then, and remained even in his later period of political engagement, essentially ahistorical. History is a meaningless evil which, at certain epochs, one is obliged to confront unwillingly. Although for a short period (1934–1937?) a member of the Communist Party in Algeria, Camus was not influenced by any Marxist historical perspective. In another essay from the period of the Absurd ("Les Amandiers," 1940), he specifically rejects any rational philosophy of history and adopts the existentialist concept of the human condition: "We have not overcome our condition, and yet we know it better." [19]

Of the three works on the Absurd, *L'Etranger* is the closest to the perspective of the earlier essays. In the first part of the novel, the hero Meursault is portrayed as a purely sensual being, in an Algerian setting. Indifferent to social norms of behavior,[20] he lives to sleep, make love, and swim under the Mediterranean sun. Swimming with his mistress Marie, from a beach near Algiers, he experiences the form of noces which creates a human bond: "The water was cold and I felt all the better for it. We swam a long way out, Marie and I, side by side, and it was a pleasant feeling how our movements matched, hers and mine, and how we were both in the same mood, enjoying every moment." [21] Yet there is no lyrical celebration of this form of communion through nature. Meursault's sensual life in nature does not come as an ecstatic escape from the anguish of absurdity, as in the early essays, but *precedes* the full awareness of absurdity. Moreover, in the two crucial scenes that determine Meursault's fate—his mother's funeral and the murder—nature shows a hostile face to him, in the form of an unbearably hot sun that precipitates the fatal killing and causes the sluggish indifference at the funeral that will sentence him to death. Once Meursault is imprisoned, the sensual link with Marie is broken and she becomes entirely foreign to him. He is alone, afraid of his coming death, until the closing moment of the novel when he accepts the absurdity of the universe, which then suddenly becomes "fraternal" for him. Only in death will Meursault recover the lost union with nature which was broken by his conflict with society (a conflict set in motion by nature itself). In death he will realize the inhuman form of noces and attain the condition of the stone.

If sensual communion with others through nature plays only a muted role in *L'Etranger*, to be destroyed by the drama that is central to the novel, in *Caligula* it has no place at all. The emperor discovers the Absurd at the opening of the play, and this discovery drives him to seek the extreme form of solitude. Friendship and love are meaningless in the face of death, and Caligula refuses them to pursue the only absolute possible—the individual's free expression of his desires. Yet the idea of the individual as a supreme value, carried to its extreme consequences, ends in the enslavement and destruction of all others. The individual's unlimited desires require total submission of others and, at the limit, their death. Caligula tells Caesonia as he strangles her:

I live, I kill, I exercise the rapturous power of a destroyer . . . And this, *this* is happiness; this and nothing else—this intolerable release, devastating scorn, blood, hatred all around me; the glorious isolation of a man who all his life long nurses and gloats over the ineffable joy of the unpunished murderer; the ruthless logic that crushes out human lives . . . that's crushing yours out, Caesonia, so as to perfect at last the utter loneliness that is my heart's desire.[22]

Within the logic of the supreme individual and his negation of others, neither form of noces is conceivable; he cannot and does not wish either to lose himself in the universe or to embrace others.

Camus' essay on the concept of the Absurd, *Le Mythe de Sisyphe*, suggests why the solution of noces is also philosophically unacceptable for him now. In the essay he places himself in the perspective of the existentialist philosophers only to part ways with them when they offer an escape (through Reason, or God, or some other transcendent principle) from the anguish of the Absurd. Camus defines the Absurd as the contradiction between man's need for meaning and the incomprehensibility of the universe. It is essentially a divorce, "that divorce between the mind that yearns and the world that disappoints, my nostalgia for unity, this scattered universe, and the contradiction that links them." [23] This divorce must be *preserved,* and the noces that unite a man with others and with the world destroy the separation on the physical level, as the existentialists do on the metaphysical Maintaining the divorce, on the other hand, condemns the Absurd man to solitude. Sisyphus' futile toil is accomplished alone.

In a third series of works, Camus attempts to break out of this isolation of the individual, not through a sensual marriage with the world this time, but rather in direct bonds of solidarity between men. In 1942 Camus began active participation in the Resistance, and his next series of writings dates from that period. With *Lettres à un ami allemand* (1943–44), the new positive value is fully asserted. Camus turns from the value of solitary defiance in the Absurd to the aid of others in human solidarity. In these published letters to a former German friend who has adopted the fascist cause, Camus recognizes that consciousness of the Absurd can lead, as it does fictionally in *Caligula* and historically in Nazism, to nihilistic destruction. He now refuses this nihilism by affirming a new value. Camus tells his German friend: "If nothing had any meaning, you would be in the right. But there is something that still has meaning." [24] The entity that has meaning for Camus is Man, the community of the human race. Further on he invokes another community as "my larger homeland": the community of Western Europe, the Occident.[25] With the location of community in mankind, and more specifically in the West, Camus places himself in a *liberal* perspective, rejecting the socialist concept of community (as a fraternity of struggle to realize a veritable, global community through social transformation), as well as the fascist (which he recognizes to be an institutionalization of solitude).[26]

The liberal definitions of community, combined with Camus' antihistorical bias, which he now projects upon the West, claiming that France was deflected from her pursuit of happiness in Nature to struggle against History in the form of Nazism,[27] will later lead him into a quandary. If solidarity comes only in an unwilling and episodic struggle against evil, it is bound to be weak and short-lived. And when that struggle is over, if community does not turn out to exist in the entities upon which he rests his faith, then for Camus man will again be faced with isolation.

Both the new value of solidarity and its inherent weakness as defined in the Camusian perspective are illustrated in *La Peste* (first version, 1943; final version, 1946). The sudden attack of plague in Oran gives the inhabitants of the city a collective destiny and struggle. But Dr. Rieux reflects the fundamental attitude of the inhabitants toward the plague when he says: "This business is stupid, I know, but it concerns us all." [28] The plague is a temporary disruption in the ordinary course of life; the solidarity so created is one which no one sought. Only Cottard, who suffered from isolation before the plague, wishes it to continue; in the plague situation, at least he shares his isolation with everyone else. For rather than being truly united, the inhabitants of Oran are *collectively isolated* by the plague.

The only bonds created between the inhabitants, finally and in spite of themselves, are negative ones. They share the same fear of death and separation from their loved ones, and this common physical separation reveals to them the psychological separations that often existed when they were with those they love. With even these imperfect ties broken, love and friendship no longer exist. Traditional groups and organizations must break up to keep the plague from spreading through them. And although people feel the need to gather for companionship in suffering, they fear and shun each other in public places, since everyone is a potential enemy, a possible plague-bearer. A team of volunteers is set up to create sanitary conditions that will limit the spread of the plague, but the exhausting work does not allow personal relationships to evolve fully; and at any rate this group—the only one that engages in common action—plays a relatively minor role beside the divisive factors in the situation. In this light, despite Camus' objections to the contrary, there are strong grounds for accepting Roland Barthes's judgment that *La Peste* "founds an antihistorical ethic and a politics of solitude." [29] It is perhaps more accurate to say that the novel repeatedly affirms the necessity of a human solidarity that never becomes a living reality.

L'Homme révolté, the last work of the third series (written from 1947 to 1951), repeats in discursive form the same pattern: beginning with an affirmation of solidarity, the essay goes on to demonstrate its nonexistence. Now a basic confusion in Camus' conceptions of the Absurd and man's revolt against it—a confusion operative in Camus' previous works and especially in his other philosophical essay, *Le Mythe de Sisyphe*—reveals its ultimate consequences. Metaphysical absurdity (death and the incomprehensible universe) is never clearly distinguished from human absurdity (murder and social evils), nor revolt against man's metaphysical condition from his social revolts. Moreover, the metaphysical is consistently given primacy over the human and social. This fusion of two terms in a hierarchical relationship explains the intellectual procedure in *L'Homme révolté*. Since Camus in this early postwar period is still seeking to posit the grounds for human community when the temporary solidarity of the Resistance is no longer available, he opens the essay with an analysis of the human revolt of the slave against his master and concludes that by its very nature this revolt creates a human community. If the Absurd is analogous to Descartes' systematic doubt, revolt is equivalent to the *cogito:* "[Revolt] is the first item that is clearly evident. But this evident thing draws the individual from his solitude. It is a bond in common that founds its primary value on all men. I revolt, therefore *we* are." [30] Here community does not lie in struggle toward the goal of realizing the *potential* union of men, but rather in the liberal concept of mankind's common essence, made palpable in the slave's demand for equality. Camus attempts in this way to integrate his liberal notion of the unity of mankind with the idea of revolt and revolution.

After positing the existence of human community in revolt, however, Camus turns to a lengthy consideration of modern metaphysical revolts in literature and philosophy, and shows that they all lead to nihilism and solitude. When he follows with a consideration of "historical revolt," the anticommunism, antihistoricism, and primacy of the metaphysical latent in his earlier works draw all of their logical conclusions (the Cold War was in full swing in France after 1947).[31] Communist revolution is interpreted as an extension of metaphysical revolt into history, an "excessive metaphysical crusade" [32] that results in monstrous evil and the solitude of dictatorship (Camus treats Stalinism as a necessary outcome rather than as a perversion of revolutionary theory).

If metaphysical nihilism and its historical extension, Stalinist dictatorship, betray the real meaning of revolt and create only solitude, then where can true revolt and community be found? Camus presents only one positive image of revolt [33] in *L'Homme révolté:* the adventure of a group of Russian terrorists in 1905, which he also dramatizes in *Les Justes* (1949). These terrorists are conscious of an insoluble dilemma: murder is necessary to revolution, but killing another human being destroys the human community. The solution they find is to join murder and suicide; in killing they must also die themselves. The only social revolt that is pure for Camus is self-negating, which turns upon itself and renders impossible its own purposes. Indeed, the "difficult fraternity" [34] that the "delicate murderers" of 1905 achieve lies precisely in their common doubts and anguish about what must be done. But this fraternity, doubly negative since the terrorists are also painfully conscious of their total separation from the "masses," must give way to the only perfect fraternity, which comes in a common death. Kaliayev sees that only death can provide the solidarity that the terrorist group finally is unable to achieve: "Those who love each other today must die together if they wish to be reunited. In life they are parted—by injustice, sorrow, shame; by the evil that men do to others . . . by crimes. Living is agony, because life separates." [35] Since the révoltés who remain true to mankind literally commit suicide, all that remains for the living is a purely theoretical, unrealizable human community.

L'Homme révolté and *Les Justes* conclude Camus' series on revolt, and from 1952 onward he entered a period of crisis. Camus himself considered that moment in his life to be a watershed, as he told Roger Quilliot. [36] The year 1952 saw his violent controversy with Sartre (and Francis Jeanson) over *L'Homme révolté*. Two years later the Algerian revolt began. In *L'Homme révolté* Camus had located true revolt in a collectivity that was self-negating, annihilating itself in favor of a disembodied idea of universal human community. He now felt personally isolated from the French intellectual community (belonging neither to the Left nor the Right) and from both the Algerian Arabs and the French Algerians. On the Algerian question he was unable to join either camp; standing between the two, he called for a French Algeria with "social justice." [37]

In this context Camus continued to affirm in his discursive writings the two liberal concepts of community which were already present in his *Lettres à un ami allemand:* the theoretical community of man (in his acceptance speech for the Nobel Prize in 1957) and the Western European community. [38] These affirmations were unsatisfactory for the creative artist, however, since they ignored the realities of fragmentation—in Algeria and in bourgeois Western society. In his new fictional works—the fourth series, terminated with his death in 1960—Camus turned back to the reality of solitude, while resituating the image of community in the lost paradise of noces.

In the collection of short stories, *L'Exil et le royaume* (1957), the image of integration with the Algerian land and people—the "kingdom"—is ephemeral if not lost forever. In one story—"Jonas"—the overall meaning is in a perspective similar to the Nobel Prize speech: the artist's solitude in his garret is necessary to his work, and through this work he affirms solidarity with man. But the other five stories take place in Algeria (or, in one instance, a similarly southern and underdeveloped country, Brazil) and concern the nature and possibility of integration in the human and natural world. Now Arabs and other natives, who were virtually absent from the Algeria of the early essays, appear as part of the human world. In one story, "Le Renégat," nature is hostile (the unbearable desert sun, as in *L'Etranger*), and the native tribe joined by the renegade priest practices the same cruelty and worship of force which Camus denounced as totalitarian solitude in *L'Homme révolté*. But in the remaining stories Algeria is still the land of noces.

The celebration of noces by the young in Camus' early essays has given way to the nostalgia of aging characters for whom integration is no longer possible or is only a momentary, unique experience. In "L'Hôte," the French schoolteacher, who has lived for years on the Algerian plateaux like a seigneur, in the end knows he is to be cut off from the land. And in spite of a momentary understanding with the Arab prisoner, the teacher is isolated from other men, like Camus himself distrusted or hated by both the French Algerians (represented by the gendarme Balducci) and the Arabs who vow to take revenge on him. The main characters of two other stories—"La Femme adultère" and "Les Muets"—are also French Algerians, one bourgeois and the other an artisan. They have lost their youthful communion with nature through years of marriage and work. Janine, in the first story, experiences a moment of ecstatic union with the desert night and the nomadic tribes living in the desert. Yet she does not make human or sensual contact with the natives (the experience is quasi-mystical), and afterwards she must return to her husband, to her guilt for having committed "adultery" and to her real relations with the impenetrable, disquieting Arabs. At the end of the second story, after the failure of the artisans to express the universal human solidarity above class, the protagonist Yvars sits looking at the sea (his weak, daily substitute for the passionate sensual pleasures of his youth on the beaches), wishing that he were young again.

With the failure of all the forms of integration, only the reality of isolation remained for Camus. Although they were published later, probably most or all of the stories in *L'Exil et le royaume* had been completed when Camus wrote *La Chute* (published in 1956).[39] The latter was to be another short story in *L'Exil et le royaume*, but developed into a short novel. *La Chute* is thus the most important, and the final, elaboration of Camus' vision in this period. In it he explores—and that he does so is certainly a mark of his artistic honesty—the real world of fragmentation and the bankruptcy of liberal solidarity.

II

Jean-Baptiste Clamence, the narrator and only developed character in
La Chute, is not a fully particularized individual, but rather a modern
Everyman. After painting his self-portrait, Clamence informs us that
its features are not strictly limited to his own idiosyncrasies: "I
mingle what concerns me and what concerns others. I choose the
features we have in common, the experiences we have endured
together, the failings we share—good form, in other words, the man
of the hour as he is rife in me and in others. With all that I construct
a portrait which is the image of all and no one" (O 139).[40] Camus
considered entitling the novel "Un Héros de notre temps" and affixing
an epigraph from Lermontov: " 'A Hero of Our Time' is in fact a
portrait, but it is not of one man. It is rather an assemblage of the
faults of our generation in all the fullness of their development." [41]
This hero, the Everyman of modern, bourgeois society, is a bourgeois
himself, or a "Sadducee," as he says (1478). The life and person of
Clamence, then, is a narrowly focused image of Camus' vision of
contemporary bourgeois existence and mentality.

Jean-Baptiste is special, however, in that he, unlike most bourgeois,
becomes conscious of the reality of his existence; he discovers a hidden
reality beneath the surface appearance of his life. This discovery is
his Fall—from the innocence that is only ignorance of evil, to knowledge of his true condition. The mechanism of discovery is set off by
the experience of a laugh coming from the Seine as Jean-Baptiste
crosses a bridge in Paris. The laugh is aimed at his entire life, revealing
its hypocritical doubleness; beneath the apparent Jean-Baptiste there
lies another self. Slowly memories of his past life come back which
allow him to reconstitute his hidden, true nature (1498). In the first
three of the six chapters of *La Chute,* Jean-Baptiste recounts his life
before the Fall, and explains what he discovered about that existence.

As he describes himself in the role he played for himself and for
others, Clamence was a perfected example of the liberal (as well as
highly cultivated) bourgeoisie. He belongs to one of the professions—
he is a lawyer [42]—which have the virtue of allowing the bourgeois to
feel he is performing a beneficial social service while at the same time
participating in the privilege and wealth of the ruling class. Jean-
Baptiste shares the liberal's concern with aiding others: his specialty
as a lawyer is "noble cases" (O 17)—that is, aiding victims of society
or misfortune. He is even concerned with the lack of good will within
his own class and holds forth before friends on "the hard-heartedness

of our governing class and the hypocrisy of our leaders" (O 38). More-over, Clamence takes pleasure in the exercise of courtesy and generos-ity with everyone. His relations with others are easy and pleasant; he lives in the glow of a "felicitous sociability" (O 28). Jean-Baptiste thus incarnates the classic liberal sensibility, which interprets its own existence (psychic as well as material) as happily unoppressed and charitable.

From the minute he hears the laugh on the bridge, Jean-Baptiste begins to understand that this liberal personality was only a social role (in which he had come to believe himself), covering a deeper and very different psychological reality. He does not, however, simply discover the avidity of the bourgeois bent on gain under his liberal facade. On the contrary, he has always simply taken his wealth for granted, and he finds a grasping mentality completely alien (1483, 1517–1518). Yet his hidden psyche nonetheless exemplifies the ego-ism, isolation, and frustrated desire for power which are hallmarks of the modern bourgeois mentality.

The central vice is egoism. In spite of his seemingly altruistic con-cern for others, Clamence is concerned solely with himself (1483–1484). Egoism goes hand in hand with vanity, the self-satisfied con-viction of his own superiority (1498). His exclusive concentration upon self causes Jean-Baptiste to find a symbol in physical heights and in islands, as concrete expressions of superiority and isolation. He is especially fond of mountains, for on these solitudes men of God received revelations, and he feels himself to be "superhuman" and "chosen" (1488). By seeking others' admiration through his acts of altruism, Clamence stands upon a metaphorical mountain, in view of the multitudes below (1486). On a mountain one can be alone, superior, and dominant, as one can on an island. Jean-Baptiste's favorite landscape combines the two (1496).

Jean-Baptiste desires that others worship him, that, at the outer limit, "all the individuals on earth, or the greatest possible number, [be] turned toward me, eternally in suspense, devoid of independent life and ready to answer my call at any moment" (O 68). He desires absolute control over other beings—a control that Ferral in *La Condi-tion humaine* discovered to be impossible when he encountered alien and autonomous lives rather than passive marionettes. Clamence dis-likes any indication that others do not consent happily to domination. He is disturbed when a maid does not serve him with a smile, and he shuns Chinese restaurants: "Why? Because Orientals when they are silent and in the presence of whites often look scornful" (O 46). Representatives of a class or nation oppressed by his own present dangerously autonomous and hostile visages.[43]

Indeed, Clamence discovers not only that he wishes to be superior and dominant, but also that he cannot actually realize his wish. His egoism, vanity, and urge to dominate give the lie to his liberal social role, but in the same way his actual impotence in action gives the lie to his dreams of grandeur and power. Two specific memories from his past life come back to him after his Fall, which reveal this second hidden truth. One day a motorcyclist insulted him and when he got out of his car to protest, a bystander punched him. He returned to his car without responding to the provocation. Jean-Baptiste is intensely humiliated by this experience, for he realizes that he had dreamed of being "a complete man who managed to make himself respected in his person as well as in his profession. Half Cerdan, half de Gaulle, if you will. In short, I wanted to dominate in all things . . . The truth is that every intelligent man, as you know, dreams of being a gangster and of ruling over society by force alone . . . one generally relies on politics and joins the cruelest party" (O 54–55). With the mention of De Gaulle and the "cruelest" political party (which for Camus would be the Stalinists), there is probably a direct allusion here to Malraux. At any rate, Jean-Baptiste fails to engage in that violent action (though incomparably less dangerous, of course) in which Malraux's characters seek to give meaning and stature to their lives.

In the second, and more crucial, incident that Clamence recalls, he again failed to act, this time in a more serious and dangerous way. A woman jumped (or possibly fell) off a bridge one night, and he was unable to make any move to save her. He was confronted with the opportunity, on the one hand, to prove by risking his life the existence of the liberal community of human beings and, on the other, to actualize his hidden self-image as a heroic, superior being. His failure to act negates both his solidarity with others and his stature as an individual. The laugh that seems to come from the river and that precipitates his Fall is an ironic comment on the discrepancy between these actual failures and both the liberal image and the heroic self-image. The liberal solidarity that was a positive value in *La Peste*, although not an accomplished reality, becomes in Clamence a mere hypocritical pretext, and Malraux's heroic, self-assertive action is no longer possible for the paralyzed will of this modern bourgeois.

If Jean-Baptiste's relations with other human beings in general are demystified in his fall from innocence, so also are his more intimate relations—with friends and lovers. While he showed great cordiality and warmth with friends and acquaintances, his exhibitions of fellowship served only to bolster his vainglorious image of himself and concealed a deeper indifference or even dislike. His greatest emotion for a friend always came at death, when a show of grief was favorably remarked upon by others and when the friend no longer imposed the responsibility to understand and aid another person. Jean-Baptiste no longer had to shift his concentration away from his own person (1490–1491).

Jean-Baptiste's relations with women reveal the same essential egoism and noncommunication. He is a Don Juan for whom love is a game with ritualized words and acts (1504–1505)—a role, like his liberalism. The appearances of love hide a sensuality that expresses on the physical level Clamence's self-love. Like Ferral in *La Condition humaine* the only real object of his love in the sexual act is himself (1503).

Women as autonomous human beings, as "others," are not just indifferent but positively threatening to Clamence, for as such they continually demand a relation that would take him out of his narcissistic self-contemplation and impose a restriction on his freedom. Sometimes he wishes their death:

In my moments of irritation I told myself that the ideal solution would have been the death of the person I was interested in. Her death would, on the one hand, have definitively fixed our relationship and, on the other, removed its compulsion. But one cannot long for the death of everyone or, in the extreme, depopulate the planet in order to enjoy a freedom that cannot be imagined otherwise. My sensibility was opposed to this, and my love of mankind. (O 67)

If "others" restrict the absolute freedom of the narcissistic individual, the only logical solution is Caligula's: the triumphant ego in a world of corpses. Here Jean-Baptiste's bloodthirsty ego reveals once again the hypocrisy of the "love of mankind" with which he decorates his liberal facade.

III

After the laugh heard from the bridge brings back the memories of his past life, Clamence fears that others will see his true nature as he does. In his fear of judgment by others he becomes distrustful of everyone and imagines that "the circle of which I was the center broke and they lined up in a row as on the judges' bench" (O 78). He finds himself dethroned from the impregnable solitude of superiority, now alone among mysterious and hostile others armed with the power to judge him.

When World War Two breaks out, Jean-Baptiste leaves Paris. He considers joining the Resistance; here the opportunity offers itself to join a common struggle. But his vanity wins the day: "I think especially that underground action suited neither my temperament nor my preference for exposed heights" (O 122). In the anonymous, collective work in clandestinity which the Resistance involves, Jean-Baptiste would not enjoy the adoration of others in the splendid isolation of grandeur. Moreover, when he continues on south into North Africa, he finds himself unable even to choose sides: "But in Africa the situation was not clear; the opposing parties seemed to be equally right and I stood aloof" (O 123).[44] The vainglorious ego of Jean-Baptiste is unable to engage itself in an action that would actualize its dreams of heroism and in a solidarity where it would transcend itself. Since it cannot distinguish in the opposing forces one side which, in spite of inevitable imperfections, is part of a positive historical struggle, it becomes the isolated victim of history, experienced as an absurd evil confronting the individual. Jean-Baptiste is taken prisoner not because of his own involvement but by association with a friend who was a resister without his knowing it.

The final failure to reach outside himself comes in the prison camp to which Clamence is sent. He is appointed "pope" by a disaffected Catholic who believes that a true spiritual leader should be an equal who would "keep alive, in himself and in others, the community of our sufferings" (O 125). Jean-Baptiste attempts to lead the group of men with whom he is imprisoned with justice and equality, but soon realizes that such impartial leadership is impossible. He favors his group against other groups in the prison camp, and he favors one of his group over another depending on their relative utility. He himself once drank the water of a dying man with the justification that the man would die anyway and he was needed by the group as leader (1539). Clamence seriously attempts to realize through his leadership the brotherhood of men which was only a liberal facade before. Still, confronted with an absolute theoretical notion of human solidarity, any action within an actual group necessarily becomes impure and negates the possibility of solidarity. If there is no perfect solidarity of all men, then there is none at all. Disillusioned by his failure to actualize absolute community, Jean-Baptiste is again thrust back into his egoism and guilt.

After the war Clamence moves to Amsterdam, where he establishes himself in the life he is leading as he narrates the novel. With the failure of his efforts to escape his isolation, Jean-Baptiste installs himself definitively in the most radical of solitudes. He now lives alone and friendless in a foreign city. As his name suggests, he is a prophet crying out in the desert solitude of the city, all the more alone as his call to men is a treacherous one, aimed at misleading and enslaving them. As a false prophet he is a true Satan, torturing others in the last circle of hell. In the Dantean hell that serves as a symbolic analogy, the last circle is the *cercle des glaces*, or the Circle of Ice in which Satan stands in frozen isolation. The French phrase, moreover, contains a double meaning: *glaces* can mean mirrors as well as ice. Thus Jean-Baptiste's symbolic realm of solitude not only denies him all human warmth but also encloses him in a narcissistic play of mirrors.

Within the city Clamence lives alone in his bare room, without even the companionship of books. He hates and distrusts other men, and obsessively guards the inviolability of his room: "Forgive me, I have the bolt complex. On the point of going to sleep, I can never remember whether or not I pushed the bolt. And every night I must get up to verify . . . I am not worried about my safety, but about myself and my presence of mind. I am also eager to block the door of the closed little universe of which I am the king, the pope, and the judge" (O 127–128). This room is filled with his own ego, unassailable by hostile "others," like Marcel's room in *Du côté de chez Swann*. But Jean-Baptiste's room is more radically solitary than Marcel's room, or for that matter the nineteenth-century poet's room or the hermit's cell. For the poet's (and Marcel's) room contains the books and writings through which he may make contact with others, and the hermit's cell, though bare like Clamence's room, may be filled with a divine presence. Jean-Baptiste's room is empty both of books and of God; it contains only his isolated and fearful self.

Jean-Baptiste does not remain defensively in the fortress of his room, however. He spends much of his time in the bar which is the location of his encounters with others. "Others" now are of two kinds. In his liberal persona he wished to treat all men as brothers, but now he distinguishes. The regular customers of the seaside bar are sailors, thieves, and pimps. Clamence cynically speaks of these lower-class men as animals or prehistoric men (1475, 1493). He no longer makes a pretense of considering them his equal, and living among them he enjoys the solitary superiority of his class and culture. But at the same time his discoveries about himself have taught him that he is no less guilty than they. He serves as legal counselor for them, not as a liberal charity to the poor and oppressed as before, but because "if pimps and thieves were invariably sentenced, all decent people would get to thinking they themselves were constantly innocent . . . that's what must be avoided above all" (O 41).

Indeed, it is only with these "decent people"—the bourgeois or Sadducees who make up the other category of men—that Jean-Baptiste has any relationship other than "professional." He frequents the bar so as to encounter the fellow bourgeois who occasionally strays into such places. In form, the novel is Jean-Baptiste's monologue to one such bourgeois. Clamence's relation with this "other" is exemplary of his relations now with all bourgeois others and, by extension, with the Sadducee readers of the novel as well. Throughout the novel, only Jean-Baptiste speaks in the text; the other makes short rejoinders to Clamence's discourse, but they are only suggested by responses Clamence makes to them. The other consequently remains entirely invisible; he exists only as a listener to Jean-Baptiste, and has no independent life of his own. As J. Cruickshank has pointed out, this "monologue masquerading as dialogue" reproduces in the form of the novel Clamence's narcissistic relation to others.[45]

Yet in spite of this self-centered discourse, Jean-Baptiste does not communicate himself as a unique person to the other (or to the reader). He does not reveal himself fraternally and trustingly; he fears the antagonistic power to judge possessed by the other, and his discourse is aimed at disarming that judgment. In the role of *juge-penitant*, Clamence treats the other as an enemy to be captured. He begins as a penitant to gain the other's sympathy. Then, as he paints a portrait that resembles the other as well as himself, he becomes a judge. The "confession" in fact hides Jean-Baptiste behind something opaque; it turns out to be a mask in a mirror rather than a transparent glass: "A mask, in short, rather like those carnival masks which are both life-like and stylized, so that they make people say: 'Why, surely I've met him!' . . . The portrait I hold out to my contemporaries becomes a mirror" (139–140). The mirror comes to symbolize not only Clamence's narcissism but also the way in which the portrait, when viewed by another, reflects the viewer himself.

Through the offices of the judge-penitant, the other is drawn into a degraded solidarity of guilt. Clamence from the very start creates an insidious community between them. They are both French, so Clamence speaks of "our beautiful capital" and calls his interlocutor "cher compatriote" (O 6, 15). As his story progresses he repeatedly asks the other to interrogate his own life, in which he will perhaps find similar occurrences and traits. The solidarity that Clamence wishes to create is not one of friendship, but of complicity in guilt. As he tells the other, "I have no more friends; I have nothing but accomplices. To make up for this, their number has increased; they are the whole human race, you first of all. Whoever is at hand is always the first" (O 73). As in Bernanos, this "solidarité dans le mal"[46] is the very opposite of communication. Its atmosphere is one of hatred, distrust, ruses, and lies. If Jean-Baptiste says he will listen to the confession of the other "with a great feeling of fraternity" (O 140), it is only because the degraded fraternity he has forced upon the other allows him to triumph again: "Once more I have found a height to which I am the only one to climb and from which I can judge everybody" (O 142). Within the degraded fraternity Jean-Baptiste remains totally isolated, but with the enemy other disarmed and humiliated, he rediscovers the mountaintop solitude that he had lost in the Fall.

In his satanic isolation Clamence still dreams of a true fraternity that exists before the Fall from innocence. In this sense, the Fall has a different meaning. It signifies separation from the state of authentic innocence, rather than mere ignorance of evil. By this definition, *all* of Jean-Baptiste's life partakes of the fallen state; for in the period before his Fall from ignorance, his existence was already "fallen" in the sense that the evil of egoism was hidden within him. The realm of true innocence is one in which perfect friendship and love exist. It is the "kingdom" of *L'Exil et le royaume*—the lost paradise of noces, the impossible image of salvation.

The land of innocence is the Mediterranean. There friends walk hand in hand, but access to this paradise is denied Jean-Baptiste, the corrupted European bourgeois (1523–1524). The self-sacrifice of true friendship is impossible for him—to be capable of it would be salvation (1489–1490). Perfect love exists only in the paradise of which he dreams: "A total love of the whole heart and body, day and night, in an uninterrupted embrace, sensual enjoyment and mental excitement—all lasting five years and ending in death" (O 135). Here, as in some of the stories in *L'Exil et le royaume*, the human communication Camus sought to establish in his "liberal" period is combined with the primordial goal of sensual union, in a single, unattainable communion.

With the combined realm of noces and true human solidarities forever closed to him, Clamence awaits the coming perfection of false solidarity in the police state: "So, after all, for want of betrothal or uninterrupted love, it will be marriage, brutal marriage, with power and the whip" (O 135). Afraid of his responsibility of decision and action as a solitary individual, afraid of dying alone, and unable to transcend his egocentric self in true community, Jean-Baptiste now seriously calls for the fascist solution which was the extreme, caricatured limit of his personality before. In the meantime, he works to spread as widely as possible the degraded fraternity of common guilt, hatred, and distrust, in his role as judge-penitant.

La Chute, like Proust's *Du côté de chez Swann*, pictures a single, isolated ego in a world of hostile "others." But Marcel's inner world was the zenith of the individual self cultivated in all its richness. After

Proust, with the crisis of individualist values, novelists like Malraux and Bernanos attempted to restore to the individual his lost meaning and stature through a community and a heroic struggle. With the failure of these attempts, the modern hero remains an isolated ego, but bereft of the intrinsic value of the Proustian individual. Since self-affirmation in solidarity has failed, the new hero's efforts at rediscovering his powers take the form of aggression uniformly exercised toward others. Yet the degraded ego is no longer capable of a heroic conquest of others; his aggression upon others is insidious, self-demeaning, and self-destructive. Jean-Baptiste can only attack others indirectly by attacking himself.

The world of *La Chute* is a wasteland of uniformly degraded human substance. The isolated person of Clamence is not analyzed inwardly in psychological complexity, for it does not possess the intrinsic value of Proust's Marcel; it is rather continually reflected out upon others, more and more broadly generalized to make of Clamence a symbol of modern bourgeois man. As we have seen, Jean-Baptiste's self-portrait is held out as a mirror. But Jean-Baptiste also explicitly and repeatedly generalizes his own experience and personality. To reflections on his own identity he adds aphorisms that define modern man; to events that purportedly happened to him he adds anecdotes about anonymous others. These aphorisms and anecdotes create a parallel portrait of modern man identical with Jean-Baptiste's. All are incapable of love or friendship, are egotistical and vain, hide their oppression of others beneath a liberal facade, assault others with their judgments to avoid being judged themselves. Finally modern men, in their ambivalent destructive and self-destructive urge, in their search for power and actual impotence, call like Jean-Baptiste for the totalitarian solution: in the radical negation of the individual they may enjoy its apotheosis *vicariously* through the dictators to whom they submit. In the meantime, the faceless isolation that Clamence experienced in Paris is their experience as well: "Then I used to wander in the streets. They wander now too, I know! They wander, pretending to hasten toward the tired wife, the forbidding home . . . Ah, *mon ami*, do you know what the solitary creature is like as he wanders in big cities?" (O 118).

8

⚜

Le Planétarium:
Solitude in the
World of Commodities

I

In addition to the increase in state intervention, another important modification occurs in the monopoly capitalism of the postwar period —a modification that, like state intervention, has its beginnings in the entre-deux-guerres but that makes its qualitative leap even later. The monopoly system itself creates a perpetual danger of overproduction and underconsumption. It needs therefore to expand its consumer markets, which it does domestically through advertising and other marketing techniques (market expansion is also effected through widening foreign outlets). Advertising creates consumer "demands" for an expanding range of products, and spreads them to wider and wider sectors of society. The development of a full-scale consumer economy, however, does not take place all at once. In Western Europe the 1930s saw an initial growth in advertising and some expansion of consumption, but the real take-off did not occur until after World War Two and the postwar economic recovery. The late 1950s and 1960s mark a qualitative transition to what in France is often called the "société de consommation." [1]

In terms of the theory of alienation in capitalist society, this qualitative change in the meaning of consumption—the central importance that commodities come to have in people's lives—adds a new dimension to the alienation of the individual. Reification, which had always been one aspect of the alienation inherent in the capitalist system, takes on a new importance and new forms. Human needs are systematically translated into needs for commodities, the perception of oneself and others continually related to commodities through advertising. Human relations therefore are reified in a new way; and the hostilities of competition are given a new form in the struggle to accumulate and conspicuously consume.

The novels of Nathalie Sarraute explore the new status of commodities in human life and the relationship between commodities and human relations. In her first book, *Tropismes* (published in 1939, written in the mid-1930s), some of the short sketches picture crowds shopping, staring into display windows; a woman dominating the members of her household through her empire over the "things" in it; and women discussing clothes they have bought.[2] But in a later work, *Le Planétarium* (1959), commodities are actually central to the semiconscious dramas, the interplay of "tropisms" between the major characters. Later still, the new hegemony of commodities and consumption in human existence will be given an even more explicit expression in *Les Choses* (1965), by Georges Perec. In this short novel, which takes as its point of departure a sociological analysis of the generation growing to maturity in the late 1950s and early 1960s, a young couple similar to the couple in *Le Planétarium* dreams of future riches that take the form of "things": spacious apartments, furnishings, bibelots and expensive books, stylish clothes. They spend their spare time in *boutiques de luxe* and department stores, looking and buying, perpetually unsatisfied because their meager earnings never match their limitless desire to consume. They and their friends work as interviewers for marketing research firms, thus helping to create the very "needs" that obsess and oppress them. Their life and their relationships with others like them are experienced as empty and unsatisfying, for they are based on the search for happiness through things—a happiness that forever remains on the horizon.

Indeed, in the postwar novel the world of things in general—the world of objects, that is—tends to take on larger dimensions and a greater independence in relation to the human world. Under the pressure both of the radical diminution of the individual's importance in the economic system, and of the new consumerism, things proliferate and confront men with an inhuman, autonomous existence. This tendency has its beginning already in Sartre's *La Nausée* and in the inhuman world of stones in Camus' early essays, but is more fully developed in the work of some of the "New Novelists," especially Alain Robbe-Grillet. One of the most radical expressions of the object world's autonomy, Robbe-Grillet's *La Jalousie* (1957), contains long, impassive descriptions of objects—and people treated externally, as objects—"registered" by a narrator who functions like a camera.

His thoughts, feelings, and obsessions are indicated almost exclusively by what he *sees* as a machine-like recorder of images. Here human beings tend to become things themselves in a world of things.[3]

Although she is older than both Sartre and Camus, and published her first work at about the same time they did theirs, Nathalie Sarraute only became recognized as an important novelist in the mid-1950s,[4] in association with others of the *nouveau roman*, especially Michel Butor and Robbe-Grillet, whose first works were published in the early and mid-1950s. Sartre and Camus dominated the literary scene during the war and in the immediate postwar period. Their work still projected "promethean" images of heroes who attempt to confront and transcend the modern condition. Sarraute, and the New Novelists in general, no longer struggle against their condition; they simply portray it. Sarraute's work began to be recognized at the moment when Camus published *La Chute*, which reflects the failure of his earlier attempts to discover a human community. At the same time, the effects of the consumer mentality were beginning to be felt. Thus, with Sarraute the "heroic" period of the entre-deux-guerres, which included Malraux and Bernanos and ended with Camus, gives way to a new portrayal of the modern world and man. The essential condition of human isolation that characterized Proust's vision at the start of the twentieth century remains central to Sarraute's vision—but solitude is now integrally related to the new domination of commodities.

The vision of solitude is characteristic of the New Novel in general, although in other novelists the connection with consumerism is not present. Moreover, in Robbe-Grillet at least, solitude is not overtly thematized; for in Robbe-Grillet the "phenomenological" trend in the new fiction—the tendency to treat the psyche at the level of its contact with concrete sensations emanating from its surroundings—takes its most extreme form. As W. M. Frohock points out, "Robbe-Grillet would carry this eventually to the point of suppressing the character altogether and presenting only the sensations registered." [5] With the elimination of the subject as a psychological entity, solitude becomes largely implicit; its existence is to be implied from external images of distance, coldness, aggressivity. The refusal of psychology, the "externality" of Robbe-Grillet's novelistic technique which has interested him in film almost as much as in the novel, is shared by Marguerite Duras (also a film scenarist as well as a novelist). Yet isolation is a central feature of Duras' fiction. Eschewing any psychological analysis of Anne Desbaresdes in *Moderato Cantabile* (1958), for instance, Duras nonetheless makes the primary focus of her novel the desperate reaching out for, and eventual failure to achieve, communication with another human being, across class lines and in the midst of a society to which communication is entirely foreign.

In Butor's novels, on the other hand, the phenomenological approach does not exclude internality. Novels such as *La Modification* (1957) and *L'Emploi du temps* (1958) are narrated by a single—and isolated—consciousness very much in the Proustian tradition. Butor's protagonists are alienated from themselves, caught in a society experienced as a "system" or "machine," and they are painfully shut off from others. Their only solution is typically Proustian: redemption through writing, through esthetic self-understanding. Here solitude is not only central but also fully thematized in the psychological dimension. Yet, like the other New Novels, Butor's novels do not link alienation and solitude with the world of consumer goods. The alienation of the narrator of *La Modification* is explicitly related to his position as executive in a commercial establishment,[6] related, that is to say, to the area of production rather than consumption.

In the quasi-sociological novel of Christiane Rochefort, *Les Petits Enfants du siècle* (1961), however, the new world of the consumer is the context in which alienation and solitude are generated.[7] Josyane, the narrator, is an adolescent girl in one of the many low-cost housing projects (H.L.M.) that began to burgeon in the suburbs of Paris in the 1950s to house the urban working class. Moreover, in an effort to expand both population and consumption, the French government had initiated a system of family subsidies and awarded monetary bonuses for each child born. Thus Josyane, like her brothers and sisters and all the children around her, is born so that the parents can get a subsidy; and what the parents want with each subsidy is a new consumer item. Each child born allows them to buy (or repair) a washing machine, refrigerator, television, car. In the forced and overcrowded togetherness of the housing project, love and communication are rare, and when they do occur they are immediately transmuted into a consumer happiness. In this novel the new form of reification—domination by things in the form of consumer goods, and also of that particular item of consumption, the housing in which leisure and consumption take place—generates the spiritual misery of the new "enfants du siècle." The fact that this linkage of consumerism and alienation/solitude occurs specifically in two women novelists—Rochefort and Sarraute—might suggest that because of their traditional social role women are particularly sensitive to this relationship.

It is generally recognized that Sarraute's novelistic vision, like Proust's or Bernanos's, has remained basically unchanged throughout her career, unlike Malraux's or Camus's. Sarraute emphasizes in her preface to the American translation of *Tropismes* that "this first book contains *in nuce* all the raw material that I have continued to develop in my later works." [8] This raw material is made up of the minute, psychological movements that precede the constitution of fully developed emotions—movements that Sarraute has called *tropismes*, "because of their spontaneous, irresistible, instinctive nature, similar to that of the movements made by certain living organisms under the influence of outside stimuli, such as light or heat." [9] The outside stimuli to which the human organism reacts come from other human beings and the world of things. Although Sarraute herself and most critics have presented the specific nature of the world and the people that stimulate the tropisms as irrelevant,[10] they do in fact determine the basic patterns in which the tropisms function. The characters of Sarraute's novels are contemporary Parisian bourgeois, of the old and the new generation, both philistines and intellectuals or artists. The world in which they live is the modern world of capitalist society, and specifically the world of the new "société de consommation." These also constitute the raw material of her work.

Yet if we consider the group of works from the early *Tropismes* to *Le Planétarium*, a subtle modification of the basic themes may be seen to take place, of which *Le Planétarium* is the culmination. In *Tropismes* there is a notable dichotomy between the bourgeois adults, with their *lieux communs* and their eternal preoccupations with shopping, money, and household things, and the children who exist silently and fearfully, pushed around by the adults. In an inauthentic bourgeois world,[11] only children have not yet been corrupted, or are just beginning to absorb their parents' commonplaces and concerns. *Portrait d'un inconnu* (1948), the first novel, opposes the narrator, a hypersensitive aesthete interested in painting, to a father and daughter whose relationship obsesses him, and to his friends who refuse to acknowledge the existence of the hidden tropisms he senses everywhere. The father, a morbidly avaricious petty bourgeois, sees his unmarried daughter as a leech sucking his lifeblood—his money and possessions, that is. The father's relationship both with his daughter, whom he goes so far as to suspect of stealing soap and to whom he begrudges money for medical attention, and with the narrator, whose "useless" aestheticism he attacks at every encounter, is as oppressive as the adult-child relation in *Tropismes*. The drama between father and daughter ends with the engagement of the daughter to a young man in the Finance Ministry, and as the novel closes the narrator renounces his authenticity of feeling to become "normal" like the others.

Sarraute's next novel, *Martereau* (1953), is also narrated by an aesthete living in a world of bourgeois values, concerns, and relationships. The main action of the novel, through which the tropisms form and reform, involves the purchase of a country house, the exchanges of money related to the purchase, the feelings and conflicts engendered by it. But now the young narrator-aesthete has become an interior decorator; he designs furniture for expositions, shops with the women in antique stores and takes an interest in clothing styles. Although he, like the narrator of *Portrait*, is psychologically oppressed by the older bourgeois in the family—especially by his uncle—and continues to represent a privileged domain of authenticity (he also is sensitive to the tropisms the others deny), his difference from the others is severely undermined. For aestheticism now takes the form of interior decoration; art becomes the design of housewares. The narrator, like the bourgeois women, is at home in the world of commodities and styles. And unlike the narrator of *Portrait*, he attempts desperately (although not always successfully) to construct for himself the hard, clearly defined exterior, the carapace that gives others a thinglike quality and that defines normality in the bourgeois world.

In *Le Planétarium* the subtle modification is completed. There is no longer a single narrator, no longer a privileged, authentic being who stands in opposition to bourgeois society. From *Tropismes* to *Le Planétarium* the dichotomy has imperceptibly but decisively shifted; the original opposition between the young and "aesthetic," not yet corrupted, and the inauthentic bourgeois world turns into an opposition between the new generation and the old, between the consumer-oriented young and their producer-oriented elders. In the novel that has been called the chef d'oeuvre of Nathalie Sarraute,[12] inauthenticity and reification exist in all the characters and their relationships.

II

As one critic of her novels has pointed out, the central theme of Sarraute's works as a whole is the urge for communication and the reality of human solitude.[13] The title *Le Planétarium* symbolizes Sarraute's basic conception of human relations, and it evidently has a special significance for her: before the war she thought of publishing another collection of short pieces similar to *Tropismes*, with the title *Le Planétarium*.[14] She explains that a planetarium is an artificial sky signifying the world of appearances.[15] The stars that shine separately, and in certain configurations, on the dome of the planetarium hide a common source of light. In the same way, although each individual, each character in her novelistic world, is isolated in "an artificial universe that he has constructed for himself to measure, where he feels sheltered but where he often suffocates and from which, at times, he would wish to escape," [16] each is driven by the same hidden tropisms. Beneath the surface of appearance, we are all the same. One of the main characters of Le Planétarium, Alain, is aware of this common human substance: "Somewhere, farther down, everyone is alike, everyone resembles everyone else . . . Then I don't dare judge . . . Right away I feel that I'm like them, as soon as I take off my carapace, this thin varnish" (J 33).[17] The primary motive force behind the tropisms shared by everyone is described by Sarraute (quoting Katherine Mansfield, in L'Ere du soupçon) as "this terrible desire to establish contact." [18]

The universal need to make contact with others does not, however, lead to union or community in the world of the planetarium. In one scene, Alain receives an affectionate gesture from his father as "one of those signs between them, infrequent, astonishing, like the flashes of light that come to us from distant stars, disclosing mysterious combustions" (J 142). But the scene is only *imagined* by Alain, and the real scene that follows brutally separates him from his father. The tropisms do not in fact reach out directly and affectionately for a contact that would unite them in an embrace. They are systematically turned from that path, molded into certain common patterns by the "appearances"—that is, by the nature of the social relationships involved and of the social world in general. One basic pattern recurs again and again in many different permutations: a struggle, or combat, of each individual against others. The tropisms engaged in these incessant psychic conflicts are characterized on the one hand by insecurity, distrust, and humiliation which at the limit become paranoia;[19] on the other by domination, manipulation, aggression. Distorted by the social world, the tropisms make only the brutal contact of attacker to attacked; they establish antagonism and separation rather than community.

For this separation to be maintained it is not necessary for the characters to remain totally mysterious to each other, as in the world of Proust. There are momentary illuminations, "an entire human being, with its myriads of little movements, which appear in a few words, a laugh, a gesture" (J 38). One character may even fully understand another, as Alain comprehends his aunt's universe and reveals it to a group of listeners (32, 34, 41–42). Many misunderstandings and distortions of others' feelings occur in the novel, but they are not essential to the maintenance of solitude. Real union with another implies a sharing, a free, equal exchange of the contents of one's inner self. This kind of entente is rendered impossible by the deflection of the tropisms into hostile and paranoic paths. True union is sometimes *imagined*, but never realized. The only solidarities that actually come to be realized are false ones based on *lieux communs* (literally the only "common place" in which characters meet),[20] especially those that unite a group *against* another person.

The social world that deforms the tropisms as they seek contact is characterized by the reign of commodities, and commodities are therefore directly related to the process that separates each person from others. In *Le Planétarium* all the important objects are commodities or are transformed into commodities. Tante Berthe, in the opening scene of the novel, translates a wheatfield and haystack she has seen on an outing in the country into a color combination for her apartment wall and curtains. This process of inner mutation is part of her personality: "She's made in such a way, and she knows it, that she can only look attentively and lovingly at what she can appropriate to herself, at what she can possess" (J 8).

At the very start, then, a scene of natural objects is made into a commodity, and this commodity—Berthe's apartment and furnishings—will reappear along with other objects of consumption throughout the novel to define the social world and determine the course of the characters' relations with each other. These objects often are used as weapons in the struggle to dominate others, and in the vain attempt to secure love or approval through their power. But the reified social world consists not only of the commodities themselves; it also contains the thinglike social "carapaces" that define the characters' apparent, exterior beings. Through stereotyped, rigidified definitions of themselves and others, the characters face each other as objects. These definitions separate the characters, rendering their relations inauthentic and molding the tropisms into poses of aggression or abjection.

As we have noted in another context, one aspect of Sarraute's novelistic technique is modified significantly in *Le Planétarium*. In both *Portrait d'un inconnu* and *Martereau*, the point of view is located in a first-person narrator. All the hidden movements of the tropisms in other characters, as well as their evident action and conversation, are reported to us by this narrator. Although the narrator in each case is a hypersensitive being particularly attuned to the perception of tropisms, it is impossible for us to test the accuracy of what he senses in others. His narration always has a quality of supposition. Sartre calls the narrator of *Portrait* "a sort of impassioned amateur detective who becomes fascinated by a banal couple . . . and spies on them, follows their trail, and sometimes fathoms them, at a distance, by a sort of thought transmission, but without ever knowing very well either what he is looking for or what they are." [21] The narrator of *Martereau*, near the end of that novel, gives four different versions of what might have taken place—and of the possible tropisms—between Martereau and his wife after the narrator's uncle has left their home. In these novels, then, the inner life of "others" has an ambiguous existence: we never know to what extent the narrator actually penetrates other characters and to what extent he is the victim of his imagination.

In *Le Planétarium*, for the first time Sarraute uses multiple points of view. Adopting a form of *style indirect libre*, she enters the consciousness and records the developing tropisms of one character after another. The ways in which the points of view alternate vary considerably. Often the point of view moves from one interlocutor to another as a scene progresses. Occasionally the entire scene is repeated from several points of view, most notably in the conversations between Tante Berthe and her brother. Sometimes a given scene is recounted from only one point of view, as in most of Alain's encounters with Germaine Lemaire. And in at least one instance, a scene reported from two points of view is recalled much later, after an interval, by a third (the scene in the bookstore between Alain, his father, and Germaine Lemaire). Thus we are usually, but not always, able to compare the contents of several consciousnesses.

As revealed through the interweaving of points of view, each character's perception of others is limited by a large measure of mystery. In scenes recounted from a single point of view, the mystery exists for the reader as well. At the end of Alain's first meeting with Germaine, he has the impression that she is anxious for him to leave (108). The scene is never repeated from her point of view, and we cannot know whether she actually felt that way or whether Alain's paranoia led him to imagine it.

In the scenes repeated from multiple points of view, it is clear that to a certain extent the characters are aware of the tropisms that move beneath the surface of another's conversation. These tropisims reach out to make contact, and a *sous-conversation* [22] takes place between the characters. Thus, as Alain and Gisèle stand looking at their aunt's apartment building Gisèle senses what Alain is thinking about her, and we are able to verify that the images in his mind are indeed identical with what she imagines them to be (131). In longer scenes with two points of view, however, such as the dialogues between Berthe and Alain or her brother, we also notice gaps in each one's knowledge of the other's unfolding inner experience. Thus Berthe is unaware that a childhood memory about her is passing through Alain's mind as he speaks with her (228–229, 246). In addition to these gaps in the perceiver's knowledge, in other cases the perceiver is simply unsure of what is happening within the other. Sometimes one character *speculates* on the feelings or motives of another; possibilities are contemplated, in constructions with *ou bien, peut-être* or *probablement* (for example, 24, 25, 50, 164, 205, 214).

More important than these gaps and speculations, however, is the fact that even when the characters are largely sensitive to each other's tropisms, their perception does not allow them to establish an entente to break their isolation. On the contrary, they are sensitive to each other *as enemies;* their knowledge of others is like the intelligence of the enemy which espionage gives, or the knowledge that comes in combat itself. The tropisms are hostile ones that bruise them, causing them to retreat or return the attack. The conversation between Berthe and her brother involves a series of painful blows and counterblows; each interlocutor strikes out at the other, locked in his egotistical concerns, his stereotypes, his hatred and bitterness.

The contact that characters make with one another, then, takes the form of psychological combat. This perpetual and extreme aggression is reflected in another important technique—the metaphors, some of which are extended and lengthily developed, with which Sarraute portrays the tropisms of her characters. Since the tropisms precede the formation of full-fledged emotions that are the object of "psychological analysis," they are best captured in metaphors; by comparing them with large-scale notions and things, they may be enlarged and rendered visible. The majority of these metaphors are frightening images of estrangement, conflict, aggression, and oppression. Berthe metaphorically experiences the workers who install the door in her apartment as hordes of barbarian conquérants, enemies from a foreign land overrunning her "civilization" (16–18). Gisèle's mother imagines herself to be a mole attacked by Alain, a swooping eagle (45–46), and later Alain sees himself pounced upon and held between the teeth of Gisèle's mother (121). The argument between Gisèle and her father is presented in the image of two swimmers grappling in the water (125); Berthe facing the judgment of others is like a wild animal confronting a pack of hunting dogs (225).

In a world that is as reified as it is fragmented and hostile, other images recur which picture tropisms as things. Tropisms reach others as cutting instruments, crushing weights, suffocating liquids. One of the most striking images decribes Gisèle's father as a sack swelling with fluid and threatening to burst over Alain, suffocating him with its burning, bitter contents (26–27). Here, as in other material images, the other is experienced as an object, and the relation between two people is a relation of object to object.

III

The relationship between Alain and Gisèle, the young married couple, embodies the inauthentic solidarity and the actual isolation discussed above, in the specific context of the new, consumer-oriented generation. On her wedding day Gisèle had for a moment seen a crack in the "edifice" of future happiness she had constructed: she overheard two old ladies exclaim about how little money Alain has. Then she ran to him, and standing beside him she again felt the strength of the entity they made up together: "Not a flaw in the hard, smooth wall. No way for others to see what was on the other side . . . Everybody kept a respectful distance and looked, with emotion, at the handsome, congenial young couple, joined together, the very image of happiness" (J 68).

From the start, then, Gisèle's union with Alain takes place within the stereotyped social image of the perfect couple—the lifeless image that is projected in cultural commodities. She maintains that false union in actual life by becoming a simple adjunct to Alain, seeing the world through his eyes and his interpretations, "confident, in abeyance, acquiescent" (J 71). She adopts his enthusiasm for beautiful furniture, and as they stand in front of a boutique looking at a Louis XV armchair (bergère), she feels that their communion is perfect: "Only marriage permits such moments as these, of fusion, of happiness, during which, leaning on him, she had gazed at the old silk with its ash-rose, its delicate gray tones" (J 72). Part of the definition of marriage for the new generation involves shopping together for beautiful objects to furnish the shared world of their apartment. They are both seized by a passion to possess the armchair (75).

But the crack in the edifice of their consumer happiness reappears and widens. As she stands in front of the shop, and again after the discussion with her mother, Gisèle feels her whole viewpoint shifting. She is unable to live as an independent being, and must see through the eyes of one person or another. Before her marriage with Alain, she saw through the eyes of her mother and father and other older, respected persons. Suddenly she again sees through their eyes (77); her life with Alain, and the total "fusion" with him, suddenly seem illusory, and Gisèle feels alone. She remembers the old ladies' judgment that Alain does not have much money, and her father's irritation with Alain's "aestheticism" (78–79). For the older, producer-oriented generation whose vision she now adopts, the primary concern for a young couple should be hard work, making a career, earning money, building a solid family; a preoccupation with buying beautiful things can only be decadent aestheticism.

The couple experiences another moment of fusion—again a false, reified communion in the common desire to possess an object—as they stand looking at Tante Berthe's apartment, which they hope to acquire. They imagine how they will arrange it, and Alain, like Tante Berthe, translates the memory of a farmhouse they once visited into an idea for their apartment (132–133). But in the end their real separation and hidden hostility reappear. In a moment of truth Gisèle realizes how she really feels about Alain. He is a spoiled child whose constant demands for approval devour her life's substance: "Why certainly, my darling . . . you are the cleverest, the most intelligent of all . . . Drawing off her sap like that . . . Sucking her life away" (J 137). Conversely, Alain, in his snobbish desire to be accepted by Germaine Lemaire, is secretly ashamed of Gisèle. In the final scene where the couple shows Germaine their new apartment, the objects that had once falsely united them now separate them. Alain forgets the loving care with which he and Gisèle chose their rustic bench; Germaine does not like it, and so he begins to alter his opinion to suit hers (301–302).

The relations of Alain and Gisèle with their older relatives, which vacillate between false union and hostile separation like the relations within the young couple, are specifically conditioned by several aspects of the "generation gap." The older relatives already possess the things and money that Alain and Gisèle desire, and they also represent an alien mentality. Alain thinks of his mother-in-law as an insensitive authoritarian (23, 72) and of his father-in-law as vain and egotistical (28); but he nonetheless seeks their acceptance and approval, to become one with them and with their friends. His personality is the extreme expression of "other-directedness," which accompanies the modern diminution of the role of the individual but which reaches its apex in the youngest generation. Alain's elders seem to have stronger personalities than he does, and he attempts at times to become an adjunct of them as Gisèle does with him. At gatherings with relatives and their friends, he performs for them:

How often he has made an exhibition of himself, has described himself in ridiculous positions, or in ludicrous situations . . . piling up disgraceful details to make them laugh a bit, to laugh with them a bit, delighted to feel that he's among them, near them, to one side of himself and quite stuck to them, clinging to them so closely, so dissolved in them that he even saw himself through their eyes. (J 23)

Like Gisèle's union with him, Alain's false fusion with these elders negates his own independent identity; he sees through their eyes and is totally dominated by them.

In the particular gathering of Gisèle's family and older friends described in the novel, Alain's performance at first seems to succeed. The group seems "fraternal" as he tells of the silly manias of his aunt (31). They are all united *against* the aunt in the secure feeling that they are not like her. Then pockets of hostility appear, first in Alain's father-in-law. Alain changes his tack, and begins to show them the inner universe of his aunt that is behind her manias: her self-imposed solitude and her fear of death (32–33). At this point an old lady laughs mockingly, and when Alain goes on to suggest that he and all of them are at bottom like his aunt, sharing her fear of others and of death, they try not to listen and finally leave, scandalized (33–34, 41–42). For a moment Alain has transcended the false solidarity to open up the domain in which they might participate in a true, human community. They are afraid, however, to recognize their common condition, to recognize that everyone is profoundly alike in the need for companionship and the failure to achieve it, as well as in the fear of death. The breach is reopened between themselves and Alain, and thenceforth in the novel parents and elders become the indefinite *ils* of established bourgeois opinion that presses him to become like them.

The fact that Alain has understood his aunt's deepest fears and seen the universality of her fate does not, though, lead him into rapport with her. Instead the level on which he situates their union is the alienated level of their common love of things. By its nature this union is doomed to be destroyed, since the aunt possesses the very thing that Alain wants: her spacious apartment. When she refuses the apartment she herself becomes a thing; she is reduced to an obstacle in his way: "Heavy. Inert. All shrunk into herself. Enormous motionless mass lying across his path. He would like to dislodge it, give it a good punch and kick it hard, to make it move" (J 219). He threatens to force her out of the apartment.

Gisèle's relationship with her parents and with Alain's father, while it too vacillates between the same poles, is especially conditioned by her stereotyped role as a submissive woman. The separation and conflict between mother and daughter come to the surface in the same question of furniture which separates Gisèle from Alain. The mother wishes to buy them leather armchairs (*fauteuils*), and Alain wants her to buy them the pink bergère. In her desire for the bergère in solidarity with Alain, Gisèle comes into conflict with her mother; when she shifts her allegiance to her mother's values and the leather chairs, they stand united against Alain. She later solidarizes herself again with her mother when Alain absently refuses a carrot dish that her mother has specially prepared for him; they share for a moment the stereotyped role of women providing food for their men (120–122). Thereafter Gisèle returns to the inauthentic marriage bond, again preferring the bergère with Alain. They succeed in winning the point and obtaining the bergère, and Gisèle's mother disappears from the novel altogether.

Gisèle's encounters with her own and Alain's father follow an identical pattern: after an initial recognition of hostility she experiences a moment of inauthentic solidarity with them, then returns to Alain. She senses in both men a humiliating definition of women as charming and beautiful creatures who would be ridiculous to pretend to an independent existence of their own, and she revolts against this definition (123–125, 136–139). Still in each case she asks their aid in acquiring Tante Berthe's apartment. In this struggle she rediscovers her solidarity with them. They are strong men and she a weak woman. The purpose of the struggle, however, is to make possible a greater "happiness" with Alain in the new apartment, and thereafter she embraces Alain's values again, in the loving decoration of their apartment.

The mentality that distinguishes the older generation from its consumer-oriented children insists on the primary value of work. Alain's father sums up this ethic:

After all, there's such a thing as order, thank God. As justice. Even in this world. It's still there, where it should be, everything upon which he has built his own life, in the name of which he has had the strength to overcome all obstacles: he has had to deprive himself, drudge, there have been of course hard moments, but he has never doubted, and that has been his salvation, he has never ceased to believe that there exists, in this world, a golden rule, a law to which all must submit . . . Order must reign, good must triumph, endeavor, work must receive their just reward, all gate-crashers must be punished. (J 261–262)

In this perspective the younger generation—Alain and Gisèle in particular—are "kids with no experience, excessively spoilt, rotten, rich kids who've never done anything except what they wanted" (J 48). In spite of their divergent ideologies, though, at a deeper psychological level, and in the functioning of their tropisms, there is no essential difference between the generations, only a difference of degree. For as we have seen, the diminution of the individual, universalized isolation, and the need to escape that condition, even the consumer culture itself, are not peculiar to contemporary, postwar youth. The first two characteristics are endemic to the entire period of monopoly capitalism, and the consumer culture has its roots in the prewar period. Therefore it is not surprising that the older generation in *Le Planétarium* exhibits the same loneliness, the same insecurity and failure of self-assertion, and in the case of the *women* a similar commodity consciousness.

Gisèle's mother, like the women in *Tropismes*, is in fact as immersed in commodities as Alain and Gisèle. As she picks up the carrot dish she has ordered the maid to prepare for Alain, the sales pitch that convinced her to buy the carrot peeler runs through her mind:

Finely chopped . . . as finely as you can . . . with that nice new gadget . . . Now . . . that certainly is tempting . . . Look, ladies, with this you get the most delicious grated carrots . . . I really must buy it. Alain will be glad, he adores them. Well seasoned . . . olive oil . . . 'La Niçoise' for him, it's the only one he likes, I buy no other. (J 115)

With her friends she discusses furniture and exchanges addresses of favorite stores. The leather chairs she admires at a friend's house and attempts to convince the young couple to accept are just as much commodities as the pink chair they want, although the fauteuils incarnate for her the ideal of solid, unpretentious bourgeois comfort, in keeping with the principles of work and relative austerity with which she has been raised (47–50, 60–63). Thus Gisèle's mother is ambivalent: preoccupied with commodities, attracted to some extent by the newer gadgets, she still attempts to reconcile her desires with traditional principles.

Moreover, although she is an authoritarian in the only domain in which the traditional female role allows her to be—food, children, the home—her attempts at domineering are undermined by an insecurity that parallels Alain's. In fact she fears Alain and, while attempting to prove to herself the contrary, she is afraid of losing the children's love, of being abandoned by them (26–27, 43 48–49). She surprises looks between Alain and Gisèle which put them in collusion against her, which seem to treat her as the enemy (64). She attempts to regain control and to reaffirm her union with them by forcing them to accept the leather chairs, and to do so she calls upon the powerful figure of her own father:

Only strong actions inspire respect. People accept you the way you are, people give in, they become docile, if you assert yourself with them, if you stand there, right in front of them, unshaken on your two feet: look at me. I don't need you to like me, I don't care a rap whether people like me or not—her father always said that when he spoke of his employees, and they all respected him . . . She should have taken a page out of his book . . . But, in reality, she's like him, she can be like him when she wants to be. (J 52)

The model she takes, then, is precisely the strong, entrepreneurial figure of earlier times; at the same time, he is a man and the father she adored in a passive, dominated role as daughter. These factors militate against her actually possessing his strength of character. She immediately begins to back down, and the couple buy their bergère.

The other important female character in the two families, Tante Berthe, is afflicted to an even larger degree by the insatiable desire to acquire commodities. As an old lady living alone, supported by the considerable fortune of her dead husband, she devotes herself entirely to "aesthetic" interior decoration and does not share the ideology of hard work and austerity. Indeed, she has used the temptation of luxury items to gain Alain's affection and draw him away from his father when he was a child (167). This transmission of mentality from herself to Alain illustrates the change that has taken place from one generation to the other. Within the older generation it is appropriate for an old lady to indulge in such desires, but in the new generation the consumer mentality spreads to the young and to men as well as women.

We have already seen Berthe's solitude and fear of death as a kind of emblem in the novel for the common condition of all human beings. She conceals beneath a seemingly strong personality—expressed in her colorful eccentricities and her stubbornness—an extreme insecurity in her relations with others which drives her to remain timorously in the solitude of her apartment while at the same time desperately desiring companionship.

Berthe also wishes to redeem her lifelong separation from her brother. In the novel she first sees him as an enemy in league with the children against her, and then is rebuffed by him when she momentarily reaches beyond her fears to the "old man, like herself lonely, neglected, her brother, her good old Pierrot" (J 207). She finally achieves the only communion possible with him: she asks her brother's advice on her stock-market transactions and creates for a moment a false, reified bond with him in a stereotyped submission to a "strong" man's advice on money matters (261–264).

In fact Berthe's brother (Alain's father) does not live up to this image which for an instant the two pretend to believe. The only important male character of the older generation (Gisèle's father appears very briefly and is not fully developed as a character) does not fulfill the forceful role of successful and self-assured entrepreneur of the preceding generation. We learn that Alain's father was never a successful businessman, as Berthe's husband was (262). Berthe knows that from the time Alain was a child his father already imagined himself as a poor old man proud of the future success of his son, "the handsome rider . . . the intrepid conqueror, hard and strong, trailing all hearts behind him . . . he's returning from a crusade, from long victorious campaigns, he believes he has lost, he has perhaps forgotten his old papa, but the poor paternal heart is bathed in joy, in pride" (J 241). Since Alain's father looked up to his own father with the same passive admiration, he never succeeded in having any exploits of his own. The conquérant is totally absent from the world of *Le Planétarium*, or more precisely he appears only in the mock-heroic metaphor for the workers who install Berthe's new door and who seem to be conquerors destroying her civilization. The only struggle waged and victory won in the novel is the conquest of Berthe's apartment by Alain and Gisèle. Alain's father remains a crusty old man, bitter at his failures, hurt by his lack of prestige with Alain and Berthe, inexorably shut off from them by his egoism and inability to express affection or aid others.

When Alain angrily leaves Gisèle after a quarrel and telephones Germaine Lemaire, "he feels like a hunted man on foreign soil, who is ringing the bell of the embassy of a civilized country, his own, to ask for asylum" (J 86). The foreign territory on which he finds himself is the bourgeois world of family, career, money, and things; the enemy inhabitants who are hunting him down to imprison him are Gisèle, his older relatives, and the vague *ils* of opinion. He seeks to return to his own country, the realm of pure Art, which Germaine's literary circle signifies in his mind. Far from saving him from the evils of the bourgeois world, however, the chic coterie of the famous woman writer reproduces them. The group is simply a snobbish enclave within the larger bourgeois culture; it is permeated with the same mentality, only expressed in a more sophisticated form.

Although Alain fears that she disdains him for revealing a base desire for such things (116–118), Germaine in fact seems to enjoy his stories of armchairs and apartments immensely, and in later encounters she and her followers themselves inevitably turn the conversation to objects. When the group pays him an impromptu visit, the conversation begins with his desk, then turns to the bergère, extends to considerations on the desirability of leather chairs, and finally stops at articles on his walls and books on his table (206–211). The group makes a veritable inventory of his apartment, judging him, Alain supposes, by the objects he possesses.

In their conversation, moreover, art objects themselves exist only as articles to ornament an apartment. When he had bought a statue of the Virgin and Child, Alain had considered with anguish whether or not part of it was a copy. His concern was not related to the statue's intrinsic beauty, but to the effect it would have when people would inspect it in his apartment. The effect would be ruined if one of them discovered it to be a fake (282–284). When Germaine does admire it, Alain suddenly doubts her artistic sense: "But she doesn't stir. She stares fixedly at the shoulder, the arm, she swallows them stolidly, her strong stomach digests them easily, her eyes maintain the calm, indifferent expression of a cow's eyes" (J 290). Here, at least as it is imagined by Alain, the relationship between Germaine and the statue is an ignominiously physical one. And indeed we discover that Germaine in her own art creates only lifeless objects. When a literary newspaper suggests that she is "our Madame Tussaud" (J 180), a maker of wax figures, she rereads what she thought to be some of her best passages and finds that the verdict is just: "Nothing. Everything is congealed . . . Frozen . . . A thin layer of shiny varnish on cardboard. Masks of painted wax" (J 182). Among the lifeless objects she has made, Germaine is alone: "It's all dead . . . A dead star. She's alone. No recourse. No relief from any one. She's pursuing her way in solitude beset with terror. She's alone on an extinguished star. Life is elsewhere" (J 183). Germaine's art prefigures the reified novel within a novel: *Les Fruits d'or*. As its title suggests, *The Golden Fruits* transforms living things into inanimate objects. The novel as a whole is inanimate and therefore exists only as a commodity on the literary market.

As we have seen, solitude and the reign of objects are linked in the world of the planetarium, and just as the latter extends into Germaine's circle, so does the former. Not only does Alain reproduce in his relations with Germaine and her group the same syndrome that isolates him as a fearful, antagonistic monad in the bourgeois world, but Germaine herself suffers the same fate. Her vanity reduces the human beings around her to the inanimate status of mirrors that reflect her own image (186). Alain obscurely recognizes that this reduction of others to objects is the key to the lifelessness of the characters she projects in her art. Thus in her actual human contacts as well as among her creations, Germaine is alone, and yet she is also dependent on the world of others for approval. She experiences an insecurity analogous to Alain's in her confrontation with his father, when he does not sing her praises as she expects (199–200). She is therefore another "strong personality" that conceals other-directedness—enslavement to the opinion of others—beneath the surface. She is only a conquérant—or a "conquistador," as Alain admiringly calls her—in the conquest of ornamental objects to decorate her apartment (102–103).

No one in the modern bourgeois world escapes the perpetual insecurity of other-directedness—not even those who contest that world. The *philosophe de gauche* who appears at the very end of *Le Planétarium* seems to Alain to stand outside the world in which others suffer, analyzing it from above. The philosopher regards (or seems to Alain to regard: the point of view is unclear) Alain and his wife as "squirrels going round and round in their golden cage" (J 274), pure products of their class and therefore incapable of any consciousness or action transcending the machinelike determinism that controls their behavior.

But the philosopher errs both in analyzing them as cogs in a social mechanism (that is, in philosophical terms, as object instead of subject) and in supposing that he is not engaged in the same social reality. For Alain is obscurely aware of his oppression, and the philosopher is unaware that he shares the same relationship to the other which afflicts all of the novel's characters. Germaine is speaking of the philosopher's relation to others—revealed in his slightly uneasy concern to read an article about himself which has appeared without his knowledge—in the crucial sentence that ends the novel: "I think we're all of us, really, a bit like that" (J 296). Others are judges and, more generally, potential enemies for the philosopher and for all men in modern society. By the nature of its construction, the planetarium separates a common source of light into isolated beams.

Afterword

To recapitulate the major lines of the historical and literary process which the book analyzes in considerable detail and in two different ways: "Solitude," in antiquity, means existence outside the bounds of society. The ancient period sees the development of a mercantile economy—based on the exchange of money and goods—which, for the first time in history, allows the individual to win some autonomy from the collectivity. At first, however, social solidarities remain primary, and complete separation of the individual from the collectivity is feared as a malediction. Thus in Greek literature solitude outside society takes the form of involuntary exile from the polis, one of the worst fates a Greek citizen may suffer.

Later in the ancient period, when the expansion of the market economy and its attendant evils begins to weaken the older solidarities, partial and sometimes even total retreat from the collectivity comes to be sought rather than shunned. Competition between men to acquire wealth and social position begins to transform the nature of relations between men in society; men flee society to escape the institutionalized conflicts within it and to realize themselves in a more valid "society" outside society. In the Roman Empire this flight takes two principal forms: the partial retreat of members of the Roman ruling classes to their farms outside the cities, and the total retreat of early Christians to monasteries or hermitages. In literature these solitudes are associated with mythical images of ideal community; and the retreats themselves—estate or monastery—are pictured as more harmonious communities than the society which is left behind. Even the isolated hermit, or the landowner alone in his study, communes with God, Nature, and other men.

With the dissolution of the Roman Empire, the mercantile, pre-capitalist economy of antiquity gives way to the household economy of the medieval period. The rural demesne and the monastery now become centers of the new social organization, and therefore cease to be "solitudes." The new feudal social order is no longer based on market exchange and competition, and it encloses the individual within a network of precisely defined human relations. The individual generally does not seek retreat from the integrated medieval community, with the exception of hermits escaping the corruption of the monasteries in the dangerous forest solitudes.

In ancien régime France, the market economy of antiquity is carried to a higher level; a new class of manufacturers and merchants begins to accumulate capital, partly through the purchase of land from nobles. The center of society shifts back to the city and the autocratic court; competition, accompanied by the growing exploitation of wage labor, again fragments social relations, now more intensely than ever, as the ancien régime moves toward the Industrial Revolution. In this context, after the medieval period of social integration, temptation to flee the antagonisms of bourgeois society again causes men to seek the solitude of the country estate as well as total religious seclusion. The classical theme of country retreat is thus one of the motifs adopted from antiquity by the Renaissance. Throughout the ancien régime, solitude on the country estate is praised by nobles, *gens de robe* and bourgeois alike, for the estates themselves are changing hands.

The theme of country solitude, in Roman antiquity as in ancien régime France, exemplifies the dialectic of ideal and ideology. It expresses on the one hand the protest of men during the prehistory and early history of capitalism and the ideal of community opposed to the new social antagonisms; on the other hand this expression of an ideal takes ideological forms. Under the ancien régime the glorification of the country retreat, to the extent that it emphasizes return to the land, reflects the ideology of the feudal aristocracy; and, to the extent that it emphasizes retreat into the individual self, it reflects the rising bourgeois ideology of individualism.

Although the flight from competition and antagonism in early bourgeois society suggests that solitude within society is already a latent condition—along with alienation and reification—the leap to the full reality of solitude in society, accompanied by the growing consciousness of it, takes place only with the advent of mature capitalism.

At the end of the ancien régime, Rousseau for the first time explicitly pictures urban society as a "solitude" and relates the inauthentic ties and communication between men in society to the existence of private property. For Rousseau it is still possible to escape society; but his hero, Saint-Preux, now seeks retreat in uncivilized Nature beyond the noble demesne. In the pre-Romanticism and Romanticism of the early nineteenth century, as the beginnings of full-scale industrialization occur and the bourgeoisie rapidly gains power, the solitude of the poetic soul within bourgeois society becomes a major theme; and, following Rousseau, the artist often seeks retreat in Nature.

The year 1830 marks the take-off of the industrial economy of advanced capitalism, and thereafter, as his isolation within society is sharpened, the Poet finds retreat into Nature less and less satisfactory. He is a product of the City and, moreover, the City is fast spreading its influence into the countryside. Now the poet retreats to his study within the city. The Romantic image of the poet alienated and alone in capitalist society, but obliged to live within it, is given dramatic expression in Vigny's *Chatterton*. In the realist novel, on the other hand, the unheroic hero is both alienated from society and corrupted by it; like the Romantic hero, he is not at home in society and retreats to his garret, but he is also drawn into the social struggle for wealth and luxury as the "pure" Romantic hero is not.

After 1848, with the disillusionment of the liberal Social Romantics in their role as inspired leaders of society, the poet's isolation comes close to complete separation. The artist now purposefully accentuates his alienation, cultivating impassivity, obscurity, and aestheticism, willfully distancing himself from the larger bourgeois public. In the works of the Symbolists and Decadents of the late nineteenth century, the theme of the isolated artistic elite finds its most extreme expressions. At the same time, the crisis of religious belief, which caused earlier nineteenth-century poets to suffer metaphysical solitude, culminates in Nietzsche's proclamation of the Death of God.

In the final decades of the nineteenth century, however, the elite conception of solitude exists side by side with a new vision which, in the twentieth century, will supersede it. First fully elaborated in the novelistic world of Flaubert, then spreading to many novelists at the end of the century, the new vision of solitude in society pictures universal fragmentation: not only the artistic elite, but all men are isolated in bourgeois society. The new vision corresponds to a basic transformation of the capitalist system; monopoly capitalism begins to displace liberal, competitive capitalism, and the individual entrepreneur is replaced by the organization. The individual's power within the social system is weakened and the ideology of individualism undergoes a crisis. Although the Romantic poet refused capitalist society and the entrepreneur ruled it, they both were elite individuals whose existence depended on the competitive structure of society and its heightened individualism. Under monopoly capitalism, with the diminution of the individual's social role, the distinction between elite and mass tends to disappear. The artist now sees his solitude as resembling that of all men in society.

The vision of universal human solitude in society is central in the French novel of the twentieth century. Proust's *Du côté de chez Swann*, written before World War One, envisions a world in which each individual is totally enclosed within his own self and unknowable to others. Proust, whose work is transitional, offers a solution to the condition of isolation which is still based on the individual: the cultivation of the self in solitude and communication with others through art. But collective solitude in a society that also takes away the individual's power calls for a collective solution. Therefore, especially between the two wars, novelists attempt to locate and portray integrated collectivities. In the 1920s a number of important authors seek reintegration in communities of action which exist on the margins of capitalist society; examples are Montherlant's communities of war and sports, Saint-Exupéry's pioneer airlines, and Malraux's revolutionary armed struggles. At the same time, Bernanos pictures the spiritual struggle, within bourgeois society itself, to recreate the lost medieval Christian community.

But Malraux's treatment of revolutionary action does not transcend Stalinist conceptions, and, as he pictures it, revolutionary solidarity fails to overcome the "human condition" of solitude. Bernanos locates his community in the unattainable past, and Montherlant's communities of sport and war inexorably turn into the false collectivity of fascism. The failure of the political and literary enterprises which, during the entre-deux-guerres, offered the individual the possibility of stature and reintegration in a collectivity, and the reinforcement of monopoly capitalism by the increase of state intervention, created a context that deepened the anguish of solitude for the new writers who began publishing at the outbreak of World War Two: Sartre, Camus, Beckett, and others. The two major figures of literary existentialism attempted to find the path to a new collectivity. Whereas Sartre drew progressively closer to a Marxist revolutionary perspective, Camus explored liberal forms of community in his Resistance and postwar works. His course ended in disillusionment and a pessimistic portrayal of the isolated, egocentric Everyman in society.

In the 1950s we encounter the *nouveau roman*, which no longer attempts to discover a way out of the modern condition of solitude; the New Novelists portray a reality in which things play an increasingly important role and in which universal isolation is either implicit or explicit. Reification is given a new importance and form in the consumer capitalism of the 1950s. The isolation of the individual is now conditioned by the domination of commodities over human life. Thus, although the essential condition of human solitude which characterized Proust's vision remains central in Nathalie Sarraute's novelistic world, the isolation of Sarraute's characters is primarily defined in terms of the reified consumer mentality.

As this brief recapitulation indicates, there is a direct relationship between the genesis and transformation of the vision of solitude in society and the evolution of advanced capitalism. Historical and sociological method enables us to comprehend a crucial constitutive element of modern literature. Conversely, the study of literary expressions as one medium through which men articulate their relation to their world and to other men contributes to our comprehension of the nature of human society at given historical moments. If through such a literary-sociological study we are led to conclude that men experience radical isolation only within the specific socioeconomic framework of advanced capitalism, then we must also argue against theories of social reintegration which do not involve the transcendence of capitalism.

In an unprecedented speech on the occasion of the twenty-fifth anniversary of the Union Nationale des Associations Familiales,[1] Georges Pompidou evoked, in language often similar to Malraux's, the modern crisis of individualism and the "gregarious solitude" of modern man. He noticed in particular the evident search of contemporary youth for new forms of solidarity and community. Pompidou interpreted the rise of individualism in the eighteenth and nineteenth centuries as a response to technological advance, and suggested to his listeners a strengthening of traditional family bonds as a remedy to social fragmentation. His explanation of individualism and solitude does not touch upon the social and economic relations of men in modern society, and he proposes the reaffirmation of an institution that has in fact proven unable to protect men from isolation.[2]

In a totally opposite perspective, futuristic rather than conservative, Marshall McLuhan reverses Pompidou's argument. For McLuhan, reintegration is made possible by technology, and in particular the "communications" revolution, which he goes so far as to claim has realized concretely the Christian dogma of the mystical body of Christ.[3]

And yet such an affirmation is harshly contradicted by the existence of a literature of solitude after World War Two, at the same time that television was introduced on a mass scale.

Both the ideologue of mass manipulation through the new "media" and the backward-looking ideologue of the bourgeois family are locked in a necessary incomprehension of the problem of solitude: they are not delving to its roots. Apart from these interpretations, however, it might be argued that modern solitude has a positive content, that the suffering it entails is a necessary counterpart to the enrichment of the individual's inner being.

It is certainly true that both the realities and the potentialities of self-development have increased enormously in historical evolution since the advent of exchange and the individual. That process of individualization neither should nor could be revoked. It is essential to the Marxist conception of revolutionary social transformation that the past is not simply annihilated but rather "transcended." The German verb *aufheben* incarnates the double, dialectical meaning of change: at the same time, the past is preserved and the new is created, for the past is transformed and carried to a higher level. Thus the transcendence of the condition of solitude in society in no way implies the abolition of individual being as it has developed historically or the return to a primitive communalism. On the contrary, the modern individual necessarily would transform, enrich, carry to a higher level the meaning of community. At the same time the individual's being would be similarly transcended if reintegrated into an authentic modern community.

There is good reason to believe that the need to transcend the isolated individual in a new community has already begun to play a major role in the opposition to capitalist society. With the demonstrated ability of advanced capitalism to survive its own economic crises and to relieve severe material penury, oppression tends increasingly to be experienced not only in economic terms, but totally—that is, in terms of the totality of social relations and the totality of the human being. Oppression is experienced in the manifold reality of alienation, and especially in the reification and fragmentation of human relations. Although economic misery remains an important factor still, the impoverishment of what has been called the "quality of life" comes more and more into concern.

It can no longer convincingly be claimed that solitude contributes to the richness of individual existence, precisely because in the twentieth century that richness has been undermined. The significance of the individual self has been undermined, and the revolt in the 1960s against isolation is linked to this decadence of individual life. The misery of solitude may seem small enough a price to pay for the over-flowing abundance of Proustian consciousness (even though such a consciousness was of course available only to the few), but not for the sterility of Camus' Jean-Baptiste or the pettiness of Sarraute's consumer couple.

There is a growing awareness of the contradiction between the needs of the individual and modern capitalist social relations that both impoverish the individual and cut him off from his matrix, his "species being" in the collective. The contradiction is analogous to the classic contradiction in the economic sphere between the forces and relations of production, which led Marx to assert that capitalism had given birth to its own gravedigger. In the same way, the very individual created by capitalist society cannot be fulfilled in that society and he experiences a growing discontent within it. Whether this discontent will effectively contribute to radical social transformation in the future is an open question. But what is clear is that the paradox of solitude in society is an essential aspect of the crisis of our culture.

NOTES

INDEX

Notes

INTRODUCTION

1. See *Alienation: The Cultural Climate of Our Time*, ed. Gerald Sykes (New York: Braziller, 1964); *Man Alone: Alienation in Modern Society*, ed. Eric and Mary Josephson (New York: Dell, 1962). The second title points up the integral relation between the two themes, solitude and alienation.

2. E.g. Louis Petroff, *Solitaries and Solitarization: A Study of the Concepts, Forms, Degrees, Causes and Effects of Isolation* (Los Angeles: University of Southern California Press, 1936), and Margaret Mary Wood, *Paths of Loneliness: The Individual Isolated in Modern Society* (New York: Columbia University Press, 1953).

3. Robert S. Weiss, *Loneliness: The Experience of Emotional and Social Isolation* (Cambridge: MIT Press, 1973), p. 17.

4. For an example of behaviorist interpretation, see Vilhelm Aubert, *The Hidden Society* (Totowa, N.J.: Bedminster Press, 1965), pp. 13–17.

5. See the preface to the 1961 edition.

6. E.g. Paul Halmos, *Solitude and Privacy: A Study of Social Isolation, Its Causes and Therapy* (London: Routledge and Kegan Paul, 1952), chaps. 7 and 8. Earlier on in the book, defining his theoretical construct as opposed to the Marxian one, Halmos writes: "Our thesis is restricted to the idea of social-cultural determination without any attempt to identify the social-cultural totality with any particular feature of it, however important; i.e., we have not asked the question, 'What determines the social-cultural determination?'" (p. 57).

7. See *Existentialism versus Marxism*, ed. George Novak (New York:

206   Notes to pages 2–6

Dell, 1966); also, Georg Lukács, *Existentialismus oder Marxismus?* (Berlin: Aufbau-Verlag, 1951).

8. Nicholas Berdyaev, *Solitude and Society* (London: Centenary Press, 1938), p. 97.

9. Bertell Ollman, *Alienation: Marx's Conception of Man in Capitalist Society* (New York: Cambridge University Press, 1971); István Mészáros, *Marx's Theory of Alienation* (New York: Harper and Row, 1972).

10. It is important to understand that the concept of "species-being" is not ahistorical: "The nature (essence) of man can be inferred from its many manifestations (and distortions) in history; it cannot be seen as *such*, as a statistically existing entity 'behind' and 'above' each separate man, but it is that in man which exists as a potentiality and unfolds and changes in the historical process": Erich Fromm, *Marx's Concept of Man* (New York: Ungar, 1961), pp. 78–79.

11. Karl Marx, *Grundrisse*, ed. and trans. David McLellan (New York: Harper and Row, 1971), p. 17 (this edition presents selections from the *Grundrisse der Kritik der politischen Ökonomie*, an unpublished manuscript written in 1857–58, preparatory to the composition of *Capital* and only recently brought to light); see also *Capital* (New York: International Publishers, 1967), I, 326, where Marx distinguishes between his general definition of man as social animal and Aristotle's definition of the *zoon politikon*, which, strictly speaking, "is that man is by nature a town-dweller."

12. Marx, *Grundrisse*, p. 17; also *Capital*, p. 334.

13. See Marx, *Pre-Capitalist Economic Formations*, ed. E. J. Hobsbawm (New York: International, 1965), esp. pp. 69–70, 80–82; *Pre-Capitalist Economic Formations* is a section of the *Grundrisse*.

14. Ibid, pp. 14, 96.

15. Marx, *The Economic and Philosophic Manuscripts of 1844* (New York: International, 1964), pp. 100–101.

16. Marx, *The German Ideology* (New York: International, 1970), pp. 68, 79n; *Grundrisse*, pp. 65–67, 72; *Manifesto of the Communist Party* (Peking: Foreign Languages Press, 1972), pp. 33–34, 46.

17. Marx, *Economic and Philosophic Manuscripts*, p. 167; also see *Grundrisse*, pp. 59–64.

18. Marx, *German Ideology*, p. 85.

19. Marx, *Capital*, p. 333; also p. 331.

20. Marx, *German Ideology*, p. 83.

21. Marx, *Grundrisse*, p. 67; also p. 71.

22. See e.g. Marx, *Manifesto*, pp. 36, 41–42, 55, 59.

23. Marx, *Grundrisse*, p. 17.

24. Friedrich Engels, *The Condition of the Working Class in England in 1844* (New York: J. W. Lovell Co., 1887), pp. 17–18.

25. Colin Wilson, *The Outsider* (New York: Dell, 1956), p. 281.

26. E.g. Winifred Dusenbury, *The Theme of Loneliness in Modern American Drama* (Gainesville: University of Florida Press, 1960), p. 1.

27. Nathan Scott, Jr., *Rehearsals of Discomposure: Alienation and*

Reconciliation in Modern Literature (New York: King's Crown Press, 1952), p. x.

28. E.g. Ralph Harper, *The Seventh Solitude: Metaphysical Homelessness in Kierkegaard, Dostoevsky and Nietzsche* (Baltimore: John Hopkins Press, 1965).

29. Scott, *Rehearsals of Discomposure*, p. 2. Similarly, Yolanda Patterson, in an unpublished doctoral thesis, "Solitude and Communication in the works of Jean-Paul Sartre and Albert Camus" (Stanford, 1964), sees World War Two as a principal determinant of Camus' and Sartre's preoccupation with the failure of communication. Colin Wilson is exceptional in refusing even the "cataclysmic" events a determining role; his outlook is aggressively ahistorical (see *The Outsider*, p. 148).

30. Fritz Pappenheim, *The Alienation of Modern Man: An Interpretation Based on Marx and Tönnies* (New York: Monthly Review Press, 1959), p. 35.

31. See Kenneth Burke, *Attitudes Toward History* (Los Altos, Calif.: Hermes Publications, 1937), and *The Philosophy of Literary Form* (New York: Random House, 1941).

32. Engels writes in a letter to Joseph Bloch: "From the standpoint of the materialist conception of history, the determining factor in history is *in the last analysis* the production and reproduction of real life. Neither Marx nor I ever affirmed anything more than that. If someone wants to deform this proposition to the point of making it say that the economic factor is the *only* determinant, he is transforming it into an empty, abstract, and absurd formula. The economic situation is the basis, but the diverse elements of the superstructure . . . also exercise their own action upon the course of historic struggles and preponderantly determine their *form* in many cases. There is action and reaction of all these factors, in the midst of which economic movement necessarily ends by marking out a path." Marx and Engels, *Sur la littérature et l'art: textes choisis* (Paris: Ed. Sociales, 1954), pp. 159–160; see also Lukács' essay, "Marx and Engels on Aesthetics," in *Writer and Critic, and Other Essays* (New York: Grosset and Dunlap, 1970).

1. ANTIQUITY AND THE MIDDLE AGES

1. Aeschylus *Prometheus Bound* 2; Sophocles *Philoctetes* 269, 487; Euripides *Bacchae* 222, 876. For these and following meanings of *eremia, eremos,* and related words, see *Dictionnaire Grec-Français,* ed. A. Bailly (Paris: Hachette, 1950).

2. Euripides *The Trojan Women* 26, 95.

3. Sophocles *Ajax* 1177.

4. *Philoctetes* 1018.

5. *Euripides,* trans. A. S. Way (Cambridge: Harvard University Press, Loeb Classical Library, 1928), IV, 305.

6. *Ajax* 652–653, 1178; cf. Epictetus' definition of solitude in *Discourses* iii.13.

7. Euripides *Alcestis* 363–368, 407–411, 606, 944.

8. Sophocles *Electra* 187–192, 948–950, 959–972.

9. Sophocles *Antigone* 806–940.

10. Georg Lukács, *Die Theorie des Romans* (Neuwied and Berlin: Luchterhand, 1963), p. 26.

11. For an account of this transformation, see Gordon Child, *What Happened in History* (London: Penguin, 1942), chap. 9; and M. Rostovtzeff, *Greece* (New York: Oxford University Press, 1963), esp. chap. 4).

12. *The Oxford Annotated Bible (R.S.V.)* (New York: Oxford University Press, 1962), p. 684 (Psalm 38:11–12, 15); see also Psalms 25, 69, 102, 142. A footnote indicates: "The psalmist's main concern is with some grave disease, but he is also troubled by enemies who are taking advantage of it. Their attack was made more plausible by the common belief that illness was a punishment for sin and therefore an indication that God was against the sick man."

13. Ibid., p. 670 (Psalm 22:1–3).

14. See Job 19:13–19.

15. Ibid., p. 672 (Psalm 23:4–5).

16. *Gospel Parallels: A Synopsis of the First Three Gospels* (R.S.V.), ed. B. H. Throckmorton, Jr. (New York: Thomas Nelson, 1952), p. 170 (Matt. 26:39). The following references to the gospels are also taken from *Gospel Parallels.*

17. *Theological Dictionary of the New Testament,* ed. Gerhard Kittel (Grand Rapids, Mich.: Wm. B. Eerdmans, 1964), pp. 658–659.

18. *The Dead Sea Scriptures,* trans. and intro. Theodor H. Gaster (New York: Doubleday, 1956), p. 4.

19. *Theological Dictionary,* p. 658. References given: Matt. 14:13; Mark 1:45; Luke 4:42; John 11:54.

20. Herbert B. Workman, *The Evolution of the Monastic Ideal* (Boston: Beacon Press, 1913), pp. 26, 79; source quoted: Tert. *Apol* 42.

21. Ibid., p. 97.

22. Ibid., p. 10.

23. Ibid., pp. 31–32; source quoted: Jerome *Ep.* 14 (10). See also pp. 34–37.

24. Ibid., pp. 33, 35.

25. Ibid., pp. 124–125.

26. Examples of these usages are given in: *Grand Dictionnaire de la langue latine,* ed. Dr. G. Freund (Paris, 1855), and *Dictionnaire illustré latin-français,* ed. Felix Gaffiot (Paris, 1934).

27. See J. Toutain, *L'Economie antique* (Paris: La Renaissance du Livre, 1927), pp. 290–299; also M. Rostovtzeff, *Rome* (New York: Oxford University Press, 1960), pp. 86–91, 149–155.

28. Toutain, *L'Economie antique,* p. 358. Quotation from Boissier, *Nouvelles Promenades archéologiques,* p. 36.

29. For the above themes, see Horace *Satires* i.1, i.6, ii.6.

30. Horace *Epodes* 2.1–8; *The Odes and Epodes,* trans. C. E. Bennett (Cambridge: Harvard University Press, Loeb Classical Library, 1947), p. 365:

Beatus ille, qui procul negotiis,
Ut prisca gens mortalium,
Paterna rura bobus exercet suis,
Solutus omni fenore,
Neque excitatur classico mile truci,
Neque horret iratum mare,
Forumque vitat et superba civium
Potentiorum limina.

31. Horace *Satires* ii.6.60–62; *Satires, Epistles and Ars Poetica*, trans. H. R. Fairclough (Cambridge: Harvard University Press, Loeb Classical Library, 1955), p. 215.

32. Ibid., p. 211.

33. See M. Rostovtzeff, *The Social and Economic History of the Roman Empire* (Oxford: Clarendon Press, 1926), pp. 61, 63. Horace's farm was worked for profit. It consisted of a section managed by a steward and worked by eight slaves, with in addition five plots leased to *coloni*.

34. Virgil *Georgics* ii.532–540.

35. Virgil *Eclogues* iv.39; *Eclogues, Georgics, Aeneid 1–6*, trans. H. R. Fairclough (Cambridge: Harvard University Press, Loeb Classical Library, 1935), p. 31.

36. The Golden Age as both a "magically self-yielding nature" and "the idea of a primitive community, a primitive communism," and also the "rhetorical contrast of town and country" crystallize in Roman literature of the period of Horace and Virgil: Raymond Williams, *The Country and the City* (New York: Oxford University Press, 1973), pp. 42, 46.

37. Pliny *Epistolae* iii.19. Concerning his properties, see ii.15, vii.11. Also Toutain, *L'Economie antique*, pp. 356–357.

38. Pliny *Epistolae*, e.g. ix.10, ii.8, vii.3; "hac turba" of Rome is contrasted with "solitudo" of country estates.

39. Ibid., i.9, v.6, v.18, ix.36, vi.14, ix.15.

40. Rostovtseff, *The Social and Economic History of the Roman Empire*, p. 95.

41. Seneca *Ad Lucilium Epistulae Morales*, trans. Richard Gummere (Cambridge: Harvard University Press, Loeb Classical Library, 1953), I, 371 (55.8); also (51.10–12, 56, 86.5, 123) and *De Vita Beata* 20.

42. Seneca *Ad Lucilium Epistulae Morales* 9.9: "Hac re florentes amicorum turba circumsedet; circa eversos solitudo est, et inde amici fugiunt."

43. Ibid., 9.10: "Ista, quam tu describis, negotiatio est, non amicitia, quae ad commodum accedit, quae quid consecutura sit spectat"; "The friendship which you portray is a bargain and not a friendship; it regards convenience only, and looks to the results" (trans. R. Gummere).

44. Ibid., 55.11 (trans. R. Gummere): "Amicus animo possidendus est; hic autem numquam abest. Quemcumque vult, cotidie videt . . . In angusto vivebamus, si quicquam esset cogitationibus clusum. Video te, mi Lucili;

cum maxime audio. Adeo tecum sum, ut dubitem, an incipiam non epistulas, sed codicellos tibi scribere."

45. See Toutain, *L'Economie antique*, pp. 341–344, and Marc Bloch, *La Société féodale* (Paris: Albin Michel, 1939), pp. 76, 99.

46. Bloch, *La Société féodale*, p. 23.

47. See Marc Bloch, *Les Caractères originaux de l'histoire rurale française* (Paris: Colin, 1952), pp. 5–14, 120–122; *La Société féodale*, pp. 100, 110–115; Maurice Dobb, *Studies in the Development of Capitalism* (New York: International, 1947), pp. 48–50.

48. *Dictionnaire de l'ancien langage françois*, ed. La Curne de Sainte-Palaye (Paris, 1881), IX, 420.

49. See examples of this usage in *Dictionnaire de l'ancienne langue française*, ed. Frédéric Godefroy (Vaduz, Liechtenstein: Scientific Periodicals Establishment, 1892), VII, 456–457.

50. For a general discussion of the transformation of medieval monasticism, see Workman, *The Evolution of the Monastic Ideal*, esp. pp. 157–158, 219–224, 245–246, 296–297; also Dobb, *Studies*, pp. 79–80; Bloch, *La Société féodale*, pp. 479–489.

51. Workman, *The Evolution of the Monastic Ideal*, pp. 248–253.

52. *Lettres complètes d'Abélard et d'Héloïse* (Paris: Garnier, 1940), pp. 16–17.

53. Ibid., pp. 33–34.

54. Ibid., p. 54 (lettre deuxième).

55. Arnold Hauser, *The Social History of Art* (New York: Random House, 1951), I, 149.

56. See Bloch, *La Société féodale*, p. 418.

57. For "pre-humanism," see J. Huizinga, *The Waning of the Middle Ages* (London: Edward Arnold, 1927), pp. 117–120.

58. See Hauser, *Social History*, I, 255.

59. *Oeuvres complètes de Eustache Deschamps* (Paris, 1880), II, 19 (CXCIX):

> Je congnois bien la paine du marchant,
> Le frait des grans et la dure finance,
> Des cardinaulx et des clers le bobant
> L'estat des Roys, des nobles la soufrance,
> Des justiciers l'avarice et grevance.

• • • • •

> Le bien commun n'est ame tant ne quant;
> L'un en l'autre ne puet avoir fiance;
> On suist l'avoir, la personne noyant
> Preudoms n'a rien et li mauvais s'avance . . .

60. *The Penguin Book of French Verse* (London: Penguin, 1961), I, 216.

61. Ibid., p. 219.

62. Bloch, *La Société féodale*, p. 110.

63. Lukács, *Theorie des Romans*, pp. 64–65.

64. *La Chanson de Roland,* ed. Joseph Bédier (Paris: L'Edition d'Art, 1921), pp. 200–201.

65. Ibid., pp. 91–95.

66. See Hauser, *Social History,* I, 202–219, and *Littérature et société* (Brussels: Editions de l'Institut de Sociologie, 1967), pp. 52–53 (Erich Koehler).

67. *Penguin Book of French Verse,* I, 96–97.

68. Ibid., pp. 108–109.

69. The version of the legend referred to is Joseph Bédier's composite rendering.

70. Huizinga, *The Waning of the Middle Ages,* p. 23–24.

71. Hauser, *Social History,* I, 228–229.

72. See Pierre Champion, *François Villon, sa vie et son temps* (Paris: Champion, 1913).

73. François Villon, *Oeuvres* (Paris: Champion, 1923), p. 9.

74. Another isolated expression of solitude—of a different sort—in this late medieval period is Christine de Pisan's well-known lament for her dead husband:

> Seulete suis et seulete vueil estre,
>
> Seulete m'a mon doulz ami laissiée
> Seulete suy, sanz compaignon ne maistre.
>
> . . . . .
>
> Seulete suy en ma chambre enserree
>
> . . . . .
>
> Seulete suy partout et en tout estre

"I am alone and I wish to be alone; my sweet love has left me alone. I am alone, without companion or master . . . I am alone, locked up in my room . . . I am alone everywhere and in all my being"; *Oeuvres poétiques de Christine de Pisan* (Paris, 1886), I, 12 (XI); see also p. 15 (XIV). This exceptionally strong expression of personal abandonment, without any mitigation (such as final union in death), shows the mark of its period when compared, for instance, with the immediate death of "la belle Aude" in *Roland* (she has no existence except through Roland) or with the death of Iseut which fulfills her soul's union with Tristan.

2. L'ANCIEN RÉGIME

1. This is the position adopted by Arnold Hauser in *The Social History of Art* (New York: Random House, 1951), e.g. II, 3. Hauser is concerned principally, however, with emphasizing the economic continuity upon which the artistic continuation from Gothic to Renaissance is based (II, 15), and he is aware of the problem of definition involved (I, 258–259).

2. Karl Marx, *Capital* (New York: International, 1967), I, 146, 336, 715; Maurice Dobb, *Studies in the Development of Capitalism* (New York: International, 1947), pp. 123, 160; Henri Hauser, *La Modernité du XVIe*

siècle (Paris: Colin, 1963), pp. 74–75; Henri Sée, *Les Origines du capital-isme moderne* (Paris: Colin, 1951), intro.

3. Dobb, *Studies*, pp. 116–120, 124, 128–129, 159; Henri Hauser, *La Modernité du XVIe siècle*, pp. 90–91, 98. This process is accompanied by division of labor; the "manufactory" and even in some cases the fac-tory increasingly replace the domestic system.

4. Concerning the above socioeconomic developments, see esp.: Bloch, *Les Caractères originaux de l'histoire rurale française* (Paris: Colin, 1952), pp. 123, 129–131; Dobb, *Studies*, pp. 120, 124–125, 180–181; Sée, *Les Origines*, p. 59; Frédéric Mauro, *Le XVIe Siècle européen: aspects économiques* (Paris: Presses Univ., 1966), pp. 154, 165, 213; Pierre de Vaissière, *Gentilshommes campagnards de l'ancienne France* (Paris: Perrin, 1903), pp. 213–241.

5. E.g. Petrarch, *Dal Canzoniere* CCLIX.

6. E.g. *Epistolae Familiares* XIII, 8, where Petrarch compares his modest house to that of Fabricius or Cato. For this and other letters related to the solitude of Vaucluse, see *Petrarch at Vaucluse*, ed. E. H. Wilkins (Chicago: University of Chicago Press, 1958).

7. E.g. *Dal Canzoniere* CXXIX.

8. Ibid., XXXV; also CXXIX, CCIX.

9. In one of the early French translations: *Le Mespris de la Court, avec la vie rustique* (Paris: 1568), p. 38 (chap. 6).

10. Ibid., p. 18 (chap. 4).

11. Ibid., p. 19 (chap. 5).

12. René Costes, *Antonio De Guevara: sa vie* (Bibliothèque de l'Ecole des Hautes Etudes Hispaniques, fascicule x, 1:1925), p. 117.

13. For the evolution of the eclogue from its introduction in France by Marot in 1531, see Alice Hulubei, *L'Eglogue en France au XVIe siècle* (Paris: Droz, 1938). For the Golden Age motif: Harry Levin, *The Myth of the Golden Age in the Renaissance* (Bloomington: Indiana University Press, 1969), esp. pp. 69–79.

14. Maurice Scève, *Saulsaye*, ed. Marcel Françon (Cambridge, Mass.: Schoenhof, 1959), p. 103 *(Saulsaye, 11.526–530)*.

> Mais acquerant on évite le vice
> D'oysiveté, dont maints grands maux procedent.
> Et puis l'acquis à ceux, qui le possedent
> Par leur vertu, un si hault bien leur fait,
> Que pour l'honneur se gardent de meffait.

15. Ibid., pp. 106, 135n *(Saulsaye, 11.613–624)*.

16. Ibid., p. 108 *(Saulsaye, 11.679)*.

17. *Saulsaye*, 1.637.

18. See Ibid., pp. 24–25, 135. Source cited: A. Kleinclausz, *Histoire de Lyon* (Lyon, 1939).

19. E.g. Noël du Fail's *Propos rustiques* (1547); Pontus de Tyard's two companion prose works, *Solitaire premier* and *Solitaire second* (1552, 1555); many poems by Ronsard—see the collection *Ronsard et sa*

province, ed. Paul Laumonier (Paris: Presses Univ., 1924); for other works, see Pierre de Vaissière, *Gentilshommes campagnards*, pp. 186–213.

20. E.g. *Les Plaisirs de la vie rustique* (1575), including poems by Guy du Faur, Seigneur de Pibrac, Philippe Desportes, and Nicolas Rapin; *La Colombière et maison rustique* (1583), including poems by Philibert Hegemon (Guide) and G. de Saluste, Sieur du Bartas.

21. E.g. in Noël du Fail's *Propos rustiques: conteurs français du XVIe siècle* (Paris: La Pléiade, 1965), pp. 601–605; and the poem by Guy du Faur in *Les Plaisirs de la vie rustique*.

22. Nicolas Rapin, "Les Plaisirs du Gentil-homme Champetre," in *Les Plaisirs de la vie rustique*.

23. *La Colombière et maison rustique* (Paris: Jamet Mettayer, 1583), pp. 35–36 (Du Bartas, "Les Louanges de la vie rustique").

24. According to the dating system of Pierre Villey: *Les Sources et l'évolution des Essais de Montaigne* (Paris: Hachette, 1908).

25. *The Complete Essays of Montaigne*, trans. Donald Frame (Stanford: Stanford University Press, 1965), p. 175.

26. Ibid., p. 177.

27. See Montaigne, *Essais* (Paris: Garnier, 1962) I, 271–272.

28. Racan, *Les Bergeries et autres poésies lyriques* (Paris: Garnier, 1929), p. 218.

29. *Les Premières Lettres de Guez de Balzac* (Paris: Droz, 1933), I, 133 (A M. de la Motte Aigron: Lettre XXXI.).

30. Ibid., p. 134.

31. *Oeuvres poétiques de Saint-Amant* (Paris: Garnier, 1930), p. 3.

32. In this period also the Spanish poet Gongora composed *Las Soledades* (ca. 1612–1613), which picture the solitudes of wild shores, mountains, and woods.

33. See Pierre de Vaissière, *Gentilshommes campagnards*, chap. 3.

34. For the evolution of absolutism in three stages from Louis XI, see Lucien Goldmann, *Le Dieu caché* (Paris: Gallimard, 1959), chap. 6.

35. See Erich Auerbach, *Scenes from the Drama of European Literature* (New York: Meridian, 1959), pp. 134–138, 150–155.

36. Ibid., pp. 171–172.

37. Ibid., pp. 169–171, for a list of writers and their class; also see Hauser, *Social History*, p. 206.

38. See La Fontaine, *Fables*, XI, 4 ("Le Songe d'un habitant du Mogol"); Boileau, *Epitres*, VI; La Bruyère, *Les Caractères*, VII, VIII ("De la Ville" and "De la Cour"). The aristocratic La Rochefoucauld also develops the theme of retreat—in a characteristically pessimistic vein—in *Réflexions diverses*, XIX ("De la retraite").

39. Fénelon, *Les Aventures de Télémaque* (Paris: Hachette, 1881), pp. 198–199.

40. Ibid., p. 200.

41. Cf. Molière's *Misanthrope*: the final word is given to the *honnête homme*, Philinte, who pledges to dissuade Alceste from his decision to leave society for a desert retreat.

42. See William Clark, *Pascal and the Port Royalists* (Edinburgh: T. and T. Clark, 1902), chaps. 4, 8. It should be noted that at different periods the Solitaires made their retreat in Port Royal-des-Champs (the original nunnery outside Paris) or in the Port Royal within Paris. In either case the retreat from active life was total.

43. Goldmann, *Le Dieu caché*, p. 133.

44. St. Jerome speaks of the "smoky dungeon of cities." Cf. in an essay on solitude by a Scotsman, Sir George Mackenzie, written in the latter half of the seventeenth century: "many great Men, who having left a pleasant Country to come to a City, cover'd with Smoak and infected with Stink." *Essays upon Several Moral Subjects* (London, 1713), p. 155: "A Moral Essay, Preferring Solitude to Publick Employment and All Its Appanages: Such as Fame, Command, Riches, Pleasures, Conversation, etc."

45. For treatment of the social history of the theme in English literature, see Raymond Williams, *The Country and the City* (New York: Oxford University Press, 1973).

46. Georg Lukács, *Die Theorie des Romans* (Neuwied and Berlin: Luchterhand, 1963), p. 103.

47. Lukács, *History and Class Consciousness*, trans. R. Livingstone (Cambridge, Mass.: MIT Press, 1971), p. 84.

48. See B. H. Wind, *Les Mots italiens introduits en français au XVIe siècle* (Amsterdam: Deventer, Kluwer, 1928), p. 174; also Hatzfeld and Darmesteter, *Dictionnaire général de la langue française* (Paris: Delagrave, 1964).

49. See Boursault, *Les Mots à la mode (Petite Comédie)* (Paris, 1694):

M. Delorme: Pour moy, mon coeur est libre encor:
            Mais à voir tant d'appas pour peu qu'il
               persévere,
            J'appréhende bien fort qu'il ne le soit
               plus guère.
Mannette: Quel plaisir de ranger sous l'amoureux lien
            De ces coeurs *Isolez* qui ne tiennent à rien!
(p. 15; scene 8).

50. La Bruyère, *Les Caractères* (Paris: Didier, 1921), p. 364; "Le favori n'a point de suite; il est sans engagement et sans liaisons; il peut être entouré de parents et de créatures, mais il n'y tient pas; il est détaché de tout, et comme isolé."

51. Mackenzie, *Essays*, p. 132.

52. Goldmann, *Le Dieu caché*, p. 42.

53. Ibid., p. 76.

54. Pascal, *Pensées* (Paris: Garnier, 1964), p. 211.

55. Ibid., p. 71.

56. Robert Mandrou, *La France au XVIIe et XVIIIe siècles* (Paris: Presses Univ., 1967), pp. 124–130, 167–168; Henri Sée, *La France économique et sociale au XVIIIe siècle* (Paris: Colin, 1925), chap. 8, pp. 83, 157; Arnold Hauser, *Social History*, III, 7, 9, 11–12.

57. Sée, *La France économique et sociale*, pp. 84–85, 162–163.

58. *Encyclopédie, ou Dictionnaire raisonné des sciences, des arts et des métiers* (Neufchastel, 1765), XV, 324.

59. Ibid., VIII, 927.

60. Robert Mauzi, *L'Idée du bonheur dans la littérature et la pensée française au XVIIIe siècle* (Paris: Colin, 1960), p. 590. The last sentence refers to Diderot's well-known dictum: "Il n'y a que le méchant qui soit seul" (*Le Fils naturel*, IV, 3).

61. See e.g. a letter in verse by Voltaire to Cideville, Sept. 1, 1758:

> Le sage fuit des grands le dangereux appui;
> Il court à la campagne, il y seche d'ennui.
> J'en suis bien faché pour le sage.

(quoted in Mauzi, from *Oeuvres*, XXXIX, 485). Montesquieu, in the first part of the century, does express the pleasure of studious country retreat in "Mes Pensées": *Oeuvres complètes* (Paris: La Pléiade, 1949), I, 973.

62. Ian Watt, *The Rise of the Novel* (Berkeley: University of California Press, 1965), chap. 3.

63. Daniel Defoe, *Works* (Philadelphia: John D. Morris, 1903), II, 5–6, 13; for the traditional argument for intervals of philosophical-religious retreat, see Dr. Johnson's essay in the *Rambler*, no. 7 (1750).

64. Ibid., pp. 3–4.

65. Ibid., p. 4.

66. Jean-Jacques Rousseau, *The Social Contract, and Discourses*, trans. G. D. H. Cole, (New York: Dutton, Everyman's Library), p. 132.

67. Ibid., p. 218.

68. J. J. Rousseau, *Julie ou La Nouvelle Héloïse* (Paris: Garnier-Flammarion, 1967), p. 163.

69. Ibid., pp. 166–167.

70. Ibid., p. 172. It is interesting to note, however, that further on (VI, 5) the city of Geneva is presented as somewhere between the fallen state of Parisian civilization and rustic simplicity.

71. *Héloïse*, IV, 10. See also V, 7, on harvest time, where life on the estate is again compared with the Golden Age.

72. Cf. Petrarch in the Vaucluse and the poems of Saint-Amant and Théophile. But the theme was strikingly original in the eighteenth century and had an important influence on the reading public and later writers: see Rousseau, *La Nouvelle Héloïse*, intro. Daniel Mornet (Paris: Hachette, 1925), I, 74–75, 265–267; this radicalized retreat is accompanied by a radicalization of the critique of society, as we have seen. Rousseau identifies himself with Molière's *misanthrope* and criticizes Molière for treating Alceste as a buffoon (see *Lettre à d'Alembert sur les spectacles*, "La comédie").

73. See *Les Rêveries du promeneur solitaire*, "Cinquième Promenade"; Bernardin de Saint-Pierre, *Paul et Virginie* (Paris: Garnier-Flammarion, 1966): "C'est un instinct commun à tous les êtres sensibles et souffrants de se réfugier dans les lieux les plus sauvages et les plus déserts" (p. 83). There is also considerable evidence of Rousseau's "romantic" solitude in the German

doctor J. G. Zimmermann's treatise on solitude, *Uber die Einsamkeit* (1784, 1786).

74. Rousseau, *Oeuvres et correspondance inédites,* as cited in Mauzi, *L'Idée du bonheur,* p. 597.

75. Mauzi, *L'Idée du bonheur,* p. 598. Two full-length studies of these themes now exist: Jean Starobinski, *Jean-Jacques Rousseau, la transparence et l'obstacle* (Paris: Plon, 1957); Bronislaw Baczko, *Rousseau: Einsamkeit und Gemeinschaft* (Vienna: Europa Verlag, 1970).

3. MODERN TIMES

1. See Charles Morazé, *Les Bourgeois conquérants* (Paris: Colin, 1957), pp. 86, 132–139.

2. See Paul Van Tieghem, *Le Romantisme dans la littérature européene* (Paris: Albin Michel, 1948), pp. 35, 37.

3. Mme. de Staël, *De l'Allemagne* (Paris: Didot, 1845), pp. 105, 107, 109.

4. See Leo Maduschka, *Das Problem der Einsamkeit im 18. Jahrhundert* (Weimar: Alexander Duncker Verlag, 1933), pp. 116–117, 119; also Lucien Goldmann, *Introduction à la philosophie de Kant* (Paris: Gallimard, "Idées," 1948), pp. 44–53; Arnold Hauser, *The Social History of Art* (New York: Random House, 1951), III, 173–174, 194.

5. From the "Preface to the Second Edition of Lyrical Ballads" (1800): *Critical Theory Since Plato,* ed. Hazard Adams (New York: Harcourt Brace Jovanovich, 1971), pp. 437, 439.

6. Hauser, *Social History,* III, 189, 193.

7. Chateaubriand, *Atala; René* (Paris: Garnier-Flammarion, 1964), p. 156.

8. Ibid., p. 157.

9. For the modern usages of *désert, solitude, solitaire,* and other related words, with quotations, see Paul Robert, *Dictionnaire alphabétique et analogique de la langue française* (Paris: Société du Nouveau Littré, 1964). During the ancien régime, a city, palace or other area within the bounds of human society was sometimes referred to as "un désert" or "une solitude" hyperbolically when someone had departed or died, or when the population was relatively low: see e.g. *Dictionnaire de l'Académie Françoise* (Paris, 1694), II, 473: "On dit qu'il y une grande solitude dans un Palais, que ce Palais est devenu une solitude, une grande solitude, pour dire, qu'Il n'est plus fréquenté comme il estoit auparavant. J'entray dans ce Palais, j'y trouvay une grande solitude. quelle solitude. on connoist bien qu'il est disgracié, sa maison est une solitude." Thus the solitude is due to a lack of people or of particular persons, rather than to the nature of their presence.

10. Part II, book 3, chap. 9: "Du Vague des passions."

11. Senancour, *Oberman* (Paris: Union Générale d'Editions, "10/18," 1965), pp. 30–31 (letter 1).

12. Ibid., pp. 31–32.

13. Ibid., p. 110 (letter 22).

14. Ibid., p. 147 (letter 36).

15. See *Oeuvres de A. de Lamartine* (Paris: Alphonse Lemerre, 1949), I, 105 (no. VI, "Le Vallon").

16. Ibid., p. 103 *(commentaire* for "L'Immortalité"); cf. "La Solitude" in *Nouvelles Méditations,* where God is present in strength and glory to Lamartine in Nature.

17. Ibid., p. 72.

18. Ibid., p. 120.

19. Ibid., p. 75.

20. Ibid., p. 260.

21. Raymond Giraud, *The Unheroic Hero* (New Brunswick: Rutgers University Press, 1957), pp. 31–32; René Canat, *Une Forme du mal du siècle: du sentiment de la solitude morale chez les romantiques et les parnassiens* (Paris: Hachette, 1904), p. 91; Hauser, *Social History,* III, 194.

22. Alfred de Vigny, *Oeuvres complètes* (Paris: Seuil, 1965), p. 40; see Canat, *Une Forme du mal du siècle,* pp. 6–8, also p. 153; cf. Victor Hugo, "Le Poète" (1823: *Les Odes et Ballades)* and "Fonction du poète" (1839: *Les Rayons et les Ombres).*

23. The term is used by W. W. Rostow in his *The Stages of Economic Growth* (New York: Cambridge University Press, 1960): see esp. table 1 of chap. 4; also E. J. Hobsbawm, *The Age of Revolution: 1789–1848* (New York: New American Library, 1962), pp. 44–46, 207.

24. See Hauser, *Social History,* pp. 4–5, 10, 12; Hobsbawm, *The Age of Revolution,* pp. 139–140; Morazé, *Les Bourgeois conquérants,* pp. 150–156.

25. Hauser, *Social History,* III, 177–178, 192–194; also Giraud, *The Unheroic Hero,* pp. 32–33.

26. See Ernst Fischer, *The Necessity of Art: A Marxist Approach* (Baltimore: Penguin, 1963), pp. 49, 54, 102; also Hobsbawm, *The Age of Revolution,* pp. 308–309.

27. Alfred de Vigny, *Stello,* trans. Irving Massey (Montreal: McGill University Press, 1963), p. 179.

28. Ibid., p. 180.

29. Vigny, *Oeuvres complètes,* p. 574 (act I, sc. 2).

30. Ibid., pp. 587–588 (act III, sc. 5).

31. Jean-Paul Sartre, "La Conscience de classe chez Flaubert," *Les Temps modernes,* nos. 240, 241 (mai-juin 1966), p. 1931.

32. Vigny, *Oeuvres complètes,* p. 92.

33. Canat, *Une Forme du mal du siècle,* p. 203.

34. "La Maison du berger," III, 6; also, from Vigny's journal of 1832: "Quand j'ai dit: la soltiude est sainte, je n'ai pas entendu par solitude une séparation et un oubli entier des hommes et de la société, mais une retraite où l'âme se puisse recueillir en elle-même, puisse jouir de ses propres facultés et rassembler ses forces pour produire quelque chose de grand."

35. Vigny, *Oeuvres complètes,* pp. 104–105.

36. Fischer, *The Necessity of Art,* p. 103.

37. Giraud, *The Unheroic Hero,* p. 185.

38. Paul Lafargue, *Critiques littéraires* (Paris: Editions Sociales, 1936), p. 182.

39. Balzac, *The Magic Skin* (New York: Charles Scribner's Sons, 1915), pp. 163–164. Amaury, the hero of Sainte-Beuve's *Volupté* (1834), stands somewhere between the Romantic and the unheroic hero, for he is partially corrupted in his relation with the *mondaine*, Mme. R. Yet he remains largely a spectator in society (he recognizes himself in René), and in the end regains his purity by becoming a priest and setting off for the solitudes of America as a missionary. George Sand's Indiana (1831), on the other hand, is a purely Romantic heroine. She retains the purity of her youth on the Ile Bourbon, as she faces alone the egoism and philistinism of her husband and her false lover, Raymon. In the end she returns to the exotic solitude of her birth with her childhood playmate Ralph, to live as Paul and Virginie might have lived if they had survived.

40. Ibid., p. 84.

41. Ibid., p. 9.

42. Balzac, *La Comédie humaine* (Paris: La Pléiade, 1949–1965), IV, 651–660, 749.

43. Stendhal, *The Red and the Black*, trans. Lowell Blair (New York: Bantam, 1958), p. 241.

44. Ibid., p. 83.

45. Balzac, *La Comédie humaine*, IV, 879; also pp. 628–629.

46. Karl Marx, *Pre-Capitalist Economic Formations* (New York: International, 1964), pp. 77–78.

47. George Sand, *La Mare au diable* (Paris: Garnier-Flammarion, 1964), p. 154; see also *Indiana* (Paris: Garnier, 1962), p. 161.

48. Balzac, *La Comédie humaine*, III, 505, 537, 583.

49. Cf. an interesting passage in *La Peau de chagrin* (*The Magic Skin*, pp. 238–239) comparing society to children in grammar school: "That will give you a society in miniature, a miniature which represents life more truly, because it is so frank and artless; and in it you will always find poor isolated beings, relegated to some place in the general estimation between pity and contempt, on account of their weakness and suffering . . . The whole world, in accordance with its charter of egotism, brings all its severity to bear upon wretchedness that has the hardihood to spoil its festivities, and to trouble its joys. Any sufferer in mind or body, any helpless or poor man, is a pariah. He had better remain in his solitude; if he crosses the boundary-line, he will find winter everywhere . . . Let the dying keep to their bed of neglect, and age sit lonely by its fireside. Portionless maids, freeze and burn in your solitary attics."

50. Hobsbawm, *Age of Revolution*, p. 140; also Morazé, *Les Bourgeois conquérants*, p. 204; Henri Sée, *Histoire économique de la France* (Paris: Colin, 1939, 51), II, 251.

51. Hauser, *Social History*, p. 62; Morazé, *Les Bourgeois conquérants*, chaps. 8–10; Ch. Morazé and Ph. Wolff, *L'Epoque contemporaine: 1852–1948* (Paris: Colin, 1948), chap. 3.

52. This difference between the first and second halves of the nine-

teenth century is emphasized by Lukács: *Studies in European Realism* (New York: Grosset and Dunlap, 1964), pp. 85–86.

53. Hauser, *Social History*, pp. 61, 64, 71.

54. Leconte de Lisle, *Poèmes antiques* (Paris: Alphonse Lemerre, 1871), p. 9.

55. See Canat, *Une Forme du mal du siècle*, pp. 207–214.

56. In addition to "L'Albatros," see "Bénédiction"; and in *Le Spleen de Paris*: "Solitude, silence, the incomparable purity of the azure! A little sail quivering on the horizon, in its smallness and isolation mimicking my irremediable existence." From "The Artist's Confiteor," in *My Heart Laid Bare and Other Prose Writings*, trans. N. Cameron (London: Weidenfeld and Nicolson, 1950), p. 128.

57. *Oeuvres complètes de Victor Hugo: Poésie—III* (Paris: Ollendorff, 1905), p. 122.

58. Baudelaire, *My Heart Laid Bare*, p. 132; see also in *Les Fleurs du mal*: "L'Examen de minuit," "La Fin de la journée." Baudelaire defends the pleasure of solitude in his room against the contemptible pleasures of a journalist, in "La Solitude" *(Le Spleen de Paris)*.

59. Baudelaire, *My Heart Laid Bare*, p. 130.

60. A. de Musset, *Poésies complètes* (Paris: La Pléiade, 1951), p. 329:

> Days of work! the only days I really lived!
> O much cherished solitude!
> God be praised, I have returned
> To this old study!
> Poor little nook, walls so many times deserted,
> Dusty armchairs, faithful lamp,
> O my palace, my little universe . . .

61. Canat, *Une Forme du mal du siècle*, p. 32. Canat does not, however, distinguish clearly enough in his study between the two general forms of solitude in the nineteenth century, the second of which only fully replaces the first at the end of the century: the solitude of the superior individual and the universal solitude of a fragmented society. For his discussion of exceptional occurrences of *solitude morale* in the ancien régime, see pp. 33–38. After pointing out that Pascal first theoretically postulated the incommunicability of thoughts and feelings, Canat adds: "Nevertheless, one mustn't exaggerate its importance in the development of solitude. It is one thing to establish philosophically that each soul is an individuality impenetrable to others, and another thing to in fact feel this isolation. What is important is not being alone, but feeling that one is alone."

62. Musset, *Théâtre complet* (Paris: La Pléiade, 1947), pp. 189–190.

63. Baudelaire, *Le Spleen de Paris* (Paris: Colin, 1958), p. 50.

64. Ibid., p. 52.

65. Charles-Victor d'Arlincourt's *Le Solitaire* (Paris: Le Normant, 1821) went through twelve editions from 1821 to 1837. D'Arlincourt was a divine-right monarchist and author of reactionary political tracts as well as medieval historical novels.

66. Sully Prudhomme, *Les Solitudes* (Paris: Alphonse Lemerre, 1894), p. 100; see also "Corps et âmes."

67. Ibid., p. 137.

68. In Flaubert's youthful works—for example in *Mémoires d'un fou* (1838) and *Novembre* (1842)—we discover the familiar lyricism of the elite soul, imprisoned in his inner world of memories and dreams, thirsting after the Infinite and despising the stupidity and insensitivity around him. Yet in these early works the poet's solitude is already as complete as the Parnassian's: the young man suffers from his disharmony with Nature, and his great love for the Woman is disappointed by the distance between ideal and reality. E.g. in "Novembre": Gustave Flaubert, *Oeuvres de jeunesse inédites* (Paris: Conard, 1910), II, 191, 197, 233. The end of the first *Education sentimentale* (1843–1845) contains a generalized statement which suggests that Flaubert already possesses the conception that will be embodied in the later novels: "Life goes on that way, with deceptive feelings of rapport, with outpourings of feeling not understood; those who sleep in the same bed have different dreams; people stifle their thoughts, repress their happiness, hide their tears; the father doesn't know his son, nor the husband his wife; the lover doesn't tell all his love to his mistress, and friend doesn't understand friend: they are all blind men who are feeling their way randomly in the dark to reach each other, and who collide with each other and hurt each other when they do meet" (III, 300).

69. Gustave Flaubert, *Madame Bovary* (Paris: Garnier, 1961), chap. vi.

70. Flaubert, *Madame Bovary*, trans. Paul De Man (New York: Norton, 1965), p. 138.

71. Ibid., p. 81.

72. For a detailed *explication de texte* of the passage describing Charles and Emma at the dinner table, each enclosed in his personal world, see Erich Auerbach, *Mimesis* (New York: Doubleday, 1953), esp. p. 431.

73. Flaubert, *Madame Bovary*, p. 109.

74. Flaubert, *Sentimental Education*, trans. Anthony Goldsmith (New York: Dutton, 1941), p. 252.

75. See *Flaubert: A Collection of Critical Essays*, ed. R. Giraud (Englewood, N.J.: Spectrum Press, 1964), pp. 162–163.

76. Flaubert, *Sentimental Education*, p. 356.

77. J. K. Huysmans, *Against the Grain* (New York: Dover, 1969), p. 6.

78. Villiers de l'Isle-Adam, *Oeuvres* (Paris: Le Club Français du Livre, 1957), p. 1037.

79. Stéphane Mallarmé, *Oeuvres complètes* (Paris: La Pléiade, 1945), p. 47; Hérodiade continues (p. 48):

> Je me crois seule en ma monotone patrie
> Et tout, autour de moi, vit dans l'idolatrie
> D'un miroir qui reflète en son calme dormant
> Hérodiade au clair regard de diamant . . .
> O charme dernier, oui! je le sens, je suis seule.

80. Huysmans, *Against the Grain*, p. 186.

81. Villiers de l'Isle-Adam, *Oeuvres*, pp. 1003–1004.

82. Huysmans, *Against the Grain*, p. 206.

83. See Hauser, *Social History*, IV, 189–193, and Edmund Wilson, *Axel's Castle* (New York: Scribner's, 1931), chap. 8.

84. For this chronology, see V. I. Lenin, *Imperialism: The Highest Stage of Capitalism* (New York: International, 1939), pp. 20–22; Dobb, *Studies*, pp. 300, 309–310; Morazé and Wolff, *L'Epoque contemporaine*, p. 33; Sée, *Histoire économique de la France*, II, 303–307.

85. Lenin, *Imperialism*, esp. pp. 34–35, 54–55, 59, 89, 100; Dobb, *Studies*, p. 311; Morazé, *Les Bourgeois conquérants*, pp. 408–411; Sée, *Histoire économique*, pp. 354–359.

86. P. A. Baran and P. M. Sweezy, *Monopoly Capital* (London: Penguin, 1968), p. 55.

87. Hobsbawm, *Age of Revolution*, p. 203; C. E. Labrousse, *Aspects de la crise et de la dépression de l'économie française au milieu du XIXe siècle, 1846–1851* (La Roche-sur-yon: Bibliothèque de la Révolution de 1848, XIX, 1956), intro.

88. Lafargue, *Critiques littéraires*, p. 183; Lafargue rightly points out that Zola portrays this power of economic organisms over individuals' lives.

89. André Gorz, *La Morale de l'histoire* (Paris: Seuil, 1959), pp. 237–238.

90. Ibid., pp. 245–246.

91. Canat, *Une Forme du mal du siècle*, p. 1; quotation from Paul Bourget, *Etudes et portraits* (1889).

92. See the short story "La Solitude" and e.g. in *Mademoiselle Fifi* (Paris: Albin Michel), p. 100: "Voyez-vous, madame, quel que soit l'amour qui les soude l'un à l'autre, l'homme et la femme sont toujours étrangers d'âme, d'intelligence; ils restent deux belligérants; ils sont d'une race différente; il faut qu'il y ait toujours un dompteur et un dompté, un maître et un esclave; tantôt l'un, tantôt l'autre; ils ne sont jamais deux égaux. Ils s'étreignent les mains, leurs mains frissonantes d'ardeur; ils ne se les serrent jamais d'une large et forte pression loyale, de cette pression qui semble ouvrir les coeurs, les mettre à nu dans un élan de sincère et forte et virile affection."

93. Canat, *Une Forme du mal du siècle*, pp. 28–29; and see the collection of poetry by E. Haraucourt, *Seul* (Paris: Charpentier, 1891).

94. Paul Valéry, *Monsieur Teste* (Paris: Gallimard, "Idées," 1946), p. 30.

95. Ibid., p. 25; also p. 21.

96. Ibid., p. 13.

97. Ibid., pp. 18, 43, 50, 63.

98. A similar attempt at living as a purely autonomous individual is to be found in Jean Prévost, *Tentative de solitude* (Paris: N.R.F., 1925). The protagonist leaves the stifling collectivities of family and job to isolate himself in a house in Normandy, where he attempts to realize in practice

the cartesian method, by eliminating all exterior interference with the free play of the intellect. He fails to make sense of anything in the absence of a context, however, and commits suicide in despair.

99. Henri Barbusse, *L'Enfer* (Paris: Albin Michel, "Livre de Poche," 1968), p. 112.

100. Ibid., p. 210.

101. Ibid., p. 226; also pp. 19, 22, 71, 224–225.

102. Romain Rolland, *Journey's End*, trans. Gilbert Cannan (New York: Holt, 1913), p. 52.

103. Jules Romain, *Les Hommes de bonne volonté* (Paris: Flammarion, 1932–1947), I, xvi.

104. Rolland, *Journey's End*, p. 451.

4. *DU CÔTÉ DE CHEZ SWANN*

1. George Painter, *Proust: The Later Years* (Boston: Little, Brown, 1965), pp. 234ff, 258–259n.

2. See Edmund Wilson, *Axel's Castle* (New York: Scribners, 1931), p. 134.

3. See Henri Bonnet, *Le Progrès spirituel dans l'oeuvre de Marcel Proust: le monde, l'amour et l'amitié* (Paris: J. Vrin, 1946), pp. 169–177; and Raoul Celly, *Répertoire des themes de Marcel Proust* (Paris: Gallimard, 1935), under "Amitié."

4. The fruitful solitude that the Vicountess Violante abandons for society is her birthright to the ancestral chateau. Thus Proust at first casts his image of solitude-as-retreat in the traditional mold of the country solitude of the aristocracy which fascinated and tempted him—see also *Jean Santeuil* (Paris: Gallimard, 1952), II, 247–248; this image is soon replaced, however, by the nineteenth-century image of the artist in his study.

5. With the exception of the critique of friendship. At the time of composition of *Les Plaisirs*, Proust still believed that a profound friendship could replace love in providing the perfect, secure affection that he once enjoyed as a child from his mother: see *Les Plaisirs et les jours* (Paris: Gallimard, 1924), pp. 192–193. But he became progressively more disillusioned with friendship, and by 1905 his attitude had changed: Painter, *Proust: The Early Years* (Boston: Little, Brown, 1959), pp. 359–360, 365–366, 386–387, 390–392; *Proust: The Later Years*, p. 66; Bonnet, *Le Progrès spirituel*, pp. 176–177.

6. Hauser, *The Social History of Art* (New York: Random House, 1951), IV, 181.

7. Ibid., p. 83.

8. There are specific references in *Du côté de chez Swann* to the philosophical problems of "Idealism" which indicate that Proust was familiar with them, largely through his year of philosophy with Alphonse Darlu at Condorcet: see Painter, *Proust: The Early Years*, pp. 74–75; Proust, *A la recherche du temps perdu* (Paris: La Pléiade, 1954), I, 94, 246, 402.

9. As cited in Erich Koehler, *Marcel Proust* (Göttingen: Vandenhoeck

& Ruprecht, 1958), p. 31: "Im Roman Joyces and Prousts—darin liegt u. a. der Schritt, der sie über Balzac und Flaubert, aber auch über Thomas Mann hinausführt—ist die Welt nicht mehr als neutraler, identischer und gemeinsamer Raum für alle vorgegeben, sondern erscheint in einer Vielzahl von Welten, die dasselbe geschichtliche Dasein widerspiegeln, ohne untereinander zu kommunizieren." Flaubert does approach such a conception late in his life: see his letter to Maupassant in 1878—*Correspondance* (Paris: Conard, 1926–33), VIII, 135. The conception is also announced in symbolist poetry: see Maurice Z. Shroder, "The Satyr and the Faun," *Symposium* (Fall-Winter 1969).

10. Wilson, *Axel's Castle*, p. 184.

11. Proust, *Pastiches et mélanges* (Paris: Gallimard, "Idées," 1919), p. 200; see also *A la recherche*, I, 26.

12. All further references to *Du côté de chez Swann* will be noted in parenthesis in the body of the text. Unaccompanied page numbers will refer to vol. I of the Pléiade edition of *A la Recherche*; page numbers preceded by the letter M will refer to vol. I of the C. K. Scott Moncrieff translation: *Rememberance of Things Past* (New York: Random House, 1934).

13. Cf. the opening pages of Edouard Dujardin's *Les Lauriers sont coupés* (1887), in which the narrator walks through the streets of Paris, a lone consciousness among anonymous "others." This novel was the first to employ systematically the *monologue intérieur*, one of the modern techniques that isolates point of view in a single consciousness. For a consideration of the modern experience of the lone "I" in the city in English literature, see Raymond Williams, *The Country and the City* (New York: Oxford University Press, 1973), chap. 20.

14. See e.g. Michel Philip, "The Hidden Onlooker," *Yale French Studies: Proust*, no. 34 (June 1965), p. 37.

15. See Jack Murray, "The Mystery of Others," *Yale French Studies: Proust*, p. 66. The hypothesis construction in Proust was first brought to my attention by the late Professor Justin O'Brien in his seminar on Proust at Columbia University in Spring 1966.

16. Murray, "The Mystery of Others," *Yale French Studies: Proust*, p. 70.

17. There is a seeming contradiction between Proust's radical assertion of the unknowable nature of others and his frequent formulation of general rules of human conduct.

18. Cf. "Présence réelle" in *Les Plaisirs et les jours*.

19. Cf. Baudelaire's prose poem, "Les Yeux des pauvres."

20. Cf. Koehler, *Marcel Proust*, pp. 29–30; "Die Einheit dieser Welt ist nur scheinhaft. Die sterile Konvention verdeckt nur notdürftig die Anarchie, die inmitten der Geselligkeitskulte und der äusseren Verbindlichkeit jedes Individuum isolieren, es zu einem *univers particulier* werden lassen. Für Proust war diese Erfahrung so grundlegend und so beherrschend, dass sie sein Menschenbild entscheidend prägte."

21. For Proust's ideas on reading in contrast with friendship, see *Pastiches et mélanges*, "Journées de lecture."

22. Koehler, *Marcel Proust,* pp. 31–33.

23. Proust himself strongly desired wide readership: Painter, *Proust: The Later Years,* pp. 184, 203.

24. Wilson, *Axel's Castle,* p. 190.

5. *LA CONDITION HUMAINE*

1. They follow the notable—although isolated—earlier examples of Zola and Barrès.

2. Jules Romains, *Les Hommes de bonne volonté,* I, xiii (preface).

3. Ibid., pp. xix–xx; for an example of Romains' portrayal of group life, see vol. I, chap. 18, "Présentation de Paris à cinq heures du soir." Although Zola's aesthetic commitment to the portrayal of group life resembles Romains', Zola pictures the process of conflict between contradictory collective forces in society, and his ideological perspective is socialistic rather than liberal.

4. World War One was experienced by many soldiers as solitude rather than solidarity. Edouard Estaunié calls his *Solitudes* (Paris: G. Cres et Cie, 1922), which portrays the isolation of ordinary people in their daily relations, "un livre de guerre." He comments in the preface: "The incredible isolation of the men of 1914 has not been sufficiently remarked upon; they were torn from their homes, thrown into a life where everything was strange to them—faces, habits, social order—and henceforth bound to chance neighbors by a shared anguish alone. And even this link is one that wears out" (p. ii).

5. Cf. the case of Jean Prévost, who after his *Tentative de solitude* turns to sports (*Plaisirs des sports,* 1926).

6. Antoine de Saint Exupéry, *Wind, Sand and Stars,* trans. Lewis Galantière (New York: Reynal and Hitchcock, 1939), p. 47.

7. Saint Exupéry, *Oeuvres* (Paris: La Pléiade, 1953), p. 148.

8. Ibid., p. 209.

9. Cf. the Communist novelist Louis Aragon, for whom violent action does not have the primary importance it does for Malraux. In *Les Beaux Quartiers* (1936), the socialist struggle is embodied in the workers' movement in France rather than in revolutionary armed conflict abroad. One of the main characters, a romantic and isolated young bourgeois from provincial Sérianne—Armand Barbentane—first experiences fraternity in the crowd at a huge socialist rally addressed by Jaurès. The novel ends with Armand joining a union strike.

10. Andre Malraux, "D'une jeunesse européenne," *Ecrits* (Paris: Grasset, 1927), p. 134.

11. *Romans d'André Malraux* (Paris: Gallimard, 1951), p. 50.

12. Malraux, *Ecrits,* p. 148.

13. Roger Stéphane, "Malraux et la révolution," *Esprit,* no. 149 (October 1948), p. 467.

14. Leon Trotsky, "La Révolution étranglée," *N.R.F.,* no 211 (April 1, 1931).

15. *Romans d'André Malraux* (Paris: La Pléiade, 1947), p. 774.

16. Ibid., p. 625.

17. Lucien Goldmann, *Pour une sociologie du roman* (Paris: Gallimard, "Idées," 1964), pp. 225–256. I am indebted in this chapter to the comprehensive study by Goldmann: "Introduction à une étude structurale des romans de Malraux"; although I am not in agreement with his interpretation in all points, my general approach is similar. For a book-length study of the theme of solitude in Malraux's novels, see the doctoral dissertation of Dietmar Eggart: "Das Problem der Einsamkeit und ihrer Ueberwindung im Romanwerk von André Malraux" (Tübingen, 1966). Eggart's approach differs from my own in that he does not study the developmental dynamic of the theme from novel to novel, but rather produces a static analysis organized by sub-themes within the larger problematic of solitude.

18. *Romans d'André Malraux* (Gallimard edition), p. 1057.

19. *Romans d'André Malraux* (Pléiade edition), p. 264.

20. Cf. Claude-Edmonde Magny, "Malraux le fascinateur," *Esprit,* October, 1948, pp. 121–122.

21. *Romans d'André Malraux* (Pléiade edition), p. 229.

22. Ibid., p. 227.

23. Malraux, *Man's Fate,* trans. H. M. Chevalier (New York: Modern Library, 1934), p. 243.

24. Ibid., p. 239.

25. Ibid., p. 243.

26. Ibid., pp. 245–246.

27. See Goldmann, *Pour une sociologie du roman,* pp. 158, 161–163; in my opinion, however, Goldmann's analysis neglects the other, isolated characters and does not sufficiently stress the limitations of the revolutionary community itself.

28. *Man's Fate,* pp. 320–321.

29. Ibid., p. 59.

30. See *Romans d'André Malraux* (Pléiade edition), p. 335.

31. *Man's Fate,* p. 319.

32. *Romans d'André Malraux,* p. 411.

33. See Goldmann's *Pour une sociologie du roman,* p. 90.

34. *Man's Fate,* p. 241.

35. W. M. Frohock, *André Malraux and the Tragic Imagination* (Stanford: Stanford University Press, 1952), p. 10.

36. See the celebrated passage on Kyo's death: *Romans d'André Malraux* (Pléiade edition), p. 406.

37. See ibid., p. 218.

38. *Man's Fate,* pp. 352–353.

6. *JOURNAL D'UN CURÉ DE CAMPAGNE*

1. François Mauriac, *Le Désert de l'amour* (Paris: Grasset, "Livre de Poche," 1925), p. 243.

2. Malraux admired Bernanos' works. He was in fact the only literary

figure at Bernanos' funeral: see the biography appended to the *Oeuvres romanesques de Bernanos* (Paris: La Pléiade, 1961), p. liv; see also Malraux's favorable review of *L'Imposture* in the *N.R.F.*, no. 174 (March 1, 1928).

3. See Gaëtan Picon's preface to the *Oeuvres romanesques de Bernanos*, p. xxxii.

4. Georges Bernanos, *Les Grands Cimetières sous la lune* (Paris: Plon, 1938), p. 14; see also pp. 32–47, on the power of money.

5. Bernanos refused to support Franco and the German and Italian fascists, gave support to the Resistance (but as an exiled nonparticipant), and later a very equivocal support to De Gaulle.

6. Bernanos, *Les Grands Cimetières*, p. 49.

7. See Bernanos, *Oeuvres romanesques*, pp. 1727–1729.

8. See R. M. Albérès, *La Révolte des écrivains d'aujourd'hui* (Paris: Correa, 1949), pp. 106–111.

9. All further references to *Journal d'un curé de campagne* will be noted in parenthesis in the body of the text. Unaccompanied page numbers will refer to the Pléiade edition of the *Oeuvres romanesques de Bernanos;* page numbers preceded by the letters PM will refer to the translation by Pamela Morris: *The Diary of a Country Priest* (New York: Macmillan, 1937).

10. The original title of *Monsieur Ouine* was *La Paroisse morte;* see p. 1855n. Bernanos' view of modern bourgeois society is close to that of another Christian reactionary of the preceding generation, Léon Bloy. Indeed, many of the thematic elements we will see in the *Journal* appear as significant motifs in Bloy's writings: the thirst for the absolute and sainthood in the degraded modern world, the glorification of poverty, and, most important for our study, the paradox of the solitude of souls within the mystical "communion of saints" (on the latter see e.g. *Pages de Léon Bloy*, ed. R. and J. Maritain [Paris: Mercure de France, 1951], pp. 371–379).

11. Cf. the gathering of *prêtres politiques* in *L'Imposture*, esp. p. 422.

12. The process of dissolution of the nobility as a semiautonomous social entity, preserving to some extent the traditional aristocratic values, is chronicled in Proust's *A la recherche*. By the 1930s the process is completed, as is reflected in Montherlant's *Les Célibataires* (1934). Now the nobleman must totally renounce the old values to become a modern capitalist (Uncle Octave the banker is an admirer of the latest American methods) or else become a marginal *épave*, totally unadapted, wretchedly poor and quasi-deranged like the célibataires themselves. In this context the idea of a return to monarchy is patently absurd; the only representative of monarchy in the novel is a stupid society lady who appears briefly and attempts in vain to recruit the célibataires for her royalist committee. The absence of a pure monarchical ideal in Montherlant contributes to explain the fact that he moved politically toward fascism with the rest of the Right when Bernanos did not.

13. Cf. the country estate of the De Clergerie in *La Joie*.

14. Cf. a minor character who is also a poor man—the sexton Arsène, whose isolated sensibility leads the curé to exclaim: "Oh, the solitude of the

poor!" (p. 1101). Although his family has always worked for the Church, he conceives of priests as functionaries like notaires, and he does not believe in an afterlife (p. 1182). On the solitude of the poor, see also p. 1070: "Amongst the poor, as amongst the rich, a little boy is all alone, as lonely as a king's son. At all events in our part of the world, distress is not shared, each creature is alone in his distress" (PM 52).

15. Chantal and Séraphita resemble the Mouchettes of *Sous le soleil de Satan* and *Nouvelle Histoire de Mouchette*. The two Mouchettes are distinct characters whose names are the same because of a basic similarity: "the same tragic solitude in which I saw them both live and die" (prefatory note to *Nouvelle Histoire*, p. 1263).

16. Cf. the adventurer in the early short story "Une Nuit," in whom the metaphysical dimension does not exist and whose adventure is devaluated because he cannot answer the spiritual call of a dying man.

17. In *Sous le soleil de Satan*, the curé Donissan shows Mouchette her solidarity with the family from which she has attempted to escape (p. 207).

18. Albert Béguin, *Bernanos par lui-même* (Paris: Seuil, 1954), p. 77.

19. Donissan of *Sous le soleil de Satan* is also tempted by Satan in the form of his double: pp. 146–147, 180.

20. E.g. *Sous le soleil de Satan*: Donissan is tempted to enter a monastery, is advised by Menou-Segrais that "your vocation is not to be cloistered," and successfully resists the temptation (p. 222); *La Joie*: after the death of Chevance, Chantal does not seek the haven of a convent (p. 560).

21. All Bernanos' saints possess this unique power—see Béguin, *Bernanos par lui-même*, pp. 70–71. For examples of the vision of souls in other novels: *Sous le soleil de Satan*, pp. 183, 188, 198–199; *L'Imposture*, pp. 347–348; *La Joie*, p. 659.

22. The same relationship exists in *Sous le soleil de Satan* between Donissan and Menou-Segrais.

23. Bernanos, *Les Grands Cimetières*, p. v.

7. LA CHUTE

1. See Andrew Shonfield, *Modern Capitalism* (New York: Oxford University Press, 1965), p. 84. Shonfield cites A. Chazel and H. Poyet, *L'Economie mixte* (Paris: Presses Univ., 1963).

2. Shonfield, *Modern Capitalism*, pp. 81–83; Dobb, *Studies in the Development of Capitalism* (New York: International, 1947), pp. 333–334.

3. Dobb, *Studies*, p. 387.

4. Ibid., p. 392; also pp. 383–384, 388. In his periodization of modern capitalism in *Pour une sociologie du roman* (pp. 290–291) and also in later essays (*Marxisme et sciences humaines* [Paris: Gallimard, "Idées," 1970], pp. 279–280, 339, 343ff.), it is clear that Goldmann conceives of postwar state capitalism as a third distinct phase, of the same nature as entrepreneurial and monopoly capitalism, rather than, as I have argued, a further reinforcement and extension of monopoly capitalism. Goldmann's allusions to the "third phase" of capitalism are sketchy and somewhat unclear; he

refs to it alternately as "capitalisme d'organisation" and "société de consommation" (Pour une sociologie du roman, p. 368), without distinguishing
the specific characteristics and effects of state intervention and consumerism.

5. Shonfield, Modern Capitalism, pp. 66–67.

6. R. M. Albérès, in La Révolte des écrivains d'aujourd'hui (Paris:
Correa, 1949), includes both Sartre and Camus among representatives of the
"Promethean" literature of which Malraux and Bernanos are also examples.

7. In an entry of June 1947: see Albert Camus, Théâtre, récits, nouvelles (Paris: La Pléiade, 1962), p. 1814 (notes by Roger Quilliot).

8. Albert Camus, Lyrical and Critical Essays, ed. P. Thody, trans. E. C.
Kennedy (New York: Knopf, 1969), p. 42.

9. Ibid., p. 43.

10. Ibid., p. 90.

11. Ibid., p. 69.

12. Ibid.

13. Ibid., p. 71.

14. E. g. Camus, Noces (Paris: Gallimard, 1950), p. 49.

15. Camus, Lyrical Essays, p. 102.

16. Ibid., p. 75.

17. See Quilliot's biography of Camus, and presentations of the works
in question, in Théâtre, récits, nouvelles d'Albert Camus.

18. Camus, Lyrical Essays, p. 139.

19. Ibid., p. 135.

20. As Conor Cruise O'Brien has shown in Albert Camus of Europe
and Africa (New York: Viking Press, 1970), pp. 21–22, 25, Meursault is
by no means hostile to the evils of society (colonialism and racism in particular), since he aids Raymond in his cruel treatment of the Arab girl and
murders an Arab without feeling in the slightest responsible for his act. He
is as indifferent to society's real relations and functioning as he is to the
ideological trappings by which it justifies tself.

21. The Stranger, trans. S. Gilbert (New York: Knopf, 1946), p. 64.

22. Caligula and Three Other Plays, trans. S. Gilbert (New York:
Knopf, 1958), p. 72.

23. Camus, Le Mythe de Sisyphe (Paris: Gallimard, 1942), p. 71.

24. Camus, Lettres à un ami allemand (Paris: Gallimard, 1948), p. 42.

25. Ibid., pp. 66–67.

26. Ibid., pp. 79–80, 87.

27. Ibid., pp. 80–81.

28. Théâtre, récits, nouvelles d'Albert Camus, p. 1287.

29. In Camus' "Lettre à Roland Barthes sur La Peste," ibid., p. 1965.
There is a striking contrast between the weakness of links of solidarity in
the Resistance for Camus and their implied efficacity in Roger Vailland's
Un Jeune Homme seul (Correa, 1951), at the end of which the isolated petty
bourgeois of the title finally enters a community and discovers "his people"
by accepting complicity with the Resistance.

30. Camus, L'Homme révolté (Paris: Gallimard, "Idées," 1951), p. 36.

31. For a critique of Camus' anticommunism and antihistoricism in

L'Homme révolté, see Francis Jeanson, "Albert Camus ou l'âme révoltée," *Les Temps modernes* (May 1952).

32. Camus, *L'Homme révolté*, p. 136.

33. Camus mentions very briefly at the end of *L'Homme révolté* (pp. 356, 359) two further examples: the Commune and syndicalism. These examples resemble the more fully developed one precisely in being enterprises that do not actually effect revolutionary social transformation. The first was brutally suppressed; the second is only reformist in its intentions.

34. Camus' "Prière d'insérer" for *Les Justes: Théâtre, récits, nouvelles d'Albert Camus*, p. 1826.

35. Camus, *Caligula and Three Other Plays*, pp. 289–290.

36. *Théâtre, récits, nouvelles d'Albert Camus*, p. 2028.

37. His position on the Algerian question is fully elaborated in *Actuelles III: chronique algérienne* (Paris: Gallimard, 1958). As O'Brien points out, in spite of his protest against some of their methods, Camus' position amounted in fact to support of the French Army's presence and activities in Algeria: *Albert Camus of Europe and Africa*, p. 90.

38. E. g. in *Franc-Tireur*, November 10, 1956; see O'Brien, *Albert Camus of Europe and Africa*, pp. 88–89.

39. See *Théâtre, récits, nouvelles d'Albert Camus*, pp. 2029–2030.

40. All further references to *La Chute* will be noted in parenthesis in the body of the text. Unaccompanied page numbers will refer to the Pléiade edition of *Théâtre, récits, nouvelles d'Albert Camus*; page numbers preceded by the letter O will refer to the translation by Justin O'Brien: *The Fall* (New York: Knopf, 1957).

41. *Théâtre, récits, nouvelles d'Albert Camus*, p. 2006.

42. Cf. the doctor Rieux in *La Peste* and the schoolteacher Daru in "L'Hôte" (*L'Exil et le royaume*). It seems likely that Camus was himself tempted by the ideology of the liberal professions. According to Quilliot, "Il aimait à dire que, s'il n'avait été écrivain, il eût aimé être medecin ou instituteur": *Théâtre, récits, nouvelles d'Albert Camus*, p. 2039.

43. Jean-Baptiste's fear of hostile and taciturn Asians probably translates Camus' own relation to Algerian Arabs (cf. the relations between French Algerians and Arabs in *L'Exil et le royaume*). O'Brien's study of *La Chute* (in *Albert Camus of Europe and Africa*) interprets the novel as Camus' complex response to his inability to come to terms with the Algerian question. This approach is valid and important, especially since next to nothing has been written about the Algerian reality in relation to Camus' fictional works. The personality and life of Clamence, however, while reflecting on one level Camus' doubts, fears, and hostilities in relation to the French Left and Algeria, has a more universal dimension. My study concentrates principally on the wider significance of Jean-Baptiste's persona as a bourgeois Everyman.

44. It is significant that Jean-Baptiste suddenly becomes unable to choose sides in North Africa. Camus *did* engage in the Resistance, unlike Clamence, but was unable to endorse either the F.N.L. or the *colons* in the Algerian war. Consequently, Clamence's failure of engagement in the Re-

sistance translates Camus' own dilemma over the Algerian question, which was foremost in his mind during the period of composition of *La Chute*.

45. John Cruickshank, *Albert Camus and the Literature of Revolt* (New York: Oxford University Press, 1959), p. 185.

46. See P. H. Simon, *Présence de Camus* (Paris: Nizet, 1961), pp. 172–173.

8. *LE PLANÉTARIUM*

1. For a full analysis of the relation between monopoly capitalism, the "sales effort," and the consumer society, see Baran and Sweezy, *Monopoly Capital* (London: Penguin, 1968), esp. chaps. 2 and 4; for the historical evolution of these trends in Western Europe, see Dobb, *Studies in the Development of Capitalism* (New York: International, 1947), pp. 321–322, 357–358, 369–371; W. W. Rostow, *The Stages of Economic Growth* (New York: Cambridge University Press, 1960), pp. 82–88.

2. Nathalie Sarraute, *Tropismes* (Paris: Ed. de Minuit, 1957), esp. nos. 1, 6, 10, 13.

3. Lucien Goldmann analyses the novels of Robbe-Grillet from this perspective in *Pour une sociologie du roman* (Paris: Gallimard, "Idées," 1964), "Noveau roman et réalité."

4. For a general outline of her life and literary career, see M. Cranaki and Y. Belaval, *Nathalie Sarraute* (Paris: Gallimard, "La Bibliothèque Idéale," 1965), "Les Jours."

5. W. M. Frohock, *Style and Temper: Studies in French Fiction, 1925–1960* (Cambridge, Mass.: Harvard Univ. Press, 1967), p. 119.

6. See Michel Butor, *La Modification* (Paris: Ed. de Minuit, 1957), p. 122.

7. Cf. Paul Guimard's *Rue de Havre* (Paris: Denoël, 1957), in which modern alienation is the central organizing theme and in which the young male protagonist is a display decorator in a department store.

8. Sarraute, *Tropisms* (New York: Braziller, 1967), p. viii.

9. Ibid.

10. See, e.g., Olivier de Magny, "Nathalie Sarraute ou l'Astronomie intérieure," in the 10/18 edition of *Portrait d'un inconnu* (Paris: Union Générale d'Editions, 1956), p. 231.

11. Sartre first emphasized the role in Sarraute's work of the *lieu-commun* and of inauthenticity; see his well-known preface to *Portrait d'un inconnu* (1947).

12. See e.g. Gaëton Picon's judgment in *L'Usage de la lecture* (Paris: Mercure de France, 1961), as quoted in Cranaki and Belaval, *Nathalie Sarraute*, pp. 236–237.

13. Léon S. Roudiez, in his review of the American translation of *Tropismes:* "The Life Beneath the Lines We Wear," *Saturday Review* (May 6, 1967), p. 35.

14. Cranaki and Belaval, *Nathalie Sarraute*, p. 16.

15. See her interview with François Bondy: ibid., p. 216.

16. In an interview with Geneviève Serreau: "Nathalie Sarraute nous parle du 'Planétarium,'" *Lettres Nouvelles* (April 29, 1959), p. 28.

17. All further references to *Le Planétarium* will be noted in parenthesis in the body of the text. Unaccompanied page numbers will refer to the Gallimard edition (Paris, 1959); page numbers preceded by the letter J will refer to the translation by Maria Jolas: *The Planétarium* (New York: Braziller, 1960).

18. Sarraute, *L'Ere du Soupçon* (Paris: Gallimard, "Idées," 1956), p. 43.

19. See Sarraute's comment in the interview for *Lettres Nouvelles*, p. 29.

20. See Sartre's preface to *Portrait d'un inconnu* (Paris: Gallimard, 1956), pp. 8–10.

21. Ibid., p. 8.

22. The term is discussed in detail in *L'Ere du soupçon*, "Conversation et sous-conversation."

AFTERWORD

1. See *Le Monde hebdomadaire*, December 3–9, 1970.

2. For a response to Pompidou's allocution in one of the publications of the Leftist youth movement in France, which affirms the primacy of the problem of isolation but emphatically refuses Pompidou's solution, see "Pompidou, nous ne serons pas tes familles!," *Tout*, December 10, 1970.

3. See *McLuhan: Hot and Cool*, ed. G. E. Stearn (New York: Signet, 1967), p. 261.

Index